Edwardian London

Volume 4

Titles available from The Village Press are:-

The London Library:

Hardback
Village London Volume I
Village London Volume II
London Recollected Volume I
London Recollected Volume II
London Recollected Volume III
London Recollected Volume IV
London Recollected Volume V
London Recollected Volume VI
Village London Atlas
Besant's History of London - The Tudors
Besant's History of London - The Stuarts

Paperback
Village London Pt. 1 West and North
Village London Pt. 2 North and East
Village London Pt. 3 South-East
Village London Pt. 4 South-West
Village London Atlas
Old Fleet Street
Cheapside and St. Paul's
The Tower and East End
Shoreditch to Smithfield
Charterhouse to Holborn
Strand to Soho
Covent Garden and the Thames to Whitehall
Westminster to St. James's
Haymarket to Mayfair
Hyde Park to Bloomsbury
Belgravia, Chelsea and Kensington
Paddington Green to Seven Sisters
Highgate & Hampsread to the Lea
Edwardian London (4 Volumes.)

Other titles published are:

The Village Atlas - Birmingham and The West Midlands
The Village Atlas - Manchester, Lancashire & North Cheshire
The Village Atlas - North and West Yorkshire
The Village Atlas - Derbyshire, Nottinghamshire & Leicestershire

Edwardian London

———•◦•◦●◦•◦•———

Volume 4

The Village Press

First published in 1902 by Cassell and Co. Ltd.,
under the title Living London in 3 volumes.

This edition published by:

The Village Press Ltd.
7d Keats Parade Ltd, Church Street,
London, N9 9DP.

September 1990

British Library Cataloguing in Publication Data
Edwardian London.
  Vol. 4
  1. London, 1901-1910
  I. Sims, George R. (George Robert), 1847-1922 II. Living London
  942.10823

  ISBN: 1-85540-014-6
  (Series ISBN: 1-85540-029-4.)

Cover Artwork by Active Art, Winchmore Hill, London.

Printed and bound in Great Britain by:
J.W. Arrowsmith Ltd, Bristol.

CONTENTS.

	BY	PAGE
MONEY LONDON.	CHARLES C. TURNER	1
LIBRARY LONDON	BECKLES WILLSON	7
LORD MAYOR'S LONDON	CHARLES WELCH, F.S.A.	14
SCENES FROM LONDON SLUM-LAND.	D. L. WOOLMER	22
TELEPHONE LONDON	HENRY THOMPSON	28
LONDON'S BREWERIES AND DISTILLERIES	C. DUNCAN LUCAS	33
IN WORMWOOD SCRUBS PRISON	MAJOR ARTHUR GRIFFITHS	39
SOME OF LONDON'S CHIEF SIGHTS	JAMES BARR	45
SCENES FROM SHOP AND STORE LONDON	P. F. WILLIAM RYAN	53
UNDERGROUND TRAVELLING LONDON	ERIC BANTON	60
SOME LONDON "DODGES"	GEORGE R. SIMS	64
IN LONDON'S LESSER CLUB-LAND	HENRY LEACH	71
COURT CEREMONIES IN LONDON	NORMAN WENTWORTH	78
LONDON'S MODEL LODGING-HOUSES	T. W. WILKINSON	84
UNIFORMED LONDON	ALEC ROBERTS	91
LONDON "UP"	GEORGE R. SIMS	96
MOTORING LONDON.	H. O TYMAN	102
SUNDAY EVENING EAST AND WEST	A. ST. JOHN ADCOCK	108
CHARITABLE AND BENEVOLENT LONDON	DESMOND YOUNG	115
LONDON'S FASHIONABLE AMUSEMENTS	GILBERT BURGESS	122
SOME FAMILIAR THINGS IN LONDON	GEORGE R. SIMS	128
SOME LONDON SHOWS	CHARLES DUDLEY	134
SOME FOREIGN PLACES OF WORSHIP IN LONDON.	F. M. HOLMES	141
INSPECTING LONDON	WILLIAM MOYLE	147
SCENES FROM SCHOLASTIC LONDON	A. E. JOHNSON	153
CYCLING LONDON	C. DUNCAN LUCAS	160
LONDON BELOW BRIDGE	R. AUSTIN FREEMAN	166
SOME LONDON CONTESTS	GEORGE R. SIMS	172
SOME LONDON STREET AMUSEMENTS	EDWIN PUGH	178

CONTENTS.

	BY	PAGE
SCIENTIFIC LONDON.	*JOHN MUNRO*	. 184
MISSIONARY LONDON	*ALEC ROBERTS*	. 191
SCENES FROM EXCHANGE AND OFFICE LONDON.	*CHARLES C. TURNER*	. 198
LONDON'S FOOD SUPPLY	*A. ST. JOHN ADCOCK*	. 205
THE LONDONER OUT AND AT HOME	*GEORGE R. SIMS*	. 212
INDIAN AND COLONIAL LONDON	*HENRY THOMPSON*	. 218
FROM LONDON TENEMENT TO LONDON MANSION	*P. F. WILLIAM RYAN*	. 224
VAN DWELLING LONDON	*T. W. WILKINSON*	. 231
BOROUGH COUNCIL LONDON	*C. DUNCAN LUCAS*	. 236
LONDON BEYOND THE PALE	*GEORGE R. SIMS*	. 241
PUBLIC OFFICE LONDON	*HENRY LEACH*	. 247
LONDON'S PLEASURE GARDENS	*I. BROOKE-ALDER*	. 253
BALLOONING LONDON	*REV. JOHN M. BACON*	. 260
LONDON AT DEAD OF NIGHT	*GEORGE R. SIMS*	. 267
EPILOGUE	*GEORGE R SIMS*	. 273

MONEY EXCHANGE DEPARTMENT (MESSRS. COOK'S, LUDGATE CIRCUS).

MONEY LONDON.

By CHARLES C. TURNER.

LONDON is the chief abode of the great god Money, whose throne, visible to all men, is in the heart of the City. From Queen Street and Guildhall to Gracechurch Street and Bishopsgate, from London Bridge to London Wall, lies a region in which the temples of the god cluster together in thick profusion. From here the greatest and the most numerous of his activities are conducted; for London, in spite of the rivalry of New York and the growing importance of Paris and Berlin as money centres, is still paramount as a headquarters of exchange and banking.

In the banking section of the " Post Office Directory" there are over 11,000 entries informing the inquirer as to the banking representation in London of practically every town in the world. With few exceptions all these references are contained in the section of London I have indicated. A walk through the miles of streets and lanes in this quarter

will not fail to reveal to the observer the vast importance of London in this respect. All the buildings, save for a sprinkling of restaurants, churches, and shops, are banks of one kind and another, insurance offices, loan agencies, offices of mortgage brokers, foreign merchants, stock and share brokers, bullion dealers, insurance brokers, investment agents, assayers, and the like.

Our faith, prompted by the traditions of the place and the sight of leagues of palatial offices, not to mention multitudes of most expensively dressed City gentlemen, begins dimly to understand that this is indeed the abode of the god Money. But it is not long before the god himself appears. We are outside a well-known joint-stock bank. A vehicle resembling a private omnibus drives up. This is the car of the god. His mightiness is heralded by a shrill whistle. Attendants appear, and, without ceremony, the god is handed in bags from one to another on his way to the bank's strong room some-where in the basement. We hear the words "All gold," "All silver," or "All copper," passed from one official to the next—whether facetiously or by rule does not appear. We were beginning to think that money existed here only in an intangible form, that it was all a matter of figures in books, standing for something far away and unrealisable, and that at the best there might be a profusion of cheques and bills of exchange. On the contrary, in this region there probably is at any time a greater amount of gold than anywhere else in the world. The Bank of England alone has always some thirty-five millions in bullion, and frequently more, a mass of gold on which the credit of the country in certain last contingencies depends. By the way, a million pounds in gold weighs about eight tons.

At the Bank of England too, other banks keep their biggest treasures, retaining only enough on hand for daily use—amounts which, however, in many cases are enormous. For not one bank is like any other as regards the nature of its business. Some need a large stock of ready money. The Birkbeck Bank, with its hosts of small accounts, is one of these. Some banks, like the London City and Midland, require, especially at the end of each week, large reserves to enable their customers to pay their *employés'* salaries.

Instinctively one would make for Lombard Street in any expedition to view the money region. For centuries Lombard Street has been sacred to the banking interest. This is still the case, though the banking interest has long since overflowed the narrow limits of one street. "Lombard Street," indeed, is now a generic term often used to signify the whole of the money region. But Lombard Street itself is an epitome of all the rest. It contains such houses as Glyn's; the London and County Banking Company; Robarts, Lubbock and Company; the Crédit Lyonnaise; the Deutsche Bank; and Lloyds, one of the finest looking banks in London. It contains specimens of every class of bank, whether banks of deposit, discount, or loan; joint-stock or private; English, or foreign, or colonial. There are over thirty great banking houses in Lombard Street alone. It is necessary to remember, too, that scarcely a house having headquarters in the heart of London is not among those of the first importance. One has only to glance at the list of their liabilities to realise this. Scores of them, such as the London and County, the London and Westminster, the African Banking Corporation, the Bank of Austra-lasia, and the National Bank of India, have liabilities of anything between twenty millions and fifty millions each. But the business of some of these banks of sounding and characteristic title is often surpassed by

UNLOADING GOLD AT A BANK IN THE CITY.

that carried on under such simple but famous names as Lloyds' or Barclay's, or again as Baring's, or Rothschild's—houses which have played some little part in European politics during the last century.

Each of these banks has its spacious strong-rooms in the basement, a large room crowded with clerks, special sanctums for manager and secretary, and somewhere upstairs a board-room. Each has its own methods, its own long list of customers, its own carefully guarded secrets, its own capital employed here or there, its own cheques. And many are the devices to safeguard against frauds with regard to the latter. But from the purely artistic point of view cheques are full of interest. The designs are elaborate, often beautiful ; and a collection of various cheques might be desirable for æsthetic, if for no other, reasons. And this applies also to banknotes ; the difficulty in this case being increased by the fact that it would be locking up so much money. Besides the Bank of England, there are over one hundred banks in the United Kingdom which issue their own notes.

After the Bank of England itself—which is

described elsewhere in this work—perhaps the most interesting place is an insignificant building hidden away in a court leading out of Lombard Street. This is the famous Bankers' Clearing House, the agency through which bankers collect the money represented by cheques and bills paid to them. Instead of presenting the cheques at each banking house, bankers settle the whole amount delivered during the day at the Clearing House, receiving or paying the difference, as the case may be, by a single cheque on the Bank of England. Obviously the alternative to this system would be an interminable round of petty transactions. The annual business at the Clearing House amounts to about ten thousand million pounds sterling, and it increases every year. In one day the amount cleared is often over £100,000,000.

The scene is remarkable. A stream of "walk clerks" is continually arriving, each man carrying a portfolio which in most cases is securely chained to him. As each arrives he hurries to one of the desks and gets the amount of his load credited. Subsequently the cheques and bills are entered against the various banks on which they are drawn.

IN THE LONDON CITY AND MIDLAND BANK (LUDGATE HILL

This applies to London banks, for which there are two clearings daily, morning and afternoon. The "country clearing," some of which is collected by post, is at noon.

The "walk clerk" has a double journey to make, that from his bank to the Clearing House, and the return journey. In the latter case his portfolio may contain a big draft on the Bank of England. It will also contain the "returns"—that is, those cheques or bills which are returned from the clearing unpaid, either from want of funds, irregularity of endorsement, or from any other cause. Occasionally a forgery is detected, in which case the word "forgery" is written across in red, and the offending paper sent back for inquiry; its final destiny in most cases is Scotland Yard.

There is nothing in the interior of the Clearing House to suggest the importance of its work. A long room filled with desks so close together that at a casual glance they remind one of the old-fashioned pews. At the back, conspicuous, a clock—most important article of furniture here. Perhaps an official calling querulously for some great banking house, meaning its representative "walk clerk." Nothing in all this to indicate a hundred million pounds changing hands; and still less does the exterior betray the importance of the Clearing House.

This brings us to that interesting bank servant known as the "walk clerk." These young men are usually those who have just commenced their business career. It is necessary that they should be not only honest, active, and trustworthy, but also that they should be of fair physical proportions. Of course, they run no great danger in a city like London, but there have been instances of the bag being snatched from their hands and the contents lost to its rightful owners. Life in a London bank offers great attractions to youth. There are many prizes to be won in the banking profession, and it is a mistake to suppose that it is all a question of family influence. For positions of trust sterling qualities are required, and it has been generally found that the best way to find these is through genuine rivalry and competition. That familiar gentleman the cashier at the bank counter has by no means a simple task, the

"WALK CLERK."

chief qualification for which is the ability to count money quickly. He is the repository of stores of knowledge as to the status of his customers and the condition of their accounts. He knows when he may pay a cheque, or when it is necessary to make inquiries before doing so. Also he knows how to institute the latter without the customer at the counter suspecting that his credit is called into question. That important individual, the chief accountant, needs to be something of a genius. On him rests the responsibility of framing a new set of books on a new system of bookkeeping adapted for any new operation. Ability to do this is not common. Naturally, banks require trustworthy guards. At the Bank of England a small body of soldiers is deemed necessary to protect it at night. At most other banks one or at most two good men, who can be depended upon for acting promptly, do all that is required. Then, in many banks, even in the centre of the City, the custom of having a resident manager is still upheld. In this case the manager has comfortable quarters in a veritable palace.

The cosmopolitan character of the London banks makes linguistic attainments decidedly in request. There is a vast amount of foreign paper money and foreign documents to be

BANK PORTER.

dealt with. There is also a great deal of foreign conversation and correspondence to be attended to. This calls for many hundreds of men having these special qualifications in addition to the ordinary abilities.

Nearly every bank does business with bills—some more, some less. The principal mode in which money is raised by traders is by bills of exchange. The estimated certainty of their being able to pay those bills on the day they fall due is the measure of their credit. Knowledge of a special kind is required for this, and the bill-broker or discount banker steps in here. The amount of bill business in England is marvellous, and there are several firms in London which count among their assets discounted bills totalling up to many millions. Bill-discounting is a form of money-lending. The system enables the man or the firm possessing but little capital to engage in undertakings that require large sums of money. In short, it is an exceedingly democratic system which prevents the growing up of an aristocracy of commerce secure from the competition of energetic plebeians.

Our facsimile illustration on this page shows the noting of a bill. This constitutes almost the entire business of certain notaries located in the money quarter.

In noting a bill the notary, having presented it at the proper place and demanded payment, attaches to it a small piece of paper on which he writes the amount of his charge and the reason the bill is not paid, such as "No effects," "No orders left," or "Will be paid to-morrow."

But there are many ways of borrowing money. Dotted all over London are humble loan offices to assist the poor man in difficulty, to enable the artisan to set up in business for himself—loan offices whose merits and demerits cannot be explained here. There are loan banks and building societies. Even insurance companies lend money on life policies. Finally, there is the society usurer, sometimes a pure aristocrat, and not always of Hebrew descent. He is to be found in the best society, doing an enormous business with lords and ladies. He is not under the painful necessity of exhibiting a brass plate on his door, or of having his drawing-room windows covered with blue muslin or wire gauze.

London yearly becomes more and more a cosmopolitan city. Londoners travel more than they ever did, and London is visited more than ever by strangers from every land. Hence the necessity for money changers, who exchange English money for foreign and foreign money for English as desired, retaining a small percentage for expenses. Everyone is familiar with the money changers' establishment at Charing Cross Station, the windows filled with a remarkable collection of foreign money, both paper and coin. The big tourist agencies have a money-changing department, and do a big business, particularly at holiday times, with English

No orders left
1/6

GRAIN & SONS, Notaries,
46, Lombard Street, E.C.

SLIP ATTACHED
TO AN UNPAID AND
NOTED BILL.

folk going abroad. The "rush" at Messrs. Cook's exchange department just before the holidays is well worth seeing. The place is besieged with applicants for francs, marks, piastres, dollars, rixdalers, schillings, and pfennigs ; while postage stamps and money orders are subject to like negotiations.

So elaborate is our civilisation that it would be easy, for several chapters, to refrain from mentioning any physical necessity of our being, and to speak of nothing else save that medium, money, which makes business between men possible, and of that section of the community, tens of thousands strong, who from habit look upon money as a mere commodity, to be weighed in scales and bought and sold like so much grocery. It is not possible to realise without much thought the industrial power that is wrapped up in Money London. Railways through Africa, dams across the Nile, fleets of ocean greyhounds, great canals, leagues of ripening corn—London holds the key to all of these, and who can reckon up what beside ?

OUTSIDE A MONEY CHANGERS' (CHARING CROSS).

LIBRARY LONDON.

By BECKLES WILLSON.

IS there any more significant feature of the capital to-day than the growth of its public libraries, with the ever-swelling list of their patrons? How very far a cry it seems from the era when a daily newspaper cost sixpence, when histories, novels, and *belles lettres* were sealed to the masses, to the present day of grace when every Londoner, from peer to pot-boy, is handed a cheque-book by his local authorities and invited to draw on the bank of Universal Literature for any sum his eyesight can spend and as often as he chooses! Yet even the middle-aged reader can recall the former straitened limits of Library London, before its first free library was established.

No great search will be required to find the heart and centre of Library London. What author, what journalist at home, what cosmopolitan scholar abroad, is not familiar with the interior of that spacious, yet—it must be confessed—somewhat stuffy vault in Bloomsbury, where an average of 650 readers daily repair to draw upon a store of 1,000,000 volumes?

But the British Museum Reading-Room has already been adequately described in the pages of "Living London"; I only mention it here in order that we may be provided with a notable starting-point in our present survey of the libraries of the Metropolis.

Letting our glance rest for a moment on the hundreds of bent, studious forms at the radiating rows of desks, catching here and there, perhaps, a glimpse of a well-known face, let us emerge, and hastening down the wide steps, turn to an altogether different scene. Different and yet the same, for a common passion animates both—the insatiable thirst for something to read.

It is near enough at hand, just the length of a block, and the contrast is amusing. For here is another great library, where the note of scholarly shabbiness is absent, where brougham and landau with their pairs of champing bays are drawn up at the portals. The world-renowned Mudie's in New Oxford Street is the literary shrine of fashion. Let us pass by the waiting footmen into the paradise of novels, and, we may add, of novelists. Behind the long rear counter numerous obsequious attendants struggle to supply the demand. Does not some such dialogue as this frequently strike the ear?

"Yes, my lady, you will find Mr. X's last book very interesting. Miss Q? Well, our patrons complain of the character of her hero. Disappointing? Yes, rather; I could recommend Mr. Z's; and, of course, So-and-so's latest is quite up to the mark."

"Thank you so much; I have been out of England so long I have quite lost track of what is being read. Please send those you mention at once. Good morning." And with a smile the aristocratic patron returns to her waiting carriage. If Mudie's does not seem a gigantic establishment externally, that is because you do not take into account the vast ebb and flow of its stock, whose channels are spread over half the kingdom. The successful volumes, in their hundreds and even thousands, are no sooner within these four walls than they speed straightway forth again to the boudoirs and drawing-rooms of the Metropolis. But after a time they have their vogue, alas! often a short-lived one, and then they descend to the "catacombs." We have said that Mudie's is the paradise of novels; it is also their purgatory. Here in the cellars are stored the thousands of "have-beens," once the talk of the town, and now despised even by the country circulating libraries "in connection with Mudie's." It is a sad sight, these tons of once-triumphant "three-deckers," now to be had almost for the price of wastepaper. Many a popular living author might come here to learn humility. Here is the country department with its countless boxes, large and small, coming and going, bringing back books from libraries, clubs, societies, and

READING ROOM, GUILDHALL LIBRARY.

EXCHANGING BOOKS AT MUDIE'S LIBRARY.

institutions, and carrying them thence ; and the export department—did not Mr. Cecil Rhodes order 15,000 volumes at once from Mudie's for the Kimberley Free Library? The bulk of the London orders come by post over night ;. by 1 p.m. those rows of waiting vans outside will be off with their cargoes to gratify the jaded literary palates of the fashion's devotees. Altogether no fewer than 4,000,000 volumes are in circulation at Mudie's.

We are in the mood for contrasts : here is the Tube station close at hand ; let us descend, and in about twenty minutes we are standing before the entrance of a free library in Mile End Road. Throngs of *habitués* are entering and departing, for it is the hour of noon, and many have come to snatch a morsel of mental pabulum for the day, along with their bread and cheese or sandwiches. Of all nationalities are they, for we are now in a cosmopolitan district, but at this moment the Hebrew element is strongest. See that eager group of men, of such recent arrival from Russia, Roumania, Germany, Austria, or

Poland that they cannot as yet read a word in our language, round the Yiddish news-papers here provided for their benefit. Over the tables in an adjoining room bend other readers absorbed in the very magazines and periodicals to which the West-End turns for instruction and entertainment. It is a signi-ficant thing—this community of literary en-lightenment ; one cannot doubt, in surveying such a scene as this, that the good worked by London's free libraries, especially in the poorer quarters, is incalculable, even if it does no more than afford innocent relaxation to these work-worn battalions of East-Enders. To see the latter under more ideal conditions, it would not be a bad idea to wend our way a little further eastward, to the Bethnal Green Free Library, which, by the way, is one of the earliest, as it is one of the most successful, institutions of its kind. No one, by any stretch of the imagination, would call Bethnal Green the abode of culture and the gentler virtues. It is quite the opposite, to speak plainly, and one which would seem at first blush both to shun and to be shunned by the muses. Yet things are not what they seem, nor is Bethnal Green the haunt of vice and terror it was prior to the library being established. Five hundred volumes it had then, from various donors, including Queen Victoria ; now it boasts over 40,000. More-over, it used to be said that the experiment of lending books in such a locality was fore-doomed to failure. On the contrary, it has proved a great success, and to-day there are many hundreds of names of borrowers on the list. It is one of the most interesting and significant sights in the whole Metropolis to see in the evening the file of young men and old, women and girls, some of them thread-bare and haggard, but whose bright intelli-gence of eye tells of a new life within, an awakened intellect fed to repletion—if their stomachs are not always satisfied—on the works of Shakespeare, Scott, Dickens, and George Eliot.

Still in the humour for contrasts? Whither, then, shall we hie? Back again to a well-ordered book emporium at the West-End, where both books and borrowers are gilt-edged and genteelly bound?

Perhaps, in a moment. But meanwhile, we have a greater dissimilarity in similar things in store. What say you to a peep at the prison library at Wormwood Scrubs? Free? Oh, yes! His most gracious Majesty, through his Prison Commissioners, makes no charge to the convicts for the literary entertainment therein afforded— perfectly free, though the readers are not. There are 20,000 volumes in the library, and every convict who behaves himself is permitted his choice. It must not be thought that all are religious homilies, for here on the shelves are Scott, Thackeray, Ballantyne, Mayne Reid, amongst others, the favourite author being, as he should be, Dr. Samuel Smiles. But there is a notable peculiarity about each

volume : each page of every volume—nay, every available inch of margin, is stamped with — the broad arrow! This precaution is taken in order that no scrap of writing paper may be afforded the enforced inmate of the establishment. The librarian tells you, moreover, that he is obliged to be very careful about the character of the works served out, despite their variety. For not long ago there was a suspicious run on a bound volume of a well-known magazine, and the discovery was made that it contained an interesting and highly useful illustrated description of the various devices resorted to by famous gaol-breakers! It is needless to add that a pair of scissors was put into immediate requisition.

Between convicts and curates a wide gulf exists. Just out of Fleet Street and news-paperdom, on the Thames Embankment, stands Sion College. Fresh from glimpses of the studious burglar at the other extremity of London, you follow a scholarly bishop up a flight of stairs, and quickly find yourself in the centre of the greatest theological library in the world. These 100,000 volumes form a collection so complete of its kind that Sion College Library should be the Mecca of the clerical profession throughout the Empire. Yet, strange to relate, by the terms of its foundation, the use of this unique library with its costly missals and rare manu-scripts was originally limited to the clergy of

AN EAST-END
NEWSPAPER READING ROOM
(FREE LIBRARY, MILE END ROAD).

the City of London ; and even now its privileges are extended only to those residing within the Metropolitan postal district. It is a common resort of prelates, and many a tired parson is glad to seek in its sequestered shelves a temporary forgetfulness of work a-day scenes in communion with bygone saints and sages.

A typical free library, perhaps the busiest

cian, the busy journalist, the foreign tourist, the cab tout, the costermonger, and the politician on his way to Westminster, may all be commonly seen scrutinising London's wonderful diurnal and weekly output, from the *Times* downwards.

It is worthy of remark that these free library newspaper rooms have quite replaced the old news rooms, although one of the

APPLYING FOR BOOKS AT A FREE LIBRARY (BRIXTON).

in London, is that of St. Martin's-in-the-Fields, hard by Trafalgar Square. It catches, as in a net, all the idle, the unemployed, the leisurely loiterers of this busy central district. The basement is devoted to current newspapers and periodicals, of which this library possesses a wide selection ; while a flight of steps brings you to the liberally-stocked reference library. Both rooms are well patronised by a mixed throng of readers. Indeed, I know of no similar place of resort where the frequenters are of such "sorts," unless it be the Westminster Free Library, in Great Smith Street, a mile away. The disengaged actor and musi-

latter is still in existence near Ludgate Circus to remind us of an institution formerly common enough. By the payment of a fee of twopence the journalist, the business man, the member of a foreign colony, is able to consult upwards of 2,000 current newspapers and periodicals. Many Fleet Street writers, it is said, earn a fair livelihood here by extracting the honey from the various provincial and foreign papers.

At many of the free libraries, sprinkled with such generous profusion over the expanse of the city, a separate room is provided, in addition to the reference and newspaper rooms, for the use of ladies. Sometimes, as at Westminster, there is, besides, a ratepayers' room, devoted to the actual residents of the parish. This differs in very few essentials from the reading room of one's club. It becomes, indeed, a sort of club, from the uniformity of the *personnel* and the attendance of the occupants.

The librarian and his staff must needs be of patient temper and capable of overlooking the short-comings and eccentricities of the strange medley of their customers, whose new-found zeal for literature is easily capable of early dis-couragement. "Characters" abound at all the free libraries of the Metropolis. Some have an almost unconquerable pro-pensity for defacing the files, either by cutting or marking. One old gentleman seeks to monopolise the *Times* by reading it through from the first column to the last, and has to be expostulated with daily on behalf of other waiting patrons. The limit of time allowed to a newspaper reader is ten minutes at nearly all the free libraries, and there are often two or three readers simultaneously occupied with the same paper. In some cases the newspaper advertisements are conveniently posted up on a separate stand—sometimes on the railings outside—and this arrangement deflects a large number of the unemployed who really mean business.

In all the great free lending libraries a by

LADIES' READ-ING ROOM AT A FREE LIBRARY (SHEPHERD'S BUSH).

no means insignificant department is that devoted to the repairing and rebinding of damaged books. When we reflect on the experiences of the borrowed volumes, in the hands of the industrious apprentice, the poor sempstress, the clerk and saleswoman over luncheon or supper, in bed, in train and omnibus, it is not surprising that "David Copperfield" or "East Lynne" should sustain certain injuries requiring a period in hospital. The very mention of such an institution reminds us that if there are hospitals for books, there are also books for hospitals, in which indeed libraries have of latter years become a noteworthy feature. That at Charing Cross was given by Mr. Passmore Edwards; Middlesex owes its collection to the late Lord Sandhurst; while St. Bartholomew's was provided by the nurses themselves. A great drawback, however, to the hospital library is the frequent painful necessity of destroying books sus-pected of infection, and in this way many promising volumes have died an early and a violent death.

Of the great subscription libraries not mainly concerned with the distribution of novels, the London Library in St. James's Square stands easily first. Its

READING NEWSPAPER ADVERTISEMENTS OUTSIDE A FREE LIBRARY (SHEPHERD'S BUSH).

numerous and important collection is as much a necessity to the scholar, literary student, and man of letters as stones are necessary to a builder or pigments to a painter. In its refined, even luxurious, appointments the London Library has the air of an expensive club, and the quiet reading room often harbours some of the most notable literary figures of the age. Ten volumes at a time are allowed each member on payment of a modest £3 a year.

The famous circulating establishment of Messrs. W. H. Smith & Son is very similar to Mudie's, except that by means of its railway bookstalls it presents unequalled facilities for supplying the latest publications to country subscribers.

No article on London's libraries would be complete without mention of the Guildhall, that studious resort of the City fathers for many generations and of all interested in the history of old-world London. As a library it never suffers from that common complaint of

libraries—want of funds for its adequate and something more than merely adequate maintenance. Consequently within its " cloistered pale " all is well-housed, well-kept, and excellently served. The choice old books and charters and MS. records, illustrating the rise and progress of the world's greatest city, are here preserved for the scholar, while a bountiful supply of current literature invites the perusal of the clerk, the artisan, and the stray visitor to the Guildhall.

The Metropolis, then, on the whole, has an abundance of libraries, great and small. Library London, too, is a cosmos in itself. It is breeding a race of reading men and women whose enlightenment is derived from the greatest and wisest writers of the day and of all time. Moreover, the extent to which the masses avail themselves of the great privileges thus thrown open to them augurs well for the future intellectual progress, as a whole, of the millions of dwellers in the capital.

READING ROOM, LONDON LIBRARY.

PRESENTATION OF AN ADDRESS TO THE LORD MAYOR.

LORD MAYOR'S LONDON.

By CHARLES WELCH, F.S.A.

ARMS AND INSIGNIA OF THE
CITY OF LONDON.

ONE half at least of the English peerage can trace its descent from past Lord Mayors or other eminent citizens of the City of London. And the Lord Mayors themselves — from what stock have they come, and how do they attain to this great municipal distinction? Many have come as country lads to our great City to prove by their industry and ability that London streets are indeed paved with gold ; but all have passed through the severest tests of citizenship prescribed for the attainment of the City's highest dignity. Our future Lord Mayor must first be a liveryman of one of the City Companies. He must then become an alderman, by receiving the suffrages of the electors in one of the City wards. The next step is to fill the office of Sheriff—an annual appointment in the gift of the entire body of the Livery assembled in common hall. The emoluments of this office—about £700—form but a small part of the expenses, which amount to about £4,000 for the year. He now offers himself in due course for election to the mayoralty at the common hall held on Michaelmas Day. After hearing a sermon by the Lord Mayor's chaplain, at St. Lawrence Jewry, the Livery elect two aldermen, of whom the Court of Aldermen elect one, usually the next in seniority. Another step remains—the presentation of the Lord Mayor Elect to the Lord Chancellor for the approval of the Sovereign.

It must be admitted that the man who passes with satisfaction through these various ordeals is well worthy of the confidence of his fellow-citizens. Though now duly elected, the Lord Mayor does not enter upon his duties for another six weeks. The installation ceremonies await him, and very quaint they are. On November 8th the Lord Mayor Elect is sworn in at the Guildhall, and on the following day he is presented as

Lord Mayor to the Barons of the Exchequer, when an oath is administered to him by the King's Remembrancer. The pomp and ceremony observed for many centuries on this occasion have created a spectacle known as "The Lord Mayor's Show." Attended by the aldermen and City officials, the Lord Mayor rides in his State coach, which has been the admiration of every City apprentice from the days of Dick Whittington. Our

CARD OF INVITATION TO A
GUILDHALL BANQUET.

photographic illustration on page 106 shows this time-honoured vehicle leaving the stables in the City Greenyard. Those City Companies of which the Lord Mayor and the Sheriffs are members usually contribute to the pageantry with military music, banners, and cars emblematical of their trades. A special welcome is given to the Lord Mayor in his own Ward, a halt being made—as shown in our photographic illustration on page 101— to present him with an address, the Lady Mayoress being usually presented with a floral offering.

Great preparations have meanwhile been going on at the Guildhall, where the crypt has

become a kitchen for preparing the banquet, and the great hall above is turned into a feasting place for some 800 guests. The hospitality is characterised by a stately old-time grandeur. The distinguished guests reflect by their dignity the splendour of the scene, and the opportunity is frequently taken by the Prime Minister of delivering an important political announcement in replying to the toast of "His Majesty's Ministers." With a lavish care begotten of long experience every detail is thought out from the specially designed card of invitation to the final touches given to the decoration of the tables. With true City benevolence the poor are also remembered, and an interesting sight it is on the morrow to see the members of the Entertainment Committee, in white aprons, carving and distributing the good things which remain from the great feast. One half of this committee is nominated by the Lord Mayor, the other half by the two Sheriffs; and the cost of the banquet and "Show"—about £4,000—is contributed by the Lord Mayor and Sheriffs in like proportion.

A semi-State coach, drawn by four horses and painted with his arms and those of his Company, is provided by each Lord Mayor, together with new State liveries for his servants. The City insignia, a group of which, around the City arms, is shown in the illustration on page 101, are of great interest. There is the famous collar of SS., bequeathed to the City by Alderman Sir John Allen, who died in 1544. A Tudor rose and a knot are alternately inserted between the letters, and the ends of the collar are joined by a portcullis. From this is suspended the beautiful jewel or badge purchased by the City in 1607 for the official use of its Lord Mayors. Of much earlier date is the ancient mace or sceptre (not shown in our picture) which is borne by the Lord Mayor at State ceremonials. The shaft and base are of crystal spirally mounted with gold, and the head is decorated with pearls and uncut stones, which indicate its ancient origin. Although it has received additions in later times, this interesting object has without doubt come down to us from the Anglo-Saxon period. Then there are the State swords: the pearl sword, which

THE KING RETURNING THE LORD MAYOR'S SWORD AT TEMPLE BAR.

ROYAL GUESTS ARRIVING AT THE GUILDHALL.

is delivered up to the Sovereign at Temple Bar when his Majesty pays a visit to the City ; the sword of State, which is carried before the Lord Mayor by the sword-bearer ; the black sword for mourning, and the Old Bailey sword. The City mace, made in 1735, is borne by the mace-bearer, whose proper title is common crier or serjeant-at-arms. The City Marshal completes the retinue of the Lord Mayor, and the three officers above named comprise all that remain of the once numerous Lord Mayor's household.

The official income of the mayoralty is £10,000, but this provides for less than one half of the expenses of the year of office. Many of the Mansion House banquets are fixtures, and incumbent upon the occupant of the civic chair. Such are those to the household and other officials on Plough Monday, to the bishops at Easter, to the judges, to the Elder Brethren of the Trinity House, and others. To these each Lord Mayor adds entertainments suggested by his personal tastes and surroundings. The illustration on page 108 depicts a scene from a famous

Mansion House banquet—one that was given to his Majesty's judges. The City plate displayed on these occasions is very rich, and contains some pieces of historic interest, but none of ancient date. The help of the Lord Mayor is eagerly sought by religious and charitable bodies, a " Mansion House meeting " being the highly-prized means of bringing a deserving society under the notice of the charitably disposed. Many important movements — the Hospital Sunday Fund, for example—owe their origin to a Mansion House gathering. But the greatest public service rendered by the Lord Mayor is the establishment of those Mansion House Relief Funds which have made British charity renowned throughout the world.

In the City the Lord Mayor takes precedence of every subject of the Crown, not excepting members of the reigning house, and holds a quasi-Royal position. By virtue of his office he is head of the City Lieutenancy, and recommends the names of persons to fill vacancies. He is *ex-officio* chairman of the Thames Conservancy and a trustee of St.

Paul's Cathedral ; he has power to close or grant the use of the Guildhall ; and the Company of which he is a member has precedence over all the other City companies during his year of office. He is expected to partake of the hospitality of most of the Companies and Corporation committees, and is much in request at public gatherings of all kinds both in suburban London and in the provinces. On Sunday he sometimes attends charity sermons in state, most of the City churches being provided with a sword-rest attached to the Lord Mayor's pew. Then there is the Spital sermon at Christ Church, Newgate Street, also official duties in connection with Queen Anne's Bounty and the Sons of the Clergy Corporation, and attendance at St. Paul's to meet his Majesty's judges.

The State functions and privileges of the Lord Mayor are many and varied. He receives the password of the Tower of London quarterly under the sign manual of the Sovereign. He is entitled to venison warrants, under which he has from the Royal forests two does in midwinter and two bucks

in the late summer or autumn. No troops may pass through the City without the consent of the Lord Mayor being first obtained ; but the regiments descended from the Trained Bands have the right to march through with colours flying and bayonets fixed. His lordship's right to the title of " Lord Mayor " dates back to the year 1354 in the reign of Edward III. He is entitled to the prefix " Right Honourable " through being summoned to attend the meeting of the Privy Council on the demise of the Crown, when he signs the Proclamation of the successor to the Throne. The ceremony of the Proclamation formerly included a picturesque scene on the herald's arrival at Temple Bar. The old procedure (somewhat modified since the removal of the Bar in 1878) was as follows : A pursuivant of arms advanced between two trumpeters, preceded by two of the Life Guards. After the trumpets had sounded thrice, he was asked by the City Marshal from within " Who comes there ? " and he replied, " The officers of arms, who demand entrance into the City to proclaim his (or her) Royal

IN THE GUILDHALL CRYPT : PREPARING THE BANQUET.

DECORATING CARS FOR THE LORD MAYOR'S SHOW.

over the south part of the City. He is also the first-named Commissioner of the Central Criminal Court in the Old Bailey, and attends at the opening of each session of that Court. The Lord Mayor and the aldermen are nominally judges of the Mayor's Court, but by long-established custom the Recorder (or in his absence the Common Serjeant) acts as sole judge of this Court.

Lord Mayor's London starts into new life at the *end* of each year. On St. Thomas's Day, December 21st, the Court of Common Council is annually elected by the City ratepayers, the returns being submitted to the Court of Aldermen at their Grand Court of Wardmote, held on Plough Monday. Committees are then appointed, and the Council is fully constituted by about the middle of January. The chairman of the leading committee—that of the City Lands—bears the courtesy title of Chief Commoner. The Lord Mayor presides over the Common Council, which is the principal governing body of the City, having under its control such widely differing departments as the City schools, markets, open spaces, library, public health, and many others. The City has independent and entire control of its own police, and the efficiency of this force has often been publicly acknowledged.

Perhaps the most interesting, if not the most picturesque, of Corporation ceremonies

Majesty." On being admitted, he was conducted to the Lord Mayor, to whom he showed the Order in Council, which his Lordship, having read, returned to him. The Proclamation was then read at the usual places in the City, and the officers of arms were afterwards entertained at the Mansion House.

On attending, with the Sheriffs, the first Levee of the year, the Lord Mayor is presented by the Prime Minister, and the Sheriffs by the Home Secretary. Addresses to the Throne from the Corporation are presented with due formality by the Lord Mayor, who, approaching the Sovereign between the Lord Chamberlain and the Recorder, delivers the address, and receives the Royal reply on bended knee. At Coronations the Lord Mayor, by long-established right, has a prominent position in Westminster Abbey, standing between Black Rod and Garter-King-at-Arms. At the State banquet which formerly followed in Westminster Hall (discontinued since the Coronation of George IV.) the Lord Mayor exercised his ancient right of assisting the chief butler, and received for his fee a golden cup and ewer.

As Chief Magistrate of the City a large part of the Lord Mayor's time is occupied in the daily discharge of his magisterial duties at the Mansion House Justice Room, which has jurisdiction

LORD MAYOR'S STATE COACH READY TO START.

is the presentation of its honorary freedom. The ante-room of the council chamber is lined with the busts of eminent personages— statesmen, warriors, philanthropists, travellers (more rarely men of letters), who have received this honour. The address on such an occasion is delivered by the Chamberlain, whilst the

nature, such as embezzlement, forgeries, etc. It is seldom that the decisions of the Lord Mayor and his brother magistrates are overruled by the superior courts. The aldermen sit in their magisterial capacity also to hear police summonses, to grant or renew licences, and for many other purposes.

PREPARING TABLES FOR THE GUILDHALL BANQUET.

Lord Mayor hands to the recipient of the honour a copy of the resolution enclosed in a gold box specially and appropriately designed. The City has two seals, one for mayoralty purposes, and the other known as the City seal, which is affixed to documents only by the direct sanction of the Common Council.

The aldermen are magistrates by virtue of their office, and preside in turn at the Guild-hall Justice Room, which shares with that of the Lord Mayor at the Mansion House jurisdiction over the whole City. The resident population being small and eminently respectable, cases of assault, drunkenness, etc., are rare, and the ordinary police court work is comparatively light. The offences dealt with are chiefly of a commercial

In his own ward each alderman has full authority, and appoints a deputy from among the ward's representatives in the Common Council. Besides being members of the latter court, the aldermen also form the ancient body known as the Court of Aldermen, which has important powers both of a judicial and an administrative character. A person who refuses to serve as alderman, when elected, is liable to a fine of £500, unless he can satisfy the Court of Aldermen that at the time of his election he was not worth £30,000.

The citizens of London are proud of the privilege which they have for centuries enjoyed of appointing their own Sheriffs. The Livery meet for this purpose at the Guildhall on Midsummer Day, when they elect to this honourable office two citizens of substance and repute, the senior being usually an alderman and the junior a commoner. The Sheriffs are sworn into office on September 28th, when they give a grand entertainment known as the Sheriffs' Breakfast at the hall of the company of the senior Sheriff. It is the painful duty of these officers as custodians of the prisoners to superintend the carrying out of sentences of capital punishment. A more agreeable task is that of presenting Corporation petitions to the House of Commons, when certain quaint formalities take place between the Speaker and themselves. The ancient Sheriffs' Courts are now merged in the modern City of London Court. The Sheriffs, with the City Remembrancer, wait upon the Sovereign to know his pleasure as to receiving an address from the Corporation.

The City officers form a large and important body, many of them having ceremonial duties besides those directly connected with their post. A curious custom, for example, which still survives is that of presenting to some State officials and to the chief City officers a few yards of "Livery" cloth shortly before Christmas.

Besides the strictly municipal gatherings at the Guildhall, many other ceremonies take place there from time to time, which give it an almost national character. High above the doorway is placed the Elcho Shield when the English team is successful at Bisley. The great banquet of November 9th is soon succeeded by the Ragged School Children's dinner and entertainment. Sometimes a public meeting of citizens gives strong support to, or leads a resolute attack on, the Government of the day; occasionally a foreign Sovereign is the honoured guest at a magnificent banquet. During the year there may be a *conversazione* of some great scientific society, or a reception of the mayors of the United Kingdom; or there may be a great flower or fruit show, or perhaps a concert in aid of sufferers from a great public calamity. These and many others too numerous to mention are among the purposes for which the Guildhall throws open its doors, and on which Gog and Magog bestow a smile of benevolent approval.

ENTERTAINING JUDGES AT THE MANSION HOUSE.

SCENES FROM LONDON SLUM-LAND.

By D. L. WOOLMER.

A BACKYARD IN SLUM-LAND.

SLUM-LAND finds no place on a map, yet the most sceptical accept its existence as an indisputable fact. What cares this land of Nod either for the acknowledgment or for the contempt of gazetteers? It thrives on neglect, and only asks to be let alone. Discoverers and explorers describe it as a product of modern civilisation, injurious to the health of the Empire, inasmuch as it lies near to its heart. Slum-land is not impressed by its scientific origin and importance, nor does it shrink into itself before contumely in the abstract; it takes things as they come. Slums may be contemptible in themselves as the backyards of a noble city and the ruins of castles in the air, but they are the scenery of life's quaintest comedies and darkest tragedies.

The curtain is drawn aside to reveal, however, not the stage paintings but the actors. The shelter of the street arab may be, like the Bedouin's tent, a relief from the ordinary; but what interest has either apart from its inmates? The importance of the one consists in its being the dwelling place of the wandering, untamed son of Ishmael; of the other, its counterpart in the city, that

it is the haunt of the homeless man, of the woman of no fixed address, and of the vagabond child. The empty tent and the narrow tumble-down court might go to the winds and the pullers-down but for the sacred humanity in possession.

The Ghetto of the East-End would be simply repulsive but for episodes in the current history which Jews and their Gentile neighbours are making between them. The leaden weight of an extensive dead level of poverty in South London would be intolerable without heroes and heroines amongst dock labourers, book-folders, fur-pullers, or "hands" in jam and other factories. The monotonous regularity of streets in the West London Avernus would be only depressing but for an exciting glimpse of the fist that smashes a window, or of an inspiring vision of the patient hand that pastes up the holes and attempts to conceal the ravages with a muslin blind or a pot of scarlet geranium. No hovel in Slum-land is incapable of containing an epic or a romance. Over no other part of the kingdom, on the trustworthy authority of registrars, do the two angels of life and death hover more continually; and nowhere, as the guardians of the public peace can testify, is the fight between good and evil more fierce and stubborn.

The sun rises and lights up the first scene; and, whether it is his lazy hour of winter or after a short midsummer night's dream, Slum-land is already astir. With one consent, its natives ignore any special times and seasons for rest, work, play, or meals. A genuine Slum-lander, like the independent youth in the tale of "Sandford and Merton," would describe his method of keeping body and soul together as, "I eat when I am hungry, and I drink when I am dry." Should he belong to the lower ranks—for it is a mistake to suppose that the country enjoys absolute social equality—he may ingenuously confess, "I am dry all hours of the day."

I. A STREET DISCUSSION. II. CRIPPLED CHILDREN AT DRILL (ST. JOHN'S INSTITUTE, WALWORTH).
III. A STREET IN NINE ELMS. IV. A FAVOURITE AMUSEMENT. V. A SULTRY AFTERNOON.

Thirst is, indeed, the chief complaint of the community. They are otherwise peculiarly content. Anxiety for the future, remorse for the past, pangs of shame and pricks of conscience, may be known to stray aliens or stragglers amongst them ; but such disturbers of the peace are excluded from the common-wealth.

The great ever-changing East-End receives the first good-morning kiss of the opening day. In a narrow room in the parish of St. Mary's, Whitechapel, a sick foreign Jew bids it welcome, though the long hours of night have brought him no rest. Four men and women share his abode. It is their practice for two to carry on the trade of making "uppers" for shoes whilst the others sleep. The noise is incessant, and the beds are seldom empty. A *Box and Cox* arrangement is, in comparison, but a mild Gentile form of making the most of a lodging. In old and respectable houses of the next parish of Spitalfields, which once held weavers and their looms, more foreign Jews and Jewesses, perhaps ten in one room, stir in the beds which they have made up on the floor. They dropped in after eleven p.m., and must be off before the inspector's hour of duty. He has an English prejudice against overcrowding, and has ruthlessly emptied a four-roomed house in which he discovered fifty-one persons sleeping ; so the occupants of staircases drag their weary limbs into the open air.

When the sun catches the golden cross of St. Paul's he gives a warm touch of colour to costers and street sellers on their way to the markets. Men and women porters, denizens of the courts of central London, compete for odd jobs, and the successful bend beneath the weight of fruit and vegetables. The whirling centre of business and amusement sweeps its residents north, south, east and west, and sets up offices and workrooms on the sites of vanished dwelling-places. Some evicted tenants resist the besom, and creep into already crowded corners of St. Luke's, St. Giles's, Clerkenwell, and Soho. Cab touts and hangers-on at theatres cannot afford to rest at night until revellers set them the example. Half or a quarter of a bed within easy reach of their means of livelihood suits men and women whose days must begin or end in the small hours of the morning better than ample space a mile away. Before five a.m. a certain proportion tramps to the docks, but a crowd from the immediate neighbourhood of the river already waits at the gates. The "ticket" men are admitted first ; a struggle for entrance between candidates for casual work ensues. The gates are closed, and many turn away disappointed to loaf about and pick up odd jobs elsewhere.

The great south—from London Bridge to Walworth, and from Wandsworth on the west to Rotherhithe on the east—offers attractions to Slum-land's colonists. Seekers for a shady retreat lurk amid the remnants of old villages hidden behind the thoroughfares in parts of each of the three boroughs of South-wark Bermondsey, and Battersea. The historic parish of St. George the Martyr is faithful to old traditions, even to that of being a harbour of crime. Various parts of it are distinguished by bearing the name of the chosen saint for " Merrie England." But Charles Dickens is a rival patron. A sick child in Dorrit Street taken to the Evelina Hospital looks out on Quilp Street (late Queen Street), and a sound child romps on the asphalt space reserved as " Little Dorrit's Playground." Little Dorrit's garret window, as it appears in the drawing by " Phiz," with the prison-born girl telling Maggie the story of the " Princess," has been kept intact by a well-known firm whose tin and iron plate manufactory occupies the site of the eastern part of the Marshalsea Prison.

The invasion from older Slum-land still continues. The shores of the river will always draw the sweepings from demolished districts. To the nostrils of out-of-works the fragrance, too, of Bermondsey's tanyards is as sweet as is that of the jam factories to multitudes of rough and homeless girls. They are human, if only " hands " ; and when the monotonous day's work is done hundreds thankfully turn for tea and recreation into clubs like that at the " Time and Talents " Settlement in Bermondsey Street. Many more get half drunk, and some often make the evening hideous with wild play or rough street fights—such as the one shown on page 114—before herding together for a few hours of darkness in close sleeping-places.

South London has other early risers and hard toilers besides dockers, wharf labourers, urchins who scarcely get a square meal once a fortnight. It has come to light that considerably over 2,000 boys and girls attending Board schools, from eight years old and upwards, are wage-earners during

A SCENE IN BRICK LANE, BETHNAL GREEN.

and factory hands. From a slum in Battersea a boy of twelve starts two mornings in the week at 2.30, the other five at 4.30, for a three miles' walk to a water-cress bed. He washes and sells "creases" every available moment between the hours in which he cudgels his brains and tries his teacher's patience in school, and manages to work for his living more than seventy hours a week. A young neighbour, who does not know his own age or any name but "Jack," knows how to catch eels with a fork. His father's coat, when too ragged to cover the manly person, drapes the boy's starving body from collar to ankles. That descent of clothing which is usually old before it reaches Slum-land is a characteristic part of its social system. Father Thames is kinder to Jack than his natural parent, and at low tide leaves him a stretch of mud in which he can wade and obtain wriggling trophies. The longest he sometimes sells for twopence-halfpenny, the smallest his mother cooks for supper. He is one of an army of little

more than nineteen hours a week. A wide margin must be left for numbers besides whose casual earnings are unknown, and for little vagrants who manage to evade the School Board officers.

Slum-land's general standard of respectability is gauged by boots. Only during the five weeks' summer holiday may children discard shoes and stockings without their parents losing caste. The founders of the Ragged School Union—Franciscans of the nineteenth century, as Sir Walter Besant called them— first broke up a barefoot brigade. In spite of these friars' anomalous achievement, remnants are still to be found hobbling on chilblains in neighbourhoods such as Nine Elms; but the fear of committal to a truant school teaches them even in this district the value of shoe leather. The State now follows in the wake of charity: it enjoins that in school hours at least the rising generation must be both shod and suitably employed.

Whilst their children work, the most hopeless part of Living London lounges through the day. The sun never loses sight of loiterers on bridges and slumberers in parks. His last look as he sinks to rest is on black patches of poverty in the rich and favoured West-End. These colonies of Slum-land have no special industries; but the neighbourhood of wealth and leisure offers them very special temptations to crime and beggary. Hereditary traditions are against them. The parish of St. Andrew's, North Kensington, was formed out of the sweepings of Tyburn when the Great Western Railway took over the grim and grisly place of executions. Even yet the name of "The Piggeries" clings to a district in Latimer Road where ejected keepers of swine settled down on plots of waste land. Westminster has benefited by the dispersion of a community who bear the stamp of descent from seekers for sanctuary in past days, though a comparatively small proportion still live under the shadow of the Abbey. The curse of heredity is not so easily cast off; it follows a floating population. The dark character of a certain district in Kensal New Town, for instance, is ascribed to the fact that the ground was once the camping place of gipsies entering London from the west. Traces of the race may be still found even in the faces of the tinkers, grinders, and members of other desultory callings which prevail.

There are always depths below depths of poverty and wretchedness. Perhaps four churches which are centres of activity in Lisson Grove, the Church Army Headquarters in Edgware Road, and the Shaftesbury Institute in Harrow Street reach some of the lowest of all. Men and women, degraded criminals, who have exhausted every other attempt to raise the fallen, are not refused a twopenny bed, breakfast, and a test of labour at the two Homes of the Shaftesbury Institute. Amongst the regular lady patrons are dustbin-rakers, whose calling may bring them in sixpence a day, match and bootlace sellers, and varieties of persons who live by their wits. Girls whose pay at the small factories of the West-End never exceeds 4s. 6d. a week, and is generally claimed by their parents, have a clubroom in the institute. Their highest matrimonial ambition is to marry a coster and to share his open-air life. What though the barrow is out early and late and in fair or foul weather! It represents emancipation from dull routine.

The day is done, but Slum-land has no taste for nestling under the wing of night. Artificial light reveals it in animation, and with all its worst aspects intensified; but it also discovers in full activity all the machinery for draining off the vile exudations that morally swamp the low districts of London. Miles have been already reclaimed, not only by razing and rebuilding, but by changing the character of the inhabitants. The means used for social uplifting are too many and

RECREATION ROOM AT THE RED HOUSE, STEPNEY.

111

various to mention. Counter attractions to the influence of the low public-houses and demoralising places of entertainment are a part of the organisation in possession of every district mentioned as deserving essentially the name of Slum-land.

The Red House, a coffee palace in connection with St. Augustine's, Stepney, is an example. It is formed on a similar model to that of the Institute for Seamen at Poplar. With a fine frontage and five storeys, it smiles cheerfully on carters, costers, loafers, and weary toilers in Commercial Road East. A surrendered "cosh," a specimen of the

FACTORY GIRLS FIGHTING.

short iron walking-stick easily concealed up a sleeve, and intended to strike down an unwary stranger, hangs in the Vicar's room. It is an eloquent though silent advocate for providing cheap and respectable accommodation for the night in poor districts.

St. James-the-Less, Bethnal Green, has a working men's hotel which already pays a profit of £100 a year, and the people of this district invest annually £2,000 in provident clubs. A parish in Shoreditch, described by newspapers in 1886 as "the sink of London," is well known through "A Child of the Jago," by Mr. Arthur Morrison, who lived for a time on the spot. The "Jago," with its awful record of a mortality four times that of the Metropolis generally, is gone. On its site stands Holy Trinity Church and Institute. Close at hand are model dwellings; but in

Brick Lane and other parts of the original parish the teeming population makes it hard to realise that any dispersion has taken place. In Slum-land open hostility to religion is the exception, not the rule, though widespread regard for it may go no farther than impressions that "A prayer cannot do any harm, especially when a person is dying," or "It is good to have some belief in Hell: it prevents a man being too obstropolous," or, perhaps, "It is well to have a child baptised for the sake of its health." Public opinion rises involuntarily as a higher standard is lifted up close at hand. Large congregations assemble round the open-air pulpits of Spitalfields Parish Church and St. Mary's, Whitechapel, where often on Saturday afternoons hundreds of Jews make an attentive congregation.

South London, with its 2,000,000 inhabitants, is, in spite of overwhelming numbers, equally resolute in changing the face of Slum-land. Churchyards have been converted into recreation grounds. The Vicar of St. Peter's, Walworth, has started a small Zoo for the children, and has opened the crypt of his church for the old folk. The Vicar of St. John's has an institute, a sort of residential club for working men, which pays its own way. In its popular gymnasium, at certain times, blind and crippled children enjoy exercise which often straightens crooked limbs, and gives health and confidence to handicapped runners in the race of life.

If such objects of compassion are transformed into self-dependent citizens, and if a new generation rises up which will regard intemperance, improvidence, and dragging on charity as a disgrace, Slum-land must disappear. This part of Living London will be no more regretted than the dismal marshes which traditions declare once occupied the site of this stately city.

IN THE ELECTROPHONE SALON (GERRARD STREET).

TELEPHONE LONDON.

By HENRY THOMPSON.

USING THE TELEPHONE.

VOICES! Voices! The voices of a mighty multitude, year in and year out, holyday and holiday, noon and night, flow over our heads, around us, and under our feet in a ceaseless, silent chorus. No whisper of them ever reaches the myriad passers-by, for, hermetically sealed in their subterranean tubes of lead or high over the roof-tops in weather-resisting cables of the stoutest insulating mediums, they pass on the electric waves to those for whom they are intended.

They may convey the City magnate's mandate that will "slump" some particular shares to the tune of several thousands of pounds, a not-to-be-refused invitation to a dinner-and-theatre party, a domestic order to the family tradesman, or an appointment with "My Lady's" *modiste*. In the still hours of the night the voices are fewer, but their messages frequently speak of life or death—the hurried call for the physician, the dread signal of "Fire," or the burglar-aroused cry for "Police." So, throughout the hundreds of miles of the metropolitan area, are these voices ever speaking; for Telephone London is never at rest.

The National Telephone Company recruit their operators from the ranks of bright, well-educated, intelligent girls, who are, in many cases, the daughters of professional men, doctors, barristers, clergymen, and others.

REPAIRING OVERHEAD WIRES.

After the preliminary examination the would-be operator goes into the telephone "school," which is fitted up as a dummy exchange, and is in charge of an experienced lady-instructor. Each pupil is furnished with a short list of terse, clear rules, and, sitting before the dummy plugs and switchboard, under the guidance of the instructor she is taught how to put these into practical use. The girls in turn act as subscribers, ringing up one another, and asking to be put on to certain numbers. An error made is pointed out, and continually questions are asked to test progress, until a pupil becomes sufficiently capable to be moved into the real exchange alongside an expert operator. A few weeks later and she becomes a fully fledged operator, whom practice and experience alone can improve. Her hours of duty are about nine daily, including the time allowed for midday dinner and afternoon tea. Few female operators work after 8 p.m., and their latest hour of duty is 10 p.m., when male operators take their places until the following morning has well begun.

With pardonable feminine vanity the majority of the young ladies wear gloves while operating, to better maintain the contour and complexion of their busily worked fingers, and often conceals her ordinary

walking habit under a loose kind of graduate's gown in dark material. This latter was a kindly idea of the N.T.C.'s administration to shield a sensitive and modestly-garbed operator from being distracted by an extra smart frock on either side of her.

In the City calls practically stop at 7 p.m., but in the West-End half the day's work may be done between 10 p.m. and 12.30 a.m. The Holborn district wakes up first, owing chiefly to the Smithfield Meat Market, and the busy life of the other exchanges follows shortly afterwards. On the arrival of the dinner hour the operators are relieved by reserves, and take their seats at the attractively arranged tables in the dining-room. At every large exchange there is a spacious, cheerful room set apart for this purpose, a kitchen, cooks, crockery, plate, furniture, etc., being provided free by the company. Here the operators dine or take afternoon tea. They provide their own food in so far as paying for what they consume, or an operator may bring in her own chop and have it grilled. The operators decide what next day's joint shall be, and this is served up with two vegetables, bread, butter, tea, etc., at a price that would bankrupt the 'cutest and largest London caterer. Before this very sensible innovation, through rain, slush, or snow the staff had to rush into the streets, hurry through a cup of tea, a scone or bun in a crowded tea-room, and then return, to faint later at the switchboard for lack of proper nourishment. Marriage terminates an operator's connection with the company, but, if specially experienced, she is registered on the reserve as a stand-by when epidemics come along.

High up on the loftiest roof-tops, their myriad wires showing in a thread-like lattice-work against the heavens, are the huge square frames and many-armed standards which bear the telephone lines and cables west, south, north, east. To gaze up at one from the pavement is for the layman to be bewildered by chaos confused, yet to the linesmen each single wire is as distinct and separate as the Strand is from Holborn.

To work on these roof standards is dangerous, but the engineers, fault-finders, linesmen, etc., are specially selected. A fire may destroy a heavily wired standard and cut off a whole district, so day or night these men must be at call to effect immediate repairs. The standard on the Lime Street exchange bears over 12,000 wires, and is one of the biggest in the world, the roof having had to be specially constructed to carry it.

Besides the graceful-looking kiosks in some of the main streets, there are scattered over the Metropolis many hundreds of "call offices" in tradesmen's establishments for the convenience of the passer-by. In any of these for twopence the telephone may be commanded with the whole service of a mighty organisation.

The silent call-room of the Stock Exchange is an impressive sight when in full swing. A score of glass-doored boxes fill the wall-spaces. At the main entrance is the switch-clerk, an electric indicator before him showing boxes engaged and empty. One of the "hatless" brigade—a stockbroker or speculator's clerk—enters, giving the number he wants. "Six-two-three?

in the 'Change, and lets "Mr. Dobearem" know he is wanted.

To the pension fund each *employé* contributes 2½ per cent. of his or her pay, the company adding an equal amount and guarantees 4 per cent. on the investments. After ten years' subscription members becoming incapacitated for work are allowed a pension which otherwise becomes due at sixty-five, and a reduced rate for life assurance has been obtained at a leading office.

A composite association, presided over by the chief officials, ensures healthy sport and recreation for the whole staff. It includes clubs for cricket, football, tennis, cycling,

OPERATORS PRACTISING IN THE NATIONAL TELEPHONE COMPANY'S SCHOOL (LONDON WALL).

photography, rambling, dancing, singing, etc. Launch trips on the Thames, lectures and lantern displays in the winter at the Association's rooms, St. George's Hall,

POST OFFICE OPERATORS AT DINNER (CENTRAL TELEPHONE EXCHANGE, ST. PAUL'S CHURCHYARD).

—4" replies the switch-clerk; and the customer enters Box 4 to find his number waiting on the line for him. When he has finished, the lad calls, "Clear 4," and Box 4 is once more disengaged. If a man in the "House" be telephoned for a commissionaire through a brass trumpet shouts down a speaking-tube, and an electric light flashes

further promote social intercourse, and the subscription is but nominal, the working expenses being provided by the presiding office-bearers.

The newer telephone organisation of the Postal Department has wisely reaped all the benefits of the experiments and experience of the pioneer company. No gown hides the

IN THE POST OFFICE CENTRAL TELEPHONE EXCHANGE (ST. PAUL'S CHURCHYARD): RECEIVING CALLS.

operator's taste in dress, but each must be in height 5 ft. 2 in. or over, and extra light-weights are rejected. She is examined by a lady physician, her eyesight tested, her teeth put in order—to avoid absence through toothache—and, if considered necessary, revaccination follows. After four to six weeks in the "school" on full wages she begins duty at 11s. weekly the first year, rising gradually to £1 a week at the end of nine years. The limit of her salary-earning capacity is about £200 per annum, and if invalided two-thirds pay is awarded her. Her dining-room, decorated with the flowers she and her comrades have brought from their own gardens, looks like a first-class restaurant, and her sumptuous dinner costs her fivepence!

The Postal Telephone service has none but underground lines and cables, and deep down in the basement of the Central Exchange flow fat, sinuous snakes of lead in wavy volumes. Each is a hermetically sealed channel kept continuously filled with dry air by a driving pump apparatus to prevent the intrusion of moisture—the enemy of a good telephone circuit. Through metal frames, meters, bridges, fuse boxes, etc., the subscriber's line reaches the operating switchboard. As he rings, a tiny pencil-sized disc lights up with electricity. The operator, wearing a light aluminium receiver and having before her lips a breastplate transmitter of the same material, sees the glow, plugs into the number, receives the order, and makes the required connection. For connecting purposes, each girl has every subscriber's number before her, but, to evenly distribute the work, the calls are apportioned among the staff. To register the penny calls, tiny meters, not unlike gas indexes, stand by hundreds in frames, and the operators' work is similarly checked. Any attempt of the electric currents to shirk their work and creep off the line into the bosom of Mother Earth is thwarted by numberless glow lights in brass frames. When one of these shines it is known that the current is playing truant, and the electricians and fault-finders soon bring it back to stern duty. All the current for working the lines is generated by powerful dynamos, which charge the accumulators. The latter have a large room to themselves and resemble zinc baths filled with a colourless, acid-smelling solution, in which are immersed strange grids of metal. Throughout the building buckets of fine, brown sand stand in readiness for an outbreak of fire. Water or chemicals for the purpose would be worse than useless, but handfuls of sand thrown with force at a blazing fuse or frame extinguish the flames and leave the instruments and wires comparatively uninjured.

The most picturesque and entertaining adjunct of Telephone London is the electrophone. There is not a leading theatre, concert-room, or music-hall but has the electrophone transmitters—in shape like cigar-boxes—installed before the footlights, out of sight of the audience. They are at the Royal Opera, Covent Garden; and in many of the principal places of worship a wooden dummy Bible in the pulpit bears the preacher's words, by means of the N.T.C. telephone lines, to thousands of invalid or crippled listeners in bed or chair in their homes or hospitals. It was thus that Queen Victoria, seated at Windsor Castle, heard 2,000 school children in Her Majesty's Theatre, in the Haymarket, cheer her and sing "God Save the Queen" on her last birthday. King Edward was likewise relieved from *ennui* at Buckingham Palace during his illness, for the brightest music, mirth, and song of London were ever on tap at his side. Queen Alexandra is also a devotee of the electrophone, more especially throughout the opera season. On the other hand, the cruel lot of certain hospital patients, of the blind, and even the deaf—for the microphonic capacity of the electrophone enables all but the stone-deaf to hear—is thus greatly brightened by science. The sadness of the bedridden, the incurable, or the sufferer from contagious disease is enlivened by sacred or secular song and story, and, as a much-to-be-welcomed addition to the alleviations of London's strenuous life, the benefits of the electrophone are innumerable. It may be added that in the imposingly decorated salon in Gerrard Street from time to time fashionable parties assemble and "taste" the whole of London's entertainments in one evening.

Thus, over mammoth aërial and subterranean wire-webs does London, annihilating distance, work and play by the aid of Science.

IN A BREWERY HOP LOFT.

LONDON'S BREWERIES AND DISTILLERIES.

By C. DUNCAN LUCAS.

METAL DISC USED
AS MONEY.

TO-DAY we have arranged to see something of London's lakes and rivers—lakes and rivers not of water, but of strong ale, brown stout, and gin, and other alcoholic beverages. Nearly every locality has its river of ale flowing on night and day as swiftly and as restlessly as its teetotal neighbour the Thames. Breweries may not be as common as churches, but they make up a formidable catalogue. In central London we have the great Horseshoe Brewery of Messrs. Meux & Co.; in the south-west the establishment of Messrs. Watney & Co., while dotted here and there are the breweries of Messrs. Courage & Co., Messrs. Barclay, Perkins & Co., Messrs. Whitbread, and Messrs. Mann & Crossman—to mention only a few of the many firms who help to swell the tide of beer demanded by London's multitudes.

Let us visit one of these breweries. The gates have just been thrown open and there is scarcely room to turn, but the sight is well worth any discomfort we may have to suffer. The average Londoner has not yet come down to his breakfast, for it is but half-past seven; but here fifty men, each with a leather apron strung round him, have been at their labours since six o'clock. Their particular mission in life is to cope with London's thirst, and the day's campaign will leave them spent and weary. They are loading a dozen drays, some with casks weighing seventeen hundredweight. Their backs are like iron, and we admire their physique almost as much as we do that of the huge glossy-skinned horses which cost the

AN ORDER FOR BEER.

brewer five and seventy guineas apiece. Round, sturdy, with arms that a professional strong man might envy, they are a type by themselves. Yet they are nimble, these latter-day Samsons, despite their ample proportions, and in an amazingly short space of time each dray with its liquid freight is ready for its journey. That one by the gate, with the three massive well-groomed horses which heads the procession, is supporting five tons of bitter beer. It is bound for Woolwich.

We will now ascend 150 steps to the top

in the distance reveals some mysterious moving objects on the floor; there is a patter of soft feet, followed by a wild, unearthly cry. But there is really nothing to be alarmed at. The disturbers of our peace of mind are the eight four-legged policemen of the loft— veteran felines of a bloodthirsty temperament retained to murder maim, and otherwise molest any mice that may attempt to dine off hops, of which there are 6,000 bulky pockets.

They are going to brew a veritable ocean of beer to-day, for it is the summer season,

FILLING PUNCHEONS AT A DISTILLERY.

of the brewery, where the malt bins are situated. The bins are fifty-eight feet in depth, and one being half empty three stout men are hauling up sacks from the yard and replenishing it. In a few hours the bin will contain 225 tons of malt.

A little care must be exercised as we enter the hop-loft, for the place is in darkness. If daylight were allowed to penetrate the apartment the hops would deteriorate, and people would anathematise their beer. So we grope stealthily forward, to be seized presently with an uncanny feeling that there are ghosts in the chamber. A faint shaft of sunshine

and orders from publicans are pouring in by every post. The managers are on the alert, determined that not a moment shall be lost. Outside the hop loft perspiring men are shooting down pockets at the rate of one a minute, while down below another battalion of weight-lifters are receiving the pockets, weighing them, and carrying them off on trolleys to a gigantic copper half full of boiling wort. In go the hops, and the contents of the copper will in due course suffice to charge 1,000 barrels.

Hard by is a regiment of men who look as if they resided in a chalk pit. They are the millers, and are shifting malt. Bag-load after bag-load is emptied into a hopper, the machinery begins to roar, and before many minutes have elapsed the malt has been ground.

On the next floor we witness what is, perhaps, the most singular sight that a brewery has to present. The gigantic tub—big enough to swim in—is called the mash-tun. The mash is a mixture of the various grains that go to make beer. Iron arms propelled by powerful engines are revolving and churning the grains. In the centre of the tub a couple of red-faced men divested of every shred of attire save their unmention-ables and their boots are furiously digging out the grains as the liquid filters through. The temperature is tropical. These two perspiring men have spent years in the mash-tun, yet the heat taxes them to the uttermost. They have a thirst that is literally chronic—an incurable, unquenchable thirst. Witness the bucket of beer in the centre of the tun. It is no tankard, but a real

bucket as large as a coalscuttle, and they dip into it every few minutes. They cannot help themselves. They must either drink or lay down their tools. Nature permits of no alter-native.

The making of beer is thirsty work, and as a consequence all brewers' *employés* are allowed a certain amount of free liquor. Some have half a dozen pots a week, some a dozen—the quantity depends on how dusty their individual occupation happens to be. But only the mash-tun men obtain beer from the brewery. The others get their liquor from certain public-houses with which the brewer does business. On Monday morning each man receives an order—similar to the one reproduced on page 120—for the measure of beer to which he is entitled. This order he presents to the publican, who gives him in exchange a number of metal discs of varying denominations. There are penny discs, three-halfpenny discs, twopenny discs, threepenny discs, and fourpenny discs. Consequently for his drinks during the week the thirsty worker does not pay in coin of the realm, but in discs. If it pleases him to have twopenny worth of beer he places a twopenny disc on the counter ; if fourpennyworth, a fourpenny disc. A point also worth noting is that in return for these discs the publican is strictly enjoined only to supply ale, porter, or stout—never spirits. The discs are available for any length of time, and are generously transferable.

A word in this connection concerning the draymen. Peep through that window at the public - house opposite. Three stalwarts are manœuvring with a barrel of pale ale weighing close upon a ton. Each one of them turns the scale at fifteen stone, and the muscles of their arms stand out like whipcords. It is frightful work, yet the men seem to enjoy it. The fact is they are favoured mortals. At every inn where they deliver beer they are welcome to a meal. It is to the large amount of food that they

EXCISE OFFICER UNLOCKING A STILL.

CLEANING AND STACKING
BEER BARRELS.

case may be, the beer flows into the
cellars.

This morning the cellars are crammed
with men. Through indiarubber pipes
beer is percolating in all directions. The
big fellows in the
white smocks and
the brown paper
caps are the tun
men. The group
on the right are
filling barrels with
India pale ale ;
that on the left
are looking after
the needs of those
whose favourite
beverage is stout.

At the back of
the premises men
are fetching away
the grains which have been used in the
making of the beer. These grains will be
ultimately eaten by cattle.

Outside in the yard the scene is equally
animated. The draymen with the day's
orders have vanished, but their place has
been taken by the barrel cleaners—a dozen
of them. There are hundreds of barrels
to clean this morning. One by one they are
rolled up and placed over steam pipes.
Through the hole in the cask the bustling
engine shoots up a cloud of steam, and in a
moment the barrel is ready for another supply
of beer.

As we wend our way out we see a dapper,
jolly-looking gentleman enter a neat brougham.
He is the collector—a responsible member of
the firm, whose business it is to call at the
various hostelries which are tied to the
brewery and bring away the money that is
owing. His rounds are long, for his brewery
has many houses under its wing. From each
one he emerges with a bag containing cheques,
bank-notes, and coin, and by the time he
reaches home in the evening he has as much
property in his possession as he knows what
to do with.

Thus is the brewing industry carried on.
For enabling us to look behind the scenes of
Beer-land, and for many useful hints on the
subject, as well as for facilities for taking
photographs, our cordial thanks are due to

consume and also to
the muscular exercise
that is involved in lowering casks into the
publican's cellar that they owe their immense
strength.

But we must hasten our steps. Our guide
is inviting us to inspect the "wort"—the
liquor is not beer until the process of ferment-
ation has begun—after it has left the mash-
tun. *En route* we obtain a glimpse of the
brewer in his office. Though not necessarily
one of the proprietors he is, perhaps, the most
important individual in the establishment,
for it is his duty to see that the beer brewed
is of the proper quality. On a shelf in his
room is a row of bottles filled with different
kinds of ale. Just now he is tasting them.
Withdrawing a sample from each bottle, he
puts it in his mouth, pauses, deliberates, and
then expels it. He never drinks it.

Presently we arrive at the beer tuns, or
settling backs—enormous metal tubs full of
frothy liquid. The froth in this one is six
inches high. It is gradually dying away and
the yeast is rising.

Further on we examine the refrigerators—
rows upon rows of pipes full of cold water.
On these coolers the "wort" drops as it flows
from the settling backs.

From the refrigerators the "wort" runs
into the fermenting tuns. Altogether there
are twenty-nine tuns, some of them capable
of holding 750 barrels. Having remained in
the tuns for a week or a fortnight, as the

Messrs. Meux & Co., of the Horseshoe Brewery, Tottenham Court Road, whose ales and stout have been second to none since the days of George IV.

We will now pay a visit to a distillery. It is needless to stay long, for much that takes place in a distillery is to be seen in a brewery. More-over, the various processes are so severely technical that we shall content ourselves with merely a general view of the operations. In the mill room they

FETCHING AWAY GRAINS FROM A BREWERY.

are grinding barley and oats as fast as they can go, while in another department we see the crushed grains passing into the mash tuns. Here the grains are subjected to the action of water and thoroughly mashed up by a great shaft which revolves by machinery. This done, the wort, as it is called, is con-veyed to a vessel where it is allowed to stand for a while when it passes through the refrigerators to the colossal fermenting squares, in which it is converted by the influence of yeast into alcohol and carbonic acid.

We will now make for a rectifying house, whither the spirit is taken from the distillery.

There is enough gin on the premises we enter to float a Thames steamer. Those great vats against the wall contain from 40,000 to 50,000 gallons of duty-paid spirit. It is the busiest hour of the day, and the whole staff is filling puncheons. These, when fully charged, are rolled to the yard adjacent to be piled on the vans, which will soon dis-tribute them over the length and breadth of London and over a considerable portion of the world as well.

Watch that excise officer with the red moustache. He seems to have eyes all over him, and his curiosity is unbounded. He can tell you to an ounce how much spirit there is in the building. For the big cask that stands beside him he has charged £70

by way of duty. The spirit, which is made from malt, maize, and oats, has come in from the grain distilleries, of which there are but three or four in London. The law does not permit of a grain distillery being erected within a mile of a rectifying house; conse-quently London's distillers are, for the most part, merely purifiers of the raw spirit.

In that big still in front of us 3,000 gallons of spirit are being rectified. When the process of purification is complete this fluid will be flavoured—in other words converted into gin—but the still is locked; and before the fluid can pass out our friend the excise officer must produce the keys. There are stills in all directions—some full, some empty—but not a drop of spirit can be touched or made without the aid of the excise man. He holds the keys of the stills, and is more the master here than the owners. Presently he appears and proceeds towards an iron box which is rivetted to the wall. The box is padlocked, and in the keyhole is a ticket made of a special kind of paper bearing certain marks. It was placed there this morning. If anyone had tampered with the lock the marks on the ticket would now be obliterated, but they are intact, and all is well. The representative of the Revenue Department slowly unlocks the padlock, and from the box withdraws his bunch of keys. This done he goes to the still, which he saw charged six hours ago, and setting the vessel free, the spirit begins to trickle down into the cellars, where it is flavoured.

From the flavouring chambers it flows through pipes into receivers, from which it is thrown up into vats by an engine at the rate of 100 gallons a minute. When the still is empty the excise officer will lock it again and replace his keys in the iron box, and put another ticket in the keyhole. He is a cautious man, the revenue officer who watches over the distilleries. Messrs. O. H. Smith & Co., Messrs. Boord, Messrs. Seager, Evans & Co., Messrs. Daun & Vallentin, Messrs. Booth, Messrs. Nicholson, and all the other London distillers are as intimately acquainted with him as they are with their own clerks, for he visits them five times a day.

As we wander here and there we come upon the great vats—twelve of them. Those half-dozen brawny men with the wooden rakes are "rousing" the vats. One of them is from the country—a new hand—and shows signs of being somewhat overcome. He is dazed, and no wonder, for he has to lean over the vats and rake the spirit, a necessary task, for the reason that if the liquid is not stirred the spirit, being lighter than the added water, comes to the top and is drawn off first in an undiluted state when the vat is tapped.

Notwithstanding the nature of the work, however, and the ease with which spirits can be obtained, intoxication is a thing practically unknown in a distillery. Observe those men sitting round that vat in the corner. They are drinking, not gin, but tea. Not that they are denied free spirits, for they get their full share, as we gather from the appended notice exhibited outside the tasting room :—

Workmen employed here are allowed drinks, if required, at the following times during the day and at no other :

6 a.m. 8 to 9 a.m. 11 a.m. 1 p.m. 4 p.m.

Further there is always on tap a glass of good beer, which the men are encouraged to drink in preference to spirits.

A visit to the sample room, in which we watch the taster at his work, and we are out in the yard once more in time to see a van drive off with 600 gallons of best London gin.

It remains to be added that for assistance kindly rendered during our tour of inspection through Spirit-land, and for permission to obtain photographs, we have to thank Messrs. Daun & Vallentin, proprietors of the famous Lambeth Distillery.

Thus does London get a great portion of her beer and spirits. That the two trades afford employment to thousands it is scarcely necessary to remark.

LOWERING CASKS INTO A PUBLICAN'S CELLARS.

IN WORMWOOD SCRUBS PRISON.

By MAJOR ARTHUR GRIFFITHS.

AS London grows crime increases, although not exactly in direct ratio ; nevertheless the processes of detection, coercion, and punishment must be constantly enlarged. While existing prisons have been greatly improved, other establishments have been added from time to time, and one of the chief of these is the great edifice on Wormwood Scrubs. It stands, with its four wings and adjacent buildings, on the fringe of that large open space, once the principal duelling ground of London, where the Duke of York shot at Colonel Lennox, and where many other quarrels, social and political, were fought out. Nowadays Wormwood Scrubs is better known to Londoners as the drill ground for Household Cavalry or as a place where Volunteers practise at rifle butts and "sportsmen" destroy pigeons. The sterner uses of the place are seen in the black vans that wend their way daily along the prison road, bringing fresh contingents of wrong-doers to expiate their offences, or, again, in the daily exodus, soon after breakfast, of the ragged riff-raff, newly released, and delighted to be once more at large.

Wormwood Scrubs is essentially a prison for "doing time"—where all incarcerated, male and female, have been sentenced to imprisonment, principally for short periods. Convicts, however, or, more precisely, penal servitude prisoners, also come for the earlier part of their penalty. Yet inmates of another entirely distinct class are detained within the walls, and for no fault of their own—the poor, blameless infants who have drawn their first breath in the prison or are so young that they cannot be separated from their mothers, and are thus cradled in crime. Convicts and children : its whole population is comprised within these two extremes—the poles of the prison world. Too often, it may be feared, the outcome is the sequel to the start. To have been born or suckled in

Photo Soper & Stedman, Strand, W.C.

WOMEN AT EXERCISE IN THE PRISON YARD : BABY PARADE.

durance is the inalienable heritage of woe. The child is father to the man ; the hapless victim to environment and early vicious associations drifts back to its birthplace, and through chance—misfortune it may be—or nostalgia succumbs to destiny. Yet in many cases the prison born are better off than the free born —more cared for, more delicately nurtured than those who have first seen the light and have been dragged up in the purlieus and dark dens of the town. Prison mothers are generally a pattern to their sex. Discipline apart, and the stimulus it gives to good behaviour, there are no disturbing emotions within the walls, no incentives to neglect of offspring, no drink, no masterful men, no temptation to thieve or go astray ; and thus their better feelings, their purer maternal instincts, have full play. So the prison baby has, for the most part, a good time. High officials, visitors, matron, warders, all are glad to pet and cosset it, there is plenty of wholesome food, it has toys to play with, fresh air and exercise in its mother's arms, while its nursery, though no doubt a cell, is bright, well-ventilated, not ill-furnished with its comfortable cot, and

is scrupulously clean. Moreover, when the prison mother is drawn elsewhere by the necessities of her daily toil, she knows that her baby will be well cared for in the prison nursery or *crèche.*

Between this embryo criminal and the finished full-blown specimen there are many degrees and categories, nearly all of them to be found in Wormwood Scrubs, their antecedents very varied, their characters dissimilar, but their condition and treatment much the same. The records show that there are thieves in all lines of business — from the pickpocket to the garroter. The burglar, the forger, the fraudulent financier, the dishonest clerk are to be found here, and every kind of felon and misdemeanant is subjected to the same *régime.* In principle the rule of "strict separation" is enforced, but not solitary confinement, for that form of torture has long been abandoned by us. We have escaped the bitter reproach contained in the well-known lines by Coleridge :—

PRISONERS GOING TO DINNER.

> As he went through Cold Bath Fields he saw
> A solitary cell ;
> And the Devil was pleased, for it gave him a hint
> For improving his prisons in Hell.

IN THE WOMEN'S WORK ROOM.

Photo, Soper & Stedman, Strand, W.C.

the hymns, which are sung with great heartiness; and, again, in the yards it is said that men can talk by the movement of their lips and without making audible sound. To see one another, to make signs, to speak together, although not, of course, freely, are so many sets-off against the irksome rule of separation imposed on them.

In those old days the victims to far-fetched theory went mad after long periods of unbroken seclusion. Now all British prisoners are segregated: they are located, each one, in a separate cell or small room; that is to say, when they are not under discipline and observation. They are alone when at leisure, when feeding, sleeping, resting from labour; alone, as a general rule when at work, although some forms of labour are now carried out in common.

The isolation is never continuous, even for those kept in cells; it is broken by constant visits. The governor comes daily and the chaplain, the doctor, and other superior officers; the trade instructors and schoolmaster also spend much time with each pupil. Then there is the break for Divine service and again for exercise, when the prisoners leave their cells to pass along the galleries and file down the light staircases out into the open yards. Silence is sternly prescribed, but it cannot be invariably maintained. In chapel especially, seated close together, it is easy to communicate. Conversation passes under cover of

Of late the prison authorities have gone further, and now permit the well-conducted, after a brief period of separation, to be associated in their daily work. This is the case at Wormwood Scrubs, where the ground floors of the great halls are converted into rough and ready ateliers, and such simple trades are prosecuted as post-bag making, mat making, basket making, and the manufacture of rope. True artisans and handicraftsmen, those who acquired their

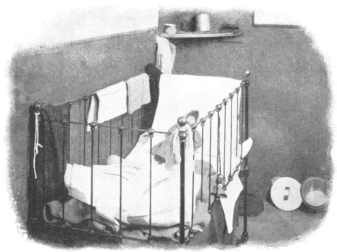

Photo: Soper & Stedman, Strand, W.C. A BABY'S COT.

skill "outside" and those who have had the wit to learn something inside, are largely utilised in the service of the State. The outcry against prison competition has limited the quantity and quality of output, but no one can complain if the Government works for itself. So you will see that much tin-ware is turned out in the "shops," that the prison carpenters produce boxes of all sorts for his Majesty's Post Office, that coal sacks for the Navy, bedding and blankets for the Army, are manufactured largely in prison. The work-rooms at Wormwood Scrubs are hives of intelligently conducted industry, and very satisfactory results are obtained. There are prison dressmakers, cutters-out, fitters, machine workers, milliners; and the female officers' uniforms, costumes, cloaks, and bonnets would not discredit a West-End place of business. In the bootmakers' shop a brisk trade is done; the tailors are genuine "snips," glad enough to be employed to keep their hands in; the bookbinder is an expert, who, although not quite a Derôme or a Grolier, deftly and neatly remedies the incessant wear and tear of the prison library. Long previous training is not needed in the kitchen: muscular strength only is indispensable for the handling of great sides of beef, for carrying heavy cans and dinner trays, but

activity and good-will are essential, and the daily toil of the prison cooks is severe. Skilled bakers may be scarce in the prison world, but the art of bread-making is kept up here by tradition, transmitted from generation to generation, and there is never much fault to find with the "whole meal" loaves that come out of the prison ovens. The prison has a claim to the best efforts of the inmates in any capacity. All the house service is performed by them — cleaning, painting, white-washing, gardening, and the removal of produce in hand carts to which they are harnessed or which they push about the enclosure.

The industrial side in Wormwood Scrubs is its pleasantest, and is rightly thrown into strongest relief. There is another aspect, the disciplinary, the methods and processes by which good behaviour is ensured, and yet another, the reformatory influences applied by religious and friendly agencies. As a rule, there is little misconduct of a serious kind in Wormwood Scrubs. The offences that mostly crop up are due to temper, too often, but not unnaturally, hot and hasty; to ingrained idleness, showing itself in a strong dislike of work. Grave acts of insubordination are rare; assaults upon warders, overt attempts at mutiny all but unknown. The

BOOTMAKING.

coercion and the penalties inflicted are mild enough, and generally limited to the reduction of diet and close confinement, although in the twelvemonth cases of corporal punishment with the birch—not the cat—may number half a dozen. The offence most ex-

IN THE KITCHEN.

cusable to the lay mind, and most heinous in official eyes—escape—is but seldom attempted, at least with success, in Wormwood Scrubs. A man on one occasion, however, broke prison by ingeniously cutting his way out, though he was captured the same evening. So little fear is there of escape that prisoners are sent to work at some distance from the prison guarded only by a couple of warders, and this within sight and earshot of London. Moral control is found to be quite as effective as bolts and bars. That crime should be prevented rather than punished is daily gaining great force as an axiom in social science. This humane view extends also to prison life. The most earnest wish of the authorities at Wormwood

Scrubs is not to force, but to persuade; to keep their charges well in hand, but to impress upon them that when their offence is once purged they should no more return to gaol. The prison chaplain, ever an active influence for good, is nowadays greatly aided by kindly folk who have made the criminal their special care, and by whose noble endeavours so many societies and institutions have been called into existence to assist the well-intentioned to go straight after release.

No description of the present palatial establishment at Wormwood Scrubs would be complete without some brief reference to its first beginnings, the manner in which it was planted and gradually grew into such imposing dimensions. The method adopted for its erection was a new departure, at least, in this country. It had been tried a century before at Sing-Sing, in the United States, and our practice has since been imitated in Austria-Hungary and in France. The whole work was executed by prison labour. The idea originated in 1874 with General Sir Edmund du Cane, an eminent Royal Engineer and publicist, at that time head of the Prison Department, who was the architect and designer of the edifice and the controlling spirit throughout The preliminaries executed by contract consisted of the shell of a small prison of corrugated iron having a wall one brick thick, and a fence or hoarding with wooden gates and a small temporary lodge. Another shed served as kitchen and lodging for the warder staff.

AT WORK OUT-OF-DOORS.

This was in the winter of 1874. Nine specially selected convicts, men of good character and within a year of release, were now lodged in the only cells with doors and locks, comparatively secure. These pioneers completed the building, and with the accommodation thus provided fifty more prison lodgers were brought in—a sufficient force to erect a second prison wing and raise the population to a hundred all told. Building operations for the great permanent prison then began in earnest. A first necessity was "ballast"—the burnt clay of the London district; it was needed for road-making and as one of the constituents of mortar. At the same time clay, dug up on the spot, was prepared and treated to form "kerf," the material from which bricks are manufactured. All this time the numbers steadily increased; there were ere long a couple of hundred hands on the job; and as the summer of 1875 advanced bricks had been burnt and stacked ready to be built into the first great block or hall, the ground floor of which was finished as winter approached. This floor, although open to the sky, was, however, used as a receptacle for convicts, only a small pent-house, with small tarpaulin roof, being put up as cover to the cell doors.

So the work proceeded steadily, without stint or difficulty, the felon bees industriously adding cell to cell in the hive, and presently the four great parallel blocks were pushed forward towards completion. Each building was a self-contained prison, and one and all had been the perfected work of convict hands; every brick having been made, every stone dressed and laid, every bar forged, every door raised and strengthened by the class for whom it has since been a place of penitence and expiation.

IN THE ARTISANS' WORKSHOP.

ST. JAMES'S PALACE: CHANGING THE GUARD.

SOME OF LONDON'S CHIEF SIGHTS.

By JAMES BARR.

TO me it came as quite a new experience. When, early in the morning, we two set out to drift through London, I understood that I was to show my friend the sights of the place. This, surely, was a natural supposition on my part, for much of my life had been spent in London, and he only arrived on his first visit the evening before. However, before I was long in the company of my Colonial friend I learned that I need not have lived in London to know her, and know her pretty thoroughly. On this day I met with the experience of being shown over the Metropolis by a complete stranger. He had, I found, studied Thackeray, learned Dickens by heart, deciphered Stow, and encompassed Besant and Cunningham, and for years had dreamed of visiting London. At length his longings were satisfied.

We were in Kensington; so early the hour that the pavement of the narrow High Street was not yet a crush of gaily dressed ladies (themselves here one of Living London's most attractive sights) gazing in at the riches of the shop windows.

The trend of vehicles and pedestrians was Citywards; loaded 'buses rocked and rattled on to the east, foot passengers hurried towards the arisen sun. We two seemed the only ones who were not obliged to hurry. My friend strolled on in silence. It seemed that the realisation of his life's dream oppressed him with overjoy.

"And this is Kensington Gardens," he said at the very earliest glimpse. It was, and we at once entered.

I hoped he would miss Kensington Palace, so that I could assert myself as really the one of us who knew London. But no. He stood for some few minutes and gazed at the building.

"Do you know that does not at all come up to my preconceived ideas of the birthplace of good Queen Victoria? I thought of a palace—there stands a home. Yet when one comes to think of it surely it is the most fitting birthplace for one whose life was of the cottage as much as, even more than, of the palace. Yes, I like the look of the place, the atmosphere and attitude of it. By the way, Queen

Victoria's rag dolls and primitive toys are shown to the public, are they not? Let us go in and see them. No doubt there will be a group of rosy-cheeked children gazing with big-eyed wonder upon a rag doll of a sort that, were one offered to them, they would push it away with scorn. Children are becoming more and more luxurious—quicker than grown-ups. Let us go in."

"Do you realise what hour in the morning it is? The official mind has not begun to wake as yet."

"Of course, you are right. There is nothing in the world that acts with such mechanical regularity as the mind of what we'll call a museum authority. It automatically opens at ten, and automatically closes at four. As ten is an hour's length distant, and we have a long drift before us—let us drift. What is that standing in front of the Palace? A statue of Queen Victoria—I know by the poise even from this distance. I want to see it."

"'By her daughter,'" mused my Colonial friend. "That must mean Princess Louise (Duchess of Argyll). A most impressive statue it is, too. The Queen at her loveliest."

"If you intend to stand all day gazing upon one statue, our drift ends here——"

"Having placed myself in your hands, I will not be bustled, you know; but if you insist, very well, we'll continue our saunter. Hullo! what's this? The

'Round Pond,' I do believe. And, yes, there are two tiny yachts slanting across followed by the admiring eyes of children and the grown-up owners striding round to meet the incoming craft. Why, I have seen this picture a thousand times since I was a boy. Every illustrated paper in the universe has reproduced the pond, its daintily-fashioned craft, and serious-faced owners of the same."

Next we made for the Albert Memorial. As we walked he talked. The huddle of fat sheep that feed in the park struck him as a quaintly countrified sight in the heart of great London; the banks of rhododendrons, flaunting their colours; the walks already crowded with clean-faced nursemaids wheeling glittering "prams" containing the youngest generation of the wealthy—every sight appealed to his heart, and each was an old acquaintance of whom he had something to tell me. He mounted the steps of the Memorial to minutely examine the sculptures of the famous ones who sit, as it were, at the feet of Prince Albert, and then stood back to gaze upon the gilded minarets.

The riders out for an exhilarating airing in Rotten Row drew my friend from his inspection of the great round hall and glittering monument. We took our time in making our way towards Hyde Park Corner, for he would peer over the stone-capped wall and in at the semi-circular windows of the mews of Knightsbridge Cavalry Barracks to catch a glimpse of a soldier attending to a charger; and paused to admire the floral decorations of the Barracks themselves. Then we cut across the Row to the Serpentine, and he quickly discovered the gipsy corner of ferns and frondose growths among

THE ALBERT MEMORIAL.

which stands the great grey stone. As we stood before this my friend suddenly turned to me and demanded :

"Are we near the statue of Achilles? Surely it is in this neighbourhood !"

And thither we proceeded.

"So that is Achilles! But where are the surging crowds of protesting people? Where are the orators haranguing the gathering from extempore platforms? This is the first thing I have seen in London which does not look quite familiar. In my mind Achilles and protest are inseparably associated. I almost wish that some great wrong was being done to the British people so that the thunderers at this moment might have gathered their hosts in angry opposition. Really there should always be a make-believe crowd about this statue, a crowd that would move on whenever genuine protesters marched in at the gates. And that's Byron over there! Well, well, he's appropriately placed in this portal of protest. We can step from here into Green Park, can we not? And that's on the way to Buckingham Palace."

After admiring Wellington's statue opposite the gates, along Constitution Hill we went, and soon came before the broad, plain face of Buckingham Palace. This, the second palace we had seen, did not appeal to my Colonial friend. It was, he said, less like a palace than Kensington Palace even. After a hasty glance at its front, he refused to look any more at it.

"No, no. Like many another plain thing, its pictures have flattered it. There is something kindly about Kensington Palace; this is both harsh and unpoetic. By the way, I have often read of the Royal Mews. I wonder if they would let us peep in for a glimpse at the horses. I have heard that the stables cover about as much ground as the Palace itself."

So round we tramped to Buckingham Gate, and to the huge delight of my friend were admitted to the model stables, clean, spacious, and occupied by beautiful horses beautifully groomed. Had it not been that time was limited, my friend would have liked to spend hours in the Royal Mews.

We were most fortunate in the hour of our arrival at St. James's Palace. Before

quitting the Mall I was able to palm off my first item of information, and this fact greatly cheered me.

"If I am not mistaken, we are just in time to witness the changing of the Guard at St. James's," I said.

The crowd had already collected, and the band, as we came up, began to play for the picturesque ceremony. In any other city on the globe this pageant would daily call forth such a concourse of people as to necessitate special regulations. But London is apathetic regarding matters musical and spectacular unless they be much heralded in the Press; and the gay scene, with its grand music, of this changing of the Guard depends for its audience upon passers-by. We stood in the gathering, and my friend followed every move of the brilliant uniformed soldiers, and drank in each strain of the swelling music.

At length I had found a palace which he agreed really looked its part. Old St. James's delighted his eye: the red brick showing the fingermarks of time, the castle-like arches and terraces, the broad-faced honest clock between the towers. Yes, St. James's Palace was indeed a palace. Then his thoughts harked back to the pageant of the changing of the Guard.

"What a vivid splash of colour in the heart of this grey old town !" was all he said as I dragged him away to catch a glimpse of the Duke of York's column, the statue of Sir John Franklin, and the Guards' Memorial in Waterloo Place. By way of Pall Mall we passed into Trafalgar Square; and, of course, I found he knew all about the statue of Charles I. that had been buried during the Commonwealth and dug up at the Restoration, and before I could point to it he had noticed the National Gallery. He decided to enter the Gallery, not with the intention of staying any great time, but only to take a glimpse at the Turner Room. Turner he named "the Hermit of London," and said that his pictures could only have been painted by one who had been bred under London's dull skies, and as a consequence relished the full glory of gorgeous sunsets and brilliant atmospheres. Into the Strand we then made our way, turning down Villiers

KENSINGTON PALACE : INSPECTING QUEEN VICTORIA'S PLAYTHINGS.

THE NATIONAL GALLERY : LOOKING AT TURNER'S PICTURES.

ST. PAUL'S CATHEDRAL: WELLINGTON'S TOMB.

doctor to take us into the quiet of St. Bartholomew's Hospital open-air enclosures. My friend would not look into Smithfield Meat Market— he disliked such sights—but carefully copied down the inscription to the martyrs who were buried here in Smithfield. We walked along Little Britain, passed the statue of Sir Robert Peel at the western end of Cheapside, and as the day proved close I was glad to get into the cool and quiet of the mighty cathedral of St. Paul's. But my friend's energy proved unflagging. Although resolved to leave the Cathedral proper for another day, he decided to descend into the crypt. So we paid our sixpences and went down.

Here we found that there were other tourists abroad. A group chiefly composed of girls stood gazing on the tomb of Wellington, and to them a young woman was talking in a low yet clear voice. And, for about the

Street for the Embankment. The instant he caught sight of the tip of Cleopatra's Needle he named it, and told me its history; Burns's statue in the Gardens he knew, having a replica in miniature of it on his desk at home; and when he was forced to admit that he did not know who the other statue in the gardens represented, and I told him it was Robert Raikes, founder of the Sunday schools, he pretended he had no interest in him, having been forced to Sunday school too often in his youth. But he took a lively interest in the Chapel Royal, Savoy Street, for the poet Wither, one of his favourites, lay buried there. By the time we had strolled through Covent Garden, gazed on the Opera and Drury Lane Theatre, and walked the length of Drury Lane, both my friend and I were hungry. So we had lunch.

We walked along High Holborn, and spent some time in examining the ancient buildings that front Gray's Inn Road; the Viaduct, too, was rich in interest to him. As soon as he had satisfied his cravings in regard to the Old Bailey, he asked for the Church of St. Sepulchre, wherein rest the remains of Captain John Smith, Governor of Virginia. Having been shown the tomb, we walked along Giltspur Street, and induced a young

Photo. York & Son, Notting Hill, W.
ON SENTRY AT WHITEHALL.

first time this day, I managed to give my companion a pleasing little piece of cheap information.

"You see the young woman conducting the party ? She is one of the lady guides of London. One hears but little of them, but they are very much sought after—for one thing, for instance, by folk who wish girls from the provinces met at the station,

"Do you know the keynote of London ? " he asked me as he ran his eye over the glorious tree. "Her rurality. I never saw a more rural city ; she is a succession of country villages, and the verdure of her is striking. I can well understand that London is the most livable, lovable city in the world."

By this time I thought we had walked a long way, but my robust friend strode on

LONDON BRIDGE AND THE RIVER AS SEEN FROM THE TOP OF THE MONUMENT.

shown through London, and safely sent on their way. Londoners know but little of these ladies, for they are quiet and unobtrusive, yet safe and pleasant guardians and guides.

"Now, if you can tear yourself away, I will show you where for so many years the Blue-coat boys were schooled."

My Colonial would not spend time in looking at the General Post Office buildings. They struck him as too modern to be interesting in London ; and consequently we pushed on along Cheapside. To be sure, his eyes could not miss the famous plane tree of Wood Street.

He insisted on remaining till Bow Bells chimed, and then we spent a quarter of an hour waiting for the figures above a watch-maker's shop hard by to strike. As he had set his mind upon seeing the Monument, I hurried him past the Mansion House and Bank, past King William's statue, and when we reached the foot of the great shaft, to my consternation, I learned that he wanted to climb to the top. My knees were already knocking together ; there was nothing for it, however, but to follow where he led. A hard climb for tired men, but a noble view ! The sky was overcast, the sun obscured and.

as we learned, the atmospheric conditions were nearly the very best for sight-seeing from a high altitude that London provides. The roar of the streets reached us not in individual notes but in a massy blend of great chords; and far down below tiny vehicles and tinier men crawled thick in the narrow streets, while the river lay like a length of

London Stone. An apple woman, old and placid of face, displayed her wares; and my friend glanced from the stone to the woman, and from the woman to the stone. As we walked away to take the Underground train he talked to me something about how he had evolved a theory which, stated briefly, was that inanimate objects through centuries of

CHANGING GUARD AT THE HORSE GUARDS.

broad, dull coloured ribbon. London Bridge was a scramble of moving midgets. Above the city of brick and stone hung a city, fantastical, ever changing, of smoke. Even I felt glad we had clambered up for the view.

When we were descending the spiral stair my friend informed me that he would like to end a day of sight-seeing by just a glimpse of London's greatest sight, Westminster Abbey.

"We have time, have we not?" he asked eagerly.

"Plenty; indeed, I can show you several other objects and scenes if you like. It is all one to me—my legs have lost feeling; I can go on indefinitely now."

I took him down Cannon Street to where, built in the wall of St. Swithin's Church, is

contact with animate took upon them something of the expression of the latter, and *vice versâ;* but, to tell the truth, I was too footsore to pay much attention to his far-drawn speculations. There being still ample time, we got out at Charing Cross so as to walk down Whitehall. Again we were in luck's way, for on coming opposite the Horse Guards we found the usual knot of interested people witnessing the relief of the guards. The precision with which the well-trained chargers turned in their movements in circumscribed space, the splendour of the troopers' uniforms, the sun glittering on the polished helmets, impressed my friend as a gorgeous little scene. More than this, a sergeant, hearing the acrid accent of my Colonial companion, and himself having been round the world with the colour, invited us to step in and make the acquaintance of the guardroom. There we found many well-set-up, clean, jolly guardsmen, and saw that they spent their time in comfort while at the Horse Guards.

We reached the Abbey in the nick of time. Indeed, I think we were included in the last group of visitors to be shown through Henry VII.'s Chapel. About twenty constituted the party, and a sombre-robed verger, with a voice that was at one and the same time resounding and subdued, gave us a concise and wholly intelligible account of the great ones who lie at rest in England's sanctuary. My friend followed the discourse in eager silence. Then he betook himself to Poets' Corner, and examined the monuments and inscriptions without missing one. It was pleasant to behold his intense yet reverent interest. He carried his hat in hand until we stood upon the pavement of Broad Sanctuary.

"Here ends the greatest day of my life," he said. "There can never be such another day for me. To-morrow I shall be abroad again in London's streets, sight-seeing; but —well, I have had my first kiss: the second cannot be so sweet."

Photo: York & Son, Notting Hill, W.

WESTMINSTER ABBEY : POETS' CORNER.

SCENES FROM SHOP AND STORE LONDON.

By P. F. WILLIAM RYAN.

COMPETITION, we are assured, is the life of trade; and reviewing the hundreds of miles of shops which form so large a fraction of the thousands of miles of streets in the Metropolis one realises its literal truth. Observe and compare shop window with shop window, beginning with the mammoth emporium and ending with the cramped shanty of the byways, and from the richest to the poorest anxiety to attract and please the class catered for is strikingly apparent.

Few women, and still fewer men, can avoid discordant combinations in the arrangement of colours. And the draper has to frame in the space behind a huge panel of glass silks, satins and velvets, carpets, dress materials and woollens, linens, art needlework and hosiery, laces, gloves and mantles, and a hundred other things in a hundred varieties so as to blend the whole into a pleasing colour scheme. The jeweller has little difficulty in arranging his stock, for he relies upon the dazzling properties of his gold and trinkets and precious stones. Mere man stands in wonder before a fashionable confectioner's window. Feminine skill alone could contrive a harmonious picture from coloured sweets, French pastry, cut glass, and gaudy chocolate boxes tied with every shade of ribbon beneath the skies. The perfumer intertwines artificial flowers with plush-covered cases and crystal bottles containing amber decoctions in a desperate attempt to obtain notice for his limited stock. The up-to-date chemist does not disdain glass and silver and velvet in the adornment of his windows. But most delightful to some eyes, at any rate, is the flower and fruit shop glowing with the treasures of garden and greenhouse.

"The stores" is a common phrase in the trivial common talk of everyday life. It is generally understood that at one of those comprehensive emporiums practically everything may be ordered. This is true to a certain extent only, for it must be remembered that there are "stores" which cater for the humblest strata of the middle class. Those are naturally less ambitious in their aims than the establishments which supply the needs of the rich and comparatively rich. Without quitting the premises of one of these latter, with their acres of warerooms, their tireless "lifts," their well-drilled assistants, it is almost impossible to ask for anything which will not be promptly yours. Do you want a house built? You have but to give the necessary instructions. Would you like to decide upon your furniture? In a moment you will find yourself inspecting improvised drawing-rooms and dining-rooms, bedrooms and billiard-rooms, studies and kitchens.

Do you want your greenhouse equipped? From where you stand possibly you can see a tangle of shrubs and plants, and nestling amidst them the flowers of the season in full bloom. Do you love animals? Then visit the zoological department, and buy a monkey or a puppy, a kitten or a canary. A lion or a tiger may not be included in the stock on hand, but if your ambition lies in that direction your order will be booked and the stores van will soon deposit the exile from African veldt or Indian jungle at your doorstep. Your wife can purchase her daughter's trousseau in one room, while in another you obtain the impedimenta incidental to a shooting expedition. Pass through the "lamp and glass" department. It reminds one somehow of a scene in a pantomime, for there are numerous lights though it is noonday, and the flood of colour is rich and dazzling. Next door are washing tubs and washing boards, pails, mangles, and ladders. Pots and pans are not far away. Move on, and you tread on a gorgeous carpet: all around are carpets stacked in huge rolls. One resembling a great green avenue is unfolded that a lady may judge of its effect. Turn in this direction, and you see silks

IN WESTBOURNE GROVE.

FLOWERS AND FRUIT (REGENT STREET).

somehow of pictures by a master of perspective with an exquisite eye for minute detail. This impression that one is looking at a canvas is heightened by the shallowness of the interior of the shops, and the subdued light which even on the hottest midsummer day gives the place an air of retirement and restfulness. The arcades at Ludgate Circus have the advantage of lying close to one of the busiest thoroughfares of the City. Here the requirements of the homely rather than of the luxurious are catered for. The partly covered Electric Avenue at Brixton resembles in many respects an arcade, and attracts patrons from the most distant quarters of the capital.

The system of payment by instalments plays an important part in modern shopkeeping, both in the west and the east. It is impossible to mark off certain districts on a map of London and assign to each a particular class of customers. Of course, those who want the best of everything without regard to cost generally find what they require without leaving the aristocratic quarter of which Bond Street and Regent Street are well-known arteries. But no lady who finds in shopping one of the pleasures of her life fails to make regular pilgrimages to Westbourne Grove. The neighbourhood has an atmosphere of its own. Here shopping assumes the dignity of a cult. The pavements are generally crowded with smartly dressed women chatting earnestly—it is all of prices, bargains, catalogues, and such things. In Westbourne Grove man realises his insignificance. That is probably the reason why his absence is so conspicuous.

The shopkeeper who makes his business pay probably devotes more of his time to his books than to his counter. His world is divided into two classes—those who pay promptly, and the others. The latter are

glistening in glorious little multi-coloured billows, where they are strewn over a long counter for the satisfaction of likely purchasers. A few steps further, and the confectionery department is in sight. Here there are many ladies having lunch. Some are indulging in the trifles on which woman alone can live and thrive—and shop! Others are enjoying fare of the more substantial sort. Full recital of the resources of the "stores" is impossible. When you have bought your medicines, your literature, your pictures, your saddlery, the latest bicycle and electric plant, flowers for the epergnes, bacon, eggs, and vegetables, fish, poultry, boots, and butter, you may, if you have time, step aside and sit for your photograph, having first made a special toilet, beginning with the bath and ending with the hairdresser and manicurist. Even then the "stores" have not been fully explored!

The arcades are an interesting feature of shop life in the Metropolis. The arcades of the west do not supply everything, but whatever they sell is of the best. The Burlington, branching off Piccadilly, is the most important. The Royal, in New Bond Street, is much smaller, but its dainty shops, bright with flowers or with the most artistically coquettish creations of the milliner's art, deserve an amount of attention inversely proportionate to their size. The Burlington reminds one

billed again and again without result. Then the assistance of the trade protection societies is invoked. The tradesman of any standing generally subscribes to one or another of these organisations. The society to which he lends his support will strive to recover his debts by sending round collectors ; and in the last resort will undertake legal proceedings on his behalf, for the shopkeeper dislikes nothing more than to have his name announced in the newspapers as plaintiff in an action for the recovery of debt : his fear is lest irresponsible gossip should brand him as a Shylock.

The shopping districts of London are as diverse, not only in their general appearance, but in their methods, their manners, and their language as though they belonged to different cities. In the west the legend " Ici on parle Français " or " Man spricht Deutsch " emblazoned on window or signboard is an invitation to foreigners to enter and purchase. But the foreigner who is well acquainted with London would not be inconvenienced if all such announcements were effaced. No matter what quarter of the world he comes from, his countrymen have a colony here, and the colony has its shopkeepers. There are shops in the neighbourhood of Leicester Square where everything sold is French, and where sellers and buyers are nearly always of the same nationality. In parts of Soho one might imagine oneself in the slums of a Continental city. Holborn is on the borders of a fashionable shopping world, and when we leave it behind in our progress towards the east we may notice that the shop assistant becomes more direct and abrupt in his manners. These are virtues he never cultivates in the west, where the customer is credited with super-sensitiveness. From Holborn pass into Clerkenwell Road—grimy even in summer. The south side is in the main occupied by warehouses. The north side is one long line of jewellers' and watchmakers' and clockmakers' shops. It is the headquarters of this trade. What wealth lies behind all their dinginess ! You pass a solitary policeman, and his solitariness is impressive when one recollects that this is one of the roughest neighbourhoods in London, and that he stands sentinel over as much gold and silver as would build a battleship. Clerkenwell Road is dull, but Old Street is lively, though the artist who paints its liveliness must not neglect to lay on the drab.

Soon we are in Shoreditch, famous for its furniture trade— furniture cheap and dear, polished and unpolished, good, bad, and

PROVISION DEPARTMENT AT A
BIG STORES (HARROD'S).

indifferent. A few minutes more, and we are in Whitechapel. In the west we bowed to shopkeepers who executed orders valued at thousands of pounds sterling. Now we can introduce ourselves to the shopkeeper whose business is done to a great extent in farthings. Take a glance at a small house in a sunless side street. Its customers are overflowing on to the pavement, for not more than half a dozen people can stand within the threshold. Peering over their heads you catch a glimpse of a room behind the shop. Its walls are

for a ha'porth of pickled onions. The next customer is no miniature, but a navvy life size of thirty years, deep chested and heavy limbed, a leather strap round his waist, a red scarf round his throat, a cap on the back of his close-cropped head. " A farthing's worth of milk." That is his order. There is a pleasant surprise here for the person who supposes the purchase of milk implies possession of a vessel in which to carry it away. The navvy has nothing at all in one of his great brown paws; between the index

BOOK DEPARTMENT AT A BIG STORES (ARMY AND NAVY).

lined with shelves. The shelves are laden with bread, for bread is the principal want here. There are two counters. A man behind one is busy cutting up loaves into small chunks. One would think these were being given away for nothing, they disappear so rapidly. The customers include men and boys, women and children. Their accents are harsh, their clothes coarse, their whole appearance rough ; but there is no pushing or elbowing. Buying and selling proceed like clockwork. A child whose chin barely reaches the counter wants a farthing's worth of sugar. A bareheaded boy of nine or ten with a soiled handkerchief round his throat— a miniature navvy in fact—hands in a plate

finger and thumb of the other he has a farthing. But civilisation in Whitechapel has risen above the tyranny of jugs and mugs and such things. A strong paper bag is slipped into another slightly larger. In this he takes his milk away. Nobody smiles—so much is humour a matter of locality.

When night descends the business of shop-keeping still goes on in all quarters of London removed from the great arteries. The baker weighs out bread. At the other side of the street a newsagent's is still open, though it is long past ten. The contents bills of the evening papers on sale within are ranged outside his door. In his window are cigarettes, notepaper, pens, ink, a piece of cardboard to

WAITING TO BUY "TRIM-
MINGS" OF MEAT.

flour, washing soda, arrowroot, blue, and starch. The little Cockney girl on marketing bent is an amusing person—she takes herself so seriously that, as she hurries from a model dwelling to the nearest ham and beef shop, or to the cooked eel house, she hardly looks to right or to left. Her juvenile friends are ignored, unless she happens to meet a young lady whose status is assured by the fact that she too is engaged on a shopping expedition.

which lead pencils are affixed, a box of Christmas cards, and scrolls emblazoned with Scriptural texts.

A few doors further on is a marine store dealer's. The light of an oil lamp reveals a curious assortment of goods. His stock includes, besides rags and bones, waste paper, old and valueless furniture, veteran bedsteads, mysterious little heaps of battered metal, bottles, and time-worn books. Dolls, wax and wooden, horses and bears, monkeys on tiny painted poles, and other wonderful creatures are in the windows of the little toy shop opposite. They seem to have been there a long time, for the sun has played strange pranks with their complexions, and some of the dolls stand sorely in need of spectacles. The small trader does not worry his soul about what the fastidious would dub incongruities. It is not unusual to come across a shop in a side street which at first sight seems to be an oil and colour store and nothing more. But closer acquaintance reveals sauce bottles with flaring red labels side by side with boot varnish and woollen thread. Beside an oil barrel is often a box of fine Spanish onions; and on the top of the barrel are sundry packages, perhaps containing corn-

Every day broken food is sold on the premises of some of the great London restaurants; and at certain big butchers' and fishmongers' shops "trimmings" of meat and odds and ends of fish, etc., are also purchasable. Such sales are very popular with the poor. On Friday night a great

A FARTHING SHOP IN THE EAST-END.

deal of shopping is done by the wives of workmen paid on that day ; but the following day is distinctly preferred by the people for marketing, and this phase of metropolitan life is described elsewhere in the article on "Saturday Night in London." The small hours of the Sabbath have arrived before Saturday night's shopping has concluded. If the butchers have not then exhausted their stock they open again on Sunday morning, when what remains is sold, even though the proverbial "song" represents the best price obtainable. But this is not the limit of Sunday's trade, for even on the first day of the week shopkeeping London does not rest absolutely. Just as many Jewish houses close on Saturday out of respect for the Hebrew Sabbath, so they open on Sunday by way of compensation. Yet it is not only in the East-End that business is done on Sunday. Some of the streets in Soho, for instance, are crowded with buyers and sellers ; and all over the capital small confectioners', tobacconists', newsvendors', fruiterers', and bakers' shops, as well as dairies and provision dealers, not to speak of licensed houses, are opened on the Sabbath.

Before taking leave of "Shop and Store London," let us turn into Oxford Street at closing time, and watch an army of shop assistants retire from the commercial battle-field after their exhausting day. Their eyes are duller, their cheeks are rather paler, than in the morning. Amongst the streams of women pouring along the footpaths there is only a sprinkling of men. Some of the "shop girls" are women far advanced in years, some are very young. Many are fashionably attired. The majority affect costumes neat and workmanlike rather than showy ; more than a few present a dowdy appearance—they are too weary to care. At the corner of Tottenham Court Road there is lively competition for seats in the omnibuses going north. Hear the sigh of relief when the competitor has been successful! The same scene is being enacted at Oxford Circus, where the lady from Finchley parts company with her sister from Putney. Hasten into Piccadilly. The spectacle here is more confusing, but more impressive for that reason. And on a smaller scale these scenes are being repeated all over London, for the shutters are up—Shopland is deserted by all save the unlucky garrison whose task is almost ceaseless.

OUTSIDE A MARINE STORE DEALER'S.

WAITING FOR THE LIFTS AT THE BANK STATION (CENTRAL LONDON RAILWAY).

UNDERGROUND TRAVELLING LONDON.

By ERIC BANTON.

LONDON is a place of such great distances, and its streets are so crowded with traffic, that the problem of locomotion is a peculiarly difficult one. You cannot drive railways through a great city, for you would destroy the city in the process ; and, pending the arrival of the flying machine, you cannot go from point to point literally " as the crow flies." But modern engineering science is making it possible for us to travel cheaply and quickly between almost any two points in the Metropolis by going beneath the surface. The extent to which underground travelling has been adopted in London is very remarkable. A single electric railway, the Central London —popularly known as the "Twopenny Tube," because it takes you all the way from the Bank to Shepherd's Bush or any intermediate distance for the uniform fare of twopence— carries more than 40,000,000 passengers every year, while the Metropolitan and Metropolitan District Railways between them carry about 130,000,000, of whom the great majority are

travellers on the underground portions of those lines.

Although new tube railways are being made in all directions, they are not likely to supersede our old and much abused friend the original Underground Railway. On the contrary, with the introduction of electric traction, which so greatly adds to the speed and comfort of underground travelling, we may reasonably expect a considerable increase in the number of passengers. It is a curious fact that, though few Londoners have a good word for the Underground, there are few who do not by their continual use of it show their appreciation of its convenience. It was, in truth, a very spirited undertaking which was begun in 1863 and not completed till 1884, the surrounding of the city with a sinuous line of underground railway connecting the principal termini and many important business centres. It involved some remarkable engineering feats, of which perhaps the most notable was that of carrying the tunnel near King's

Cross over the existing tunnel of the Great Northern Railway. For convenience, and to distinguish it from the suburban lines of the same companies, we call this line the "Inner Circle," though it is very far from being a circle in the Euclidian sense.

Watch the throngs of business men from the Great Northern trains as they hasten through the subway at King's Cross to take their tickets at the Metropolitan booking office on their way to business in the morning; stand on the platform at the Mansion House Station—a station which by reason of its position in the very heart of the City forms the starting point and destination of an immense number of journeys daily; and note how almost endless is the stream of arrivals and departures. Or go to a station like Sloane Square, where comparatively few passengers enter or alight, and observe in what quick succession the trains follow each other, emerging from the tunnel at one end of the station and after the briefest stop disappearing in the tunnel at the other end;

IN THE SUBWAY, KING'S CROSS.

journey over the most frequented parts of the Circle in a third-class carriage at the busiest time of the day (say, nine in the morning or six in the evening), when the compartment designed to seat ten is made to accommodate sixteen. In each case you will have a glimpse of the characteristic life of the oldest of London's underground railways, and be helped to realise the important part it still plays in the daily drama of the great city's life.

And what of the dangers and discomforts of travelling on the Underground? As to the former, the Metropolitan District Railway, which controls the southern half of the Inner Circle, once claimed that they had carried more than 700,000,000 passengers without the loss of a single life for which the company could fairly be held responsible.

And there is little doubt that the other underground railways could, without exaggeration, make very similar claims. It is true that the sulphurous atmosphere is far from pleasant, but there is no reason to suppose that it is seriously injurious to health. In fact, there are those who have discovered medicinal virtues in it, and, although the Inner Circle has not yet become a resort of valetudinarians, the experience of the companies' servants tends to show that there is nothing specially deleterious in the conditions of their labour.

The occasional passenger, as he staggers gasping into the fresh air after a quarter of an hour spent on the Underground, may be disposed to think that there could be no industrial lot more horrible than that of the engine-drivers who spend the greater part of their working days in the sulphurous tunnels, the signalmen immured in the little boxes at the end of the platforms or, in one or two instances, right in the tunnels themselves, and of the porters on duty at underground stations like Baker Street and Gower Street. Yet the engine-drivers would probably agree that their lot is in some respects to be preferred to that of their comrades on other lines—notably, in their immunity from the effects of boisterous weather—and there are other officials just as content with their lot as the majority of railway servants; at any rate, many of them would be found on inquiry to have survived the hardships of their present occupation for twenty, twenty-five, or thirty years.

By the old system of underground railway construction, of which the Metropolitan and District Railways are the most notable examples, it would have been impossible for London ever to obtain a complete system of intercommunication between all parts. It is obvious that tunnelling which involves the buying and pulling down of houses under which the tunnel is to pass and the closing of public thoroughfares must be extremely limited in extent. The projectors of the newer style of tube railways, however, have been subject to no such limitations. To the engineer of the tube railway, as to the passengers who travel through it, the buildings overhead are a matter of supreme indifference. Eighty or a hundred feet beneath the surface, under the foundations of the houses, the bed of the river, the gas and water pipes, and the older underground railways, he worms his way through the earth, leaving a section of iron tube behind him at every yard of his advance. To the City and South London Railway Company, whose line extends from Clapham Common to Islington, belongs the credit of having first demonstrated in London the practicability in an engineering and commercial sense of the new mode of locomotion.

Let us glance for a moment at this curious subterranean work, which is likely to be going on in one part or another of the Metropolis for a good many years to come. Descending the shaft in an iron cage, lowered by the crane, we grope our way through such portion of the tunnel as has already been made till we reach the "shield," where the boring is being carried on. The shield is a great circular iron structure, in the face of which men are at work hacking away with pickaxes at the earth in front of them, while

others shovel the displaced clay or ballast into trucks for removal to the surface. At intervals the shield, which is provided on its outer face with cutting edges, is forced forward a couple of feet by means of powerful hydraulic jacks, and one of the iron rings which form the tunnel is placed in position, segment by segment, and then bolted together.

IN A SUBWAY NEAR THE BANK OF ENGLAND.

It is rather an eerie sight in the dimly lighted tunnel—the gangs of stalwart navvies plying pickaxe and spade unceasingly day and night, while the iron shield slowly, resistlessly forces its way, like a great scientific mole, through the bowels of the earth, and the slowly lengthening tube of iron approaches daily, in obedience to calculations of the most marvellous precision and accuracy, nearer to its unseen goal.

Very different will be the scene when the railway is completed, and the well-upholstered, brightly lighted electric trains follow one another through the tunnel at intervals of two or three minutes throughout the day, and perhaps also at somewhat less frequent intervals throughout the night. These tube railways have revolutionised the Londoner's ideas of railway travelling. At first we did not know what to make of them ; but we have decided that they are all right, and are patronising them in our thousands every day. The retiring man, looking for an empty carriage, has found that the little compartments designed to seat ten uncomfortably have given place to roomy carriages in which forty or fifty people ride together, and he has learnt to tolerate the presence of his fellow creatures. The City magnate, failing to find a first-class carriage, has found that the single-class trains on the electric lines provide a means of travelling scarcely less comfortable than that to which he has been accustomed, and as a business man he does not fail to appreciate the cheapness of the fares. The office boy, finding that these trains have no third-class carriages, has sat him down in great content beside the City magnate, and still the heavens do not fall!

To obtain a good idea of the characteristic life of the underground electric railways one cannot do better than visit the Bank Station, one of the most remarkable railway stations in the world. Built entirely underground, it forms the point of junction for three railways, and is at all times of the day a scene of varied and ever-changing life. Immediately below the roadway between the Bank and the Mansion House, perhaps the busiest spot in all London, lies the booking-hall, sur-

rounded by the high-level subways—well-lighted thoroughfares lined with white glazed bricks, through which circulates continuously a kaleidoscopic procession of pedestrians avoiding the crowded streets above, as well as of passengers for the trains. At a lower level lie the platforms, which are reached by a number of commodious and smoothly working lifts.

A further development of facilities for underground travelling is promised in the future in the shape of electric tramways passing under some of the principal thorough-fares. These tramways will adopt the principle of the tubular tunnel, but they will not be at so deep a level, and will connect by a slight incline with some of the existing above-ground tramways. By the time all the projected schemes for tramways and railways are completed London will have a perfect network of underground thorough-fares which will make the city one of the best equipped in the world in respect to internal locomotion.

Photo: Messrs. Pearson & Son, Ltd.

EXCAVATING A TUBE RAILWAY: AT WORK IN THE "SHIELD" (GREAT NORTHERN AND CITY RAILWAY).

THE BEGGING LETTER WRITER AT WORK.

SOME LONDON "DODGES."

By GEORGE R. SIMS.

THE word "dodge" has many meanings. You may dodge a brickbat at an election meeting, and still retain the good opinion of the rector of your parish who is in the chair. You may dodge a bore or an importunate creditor in quite another way, and not forfeit your self-esteem. In perfectly good society men occasionally put each other up to "clever little dodges" which are quite innocent; and the young married clerk, saturated with the argot of the City, may, without causing his little wife's smile to disappear for a second, describe the new baby boy as a "knowing little dodger." When Captain Smith, of the Royal Something Fusiliers, says to his brother the curate, "Look here, Tom, I can put you up to an awfully good dodge," he is not in any way attempting to urge upon him conduct unbecoming a clergyman.

"Dodge" in this sense is merely a harmless way of accomplishing something with ingenuity, or by a method which saves time and money.

The dodges which have suggested this article are of a less innocent kind. They are the "tricks" daily practised by cunning, unscrupulous men and women—sometimes, alas! children—in order to deceive and cheat. There are dodges practised in Society and the City; there are dodges in the arts and professions which it would be difficult to defend in a court of high morality. There are dodges in the retail trade and in the labour world which, though they are practised to the detriment of the public and the employer, are accepted as "custom," and winked at. There are even, be it whispered with bated breath, little dodges practised in connection with Cabinet Councils, Parliamentary debates, trials by jury, and the proceedings of the Bench of Bishops. The dodges of railway directors are usually dignified by the name of "byelaws," and the dodges of the Press bear the high-sounding alias "the policy of the paper."

The advertising dodge is, perhaps, *the* feature of twentieth century civilisation ; and the "party dodge" of the Government under which we live frequently takes the form of a measure which a constitutional Sovereign has to mention in his speech at the opening of Parliament, immediately after prayers.

It would be delightful to take these dodges and scourge them with the lash of righteous wrath, in the manner which is sometimes uncharitably described as "the sensational dodge" or "the indignation dodge," but it would lead too far afield. Let us therefore confine ourselves to the dodges of London as practised by the tricksters, beggars, vagrants, rogues, thieves, and common cheats of the capital.

The householder and the shopkeeper are the victims of dodges purposely arranged for their despoiling. One of the commonest dodges from which the innocent householder suffers is the bogus collector—the man who

is quickly handed over as the price of peace. And they are always most particular that the donor should sign his name and enter the amount of his subscription.

The dodges to get into a house and make a profit on the transaction are not confined to fraudulent collectors. There is a man who calls with gas-burners, and hands your servant a sample and a printed sheet of testimonials. If you admit the gentleman—who is going to save you fifty per cent. on your gas bill with his new burners—he will

THE RING DODGE.

calls with a book, already half filled with the signatures of benevolent people who have given sums varying from a pound to a shilling for the relief of disabled firemen, for the repairing of churches, the establishment of soup kitchens, or perhaps the preservation of an open space. Women occasionally take to bogus collecting for a dishonest livelihood, and they are the most successful where the male householder is concerned. These ladies have always an insinuating manner and a sympathetic voice, and once they obtain a foothold in the hall they are very difficult to dislodge. When, by the ambiguity of their message, they have succeeded in getting into the presence of the master himself, a shilling or half-a-crown

fit up one gas bracket or chandelier for you, and give you ocular proof of the value of his wares. Then he will sell you sufficient burners for the rest of your gas-fittings, take your money and his departure. His wares are valueless. The only genuine gas saving burners are the ones he let you see at work, and which he carefully removed, afterwards replacing your old ones. He has swindled you out of everything you have paid him, except the bare value of the metal.

There are the ladies who call with furniture polish. Some of them may be genuine travellers in the article, but there are plenty who are simply "dodgers." The furniture polish lady sends in a visiting card. It is an elegant card, and the address on it is a good

A TEST OF HIS WARES.

at all. It is simply a brown liquid; the "half-dozen" have cost the vendor, perhaps, twopence, and she has received either a shilling or eighteenpence a bottle.

The street dodges prepared for the trapping of the unwary pedestrian are great in number and extensive in variety. There is the poor labouring man who suddenly kicks against a ring, stoops down astonished, and picks it up. He looks at it, and says, "Hullo, what's this? I wonder if it's a good 'un?" A little crowd has come round him. When you pick up anything in the street most people stop to see what the lucky find is. The poor labouring man is not an expert in precious metals. He "dunno" if the treasure trove is brass or gold. At any rate, it is no good to him. He'll take "five bob" for it. Now, it is a genuine gold ring that he picked up, and that, perhaps, someone in the crowd (generally a confederate) has already examined and given back to him; but when the speculator who gives five shillings for the ring receives it in exchange for his money a worthless ring is "palmed" upon him. Everything he has paid over a penny is the trickster's profit.

The "soap fit" is not so common as it used to be in the days of the "Soap King." To put a piece of soap in your mouth, chew it till your lips are covered with froth, and then fall down and roll up your eyes and kick, is an easy way of earning a living. The sham fit dodge gets a great deal of sympathy —which the sufferer does not want. But it also gets brandy, which he *can* do with, and as often as not a little pecuniary assistance to enable the poor fellow to get into a cab and go home when he is better.

The sham sailor generally hangs about the City on winter evenings when young clerks are on their way home. Near a railway station is his favourite pitch. He stops you, and asks you if you know anything about foreign coins. If you talk to him, he tells you a wonderful tale. On his last voyage a cabin passenger got "D.T.," and one or two of the sailors had to look after him. He used to give them handfuls of gold and silver. The sailor who is talking to you got some,

one. The mistress of the house, as a rule, falls a victim, even if the servant has not already shown the well-dressed lady in. When Mrs. Jones enters her drawing-room, wondering what her visitor can want, the visitor rises, and says she has been recommended by Lady This or the Hon. Mrs. That to call on Mrs. So-and-So, and introduce her famous furniture polish.

Before there is time for protest she has a bottle and a rag out, and is polishing the back of a chair or the top of a cabinet—anything that may be handy.

Now, the sample bottle is *good* polish, the woman is an expert polisher, and the result is excellent. The unwary housewife is taken in the toils. She says she will take a bottle, or half-a-dozen bottles, as the case may be. Madam has them in a black bag, which she has left in the hall. The sample bottle being only half full, of course she does not include that. Mrs. So-and-So pays for the bottles, and her visitor departs. When Mrs. So-and-So later on tries this remarkable polish herself, she finds that it produces no effect

but he can't spend them. They are Spanish or Greek or "summat o' that sort." Can you tell the sailor, who is a stranger to London, where he can sell them? He'd part with the lot for an honest English "quid."

If the young clerk is green, he takes the bait. There are three or four foreign gold coins each bigger than a sovereign. If he has his week's money on him, he buys the lot. If he hasn't a sovereign, he buys two for ten shillings, or one for five shillings. He takes them home, and when he looks at them finds them a bit greasy. He "rings" them on the table, and the dull sound goes to his heart. It does not need an expert to tell him that he has been swindled. The coins are "duffers," artfully prepared for the cheat's market.

The confidence dodge is known to every man who reads a newspaper. Yet the confidence dodge is practised with perfect success every day of the week in London. There is no need to go into details. You have read the story again and again. The man up from the country, or the foreigner speaking a little English, meets with a man who has just come from America or Australia with a pocket full of banknotes. The adjournment to a public-house; the arrival of a third party; the conversation. The third party has banknotes also. He trusts them to the rich stranger to show his confidence in him. The rich stranger walks away with them and brings them back. The other millionaire gives him ten pounds as a present. Then the "countryman" is asked also to show his confidence. He hands over his pocket-book full of banknotes. It is taken away. The rich stranger fails to return. The other man gets nervous, and says, "By Jove! I'll go and look for him." He also fails to return. That is one form of the confidence dodge. It is played in a dozen different ways, but the last act is invariably the same.

The sham row between men—sometimes between women—is generally a dodge of the evening. A great crowd gathers round the combatants, who keep the fun going merrily while two or three of their confederates collect the purses, watches, and pins of the bystanders. Many of the leading pickpockets and swell mobsmen of London have con-

federates whose quarrels are acted with a skill which would not disgrace the boards of a first-class theatre. If the dialogue is not exactly that which would be passed by the Examiner of Plays, it is generally witty, and keeps the crowd in roars of laughter until the purses and watches are missed.

The slang name for a worthless cheque is "stumer." The changing of "stumers" is a dodge which brings many men of a superior class before the magistrates for explanations. The tradespeople, restaurant keepers, and publicans of the west are continually being victimised by the cheque-changing dodge. It is frequently the last resource of men about town who have squandered fortunes or brought themselves to poverty. They pay small accounts and dinner bills with a cheque, and ask for the change. The cheque is returned marked "N/S"—"Not sufficient" —or "Refer to drawer." In many cases the changer retains the cheque, and the gentleman in whose pass-book it should repose makes no effort to redeem it.

THE "SOAP FIT" DODGE.

The telephone has been used to prepare the way for the cashing of a "stumer." Some little time since the proprietors of a well-known restaurant in Great Portland Street were asked by telephone if they would change a cheque for me for £20. They replied, thinking they were talking to me, "Certainly." "Then," said (the supposed) I, "I'll send it down in an hour." The proprietors, thinking things over, thought it odd that I should send my cheque to them instead of to the bank, seeing that it was still before banking hours, and so a little later they rang my number up. "How will you have that cheque?" they asked: "gold or notes?" "What cheque?" said I. Then the conspiracy was discovered. An hour later a boy came to the restaurant and handed in an envelope. It contained a forged cheque for £20 drawn by a theatrical manager in my favour. The boy said that I had sent him with it. Questioned, the boy answered that I had given him the envelope in the street, and told him to bring the money back to my house. He gave my correct address. He didn't get the money, but a note in a sealed envelope. He was followed, but nobody met him. He brought the note back to me. The contrivers of this clever dodge had, in the expressive language of the fraternity, "smelt a rat," and kept discreetly in the background. Telephoning to the victim to "ready" him for the cashing of a forged cheque is a modern departure in London dodgery.

The begging dodges of London would require not an article but a volume. The blind beggars who can see, and the dumb beggars who can talk, and the lame beggars who dispense with their wooden legs and crutches out of "business" hours are notorious London characters. The woman with the borrowed baby and the man who stands about in the cold weather in the thinnest rags he can find are well known to the Mendicity officials; so is the poor little girl who lets her milk jug or her beer jug fall and break, and is afraid to go home because father will "kill" her. If the child is a good actress she will get sometimes two or three shillings in coppers before the "incident" is closed.

A SHAM QUARREL : THE PICKPOCKETS' OPPORTUNITY.

But of all the dodges of London the most carefully planned and systematically carried out is the begging letter. The begging letter impostor who conducts affairs in a grand manner often nets an income of several hundreds a year. The proprietors of sham charitable "homes" and bogus institutions have been proved to have successfully appealed to the public for support to the tune of many thousands of pounds before they were exposed.

The humbler begging letter writer is satisfied with less, but he makes a fair living if he is in the right set. There are syndicates of begging letter writers, and lodging-houses where the inmates pool their receipts. One notorious begging letter "firm" has its clerk, its ledgers, and its staff of collectors. The writer, or "screever" as he is called, does not make any personal calls. He smokes his pipe comfortably at home, and concocts the epistles, which are signed by various names at different addresses.

I have seen a begging letter writer's ledger, with spaces ruled for three applications, the date of sending being against each name. The "screever," who takes his share of results, has a list of charitable people, "likely parties," in his possession, and against each is a memorandum of the best sort of tale to tell in order to win solid sympathy. Once in a weak moment I gave a foreigner, who said his wife was dying in Berlin and he wanted to see her before she breathed her last, his fare. During the next three months I had a succession of foreigners with dying relatives in various parts of the world. They wrote first in foreign English, and then called. No begging letter is ever favourably answered but it brings a succession of similar appeals. The successful impostor gives your address and information as to the best method of attack to members of the fraternity, and shares in the proceeds.

The sham pawnticket dodge is played in two ways. In the street you are stopped by a seedy man, who has pawned a diamond ring, a watch, or some article of jewellery. He shows you the ticket. It is within a few days of running out. He cannot find the interest. You shall have the ticket for ten shillings. If you buy it, you generally find

THE BROKEN JUG DODGE.

that the dates have been artfully altered. The pledge has long since run out. All you have for your ten shillings is a bit of cardboard. These lapsed tickets are bought for a copper or two the dozen for the purposes of fraud.

The other dodge is to enclose a little bundle of pawntickets in a pitiful letter The pawntickets are of recent date. They represent the clothing of the poor person who is writing to you; sometimes his sheets and blankets are also included. Very few people care to retain these pawntickets and to make no reply. As a rule they send them back with a shilling or half-a-crown. The pawntickets are "fakes"—that is to say, specially printed—and represent nothing but the ingenuity of the rogue who encloses them.

There are scores of dodges of a distinctly criminal character practised daily to the detriment of tradespeople. There is a trick called "ringing the changes," the victim of which is generally a publican. There is the "Bank of Elegance" note, dexterously substituted for a genuine Bank of England one at the psychological moment ; there is the lady who suddenly faints in a jeweller's shop while a confederate is examining some rings with a view to purchase.   There is the "wet paint" dodge, the well-dressed man who deliberately gets his clothes damaged and threatens legal proceedings ; there is the poor little boy who gets his trousers torn by the " savage " dog you are in the habit of letting out for a run in the morning.   The boy is brought to your house in tears by an indignant working man who was passing. The little boy's trousers are certainly torn, and there are teeth marks in the calf of his leg.   You look for yourself.   If you are nervous and love your dog, dread the police courts and perhaps an order to have your dog destroyed, you probably present the little man with a sovereign to settle the matter.   Of course, you would not have done so had you known that the trousers were bitten by that indignant working man's own

dog, who is specially trained to do the work, and that it is he who also playfully nips the little boy's leg to leave teeth marks before father and son set out on what is known as the "hydrophoby lay."

One may smile at the originality of the rogues and rascals who practise the dodges of London, but only for a moment.   For it must on reflection appear to all right-minded people that they are trading on the better feelings of humanity.   The impostors of London have fouled the pure stream of charity.   They have kept thousands of honest folk from receiving the temporary relief which would have put them on their legs again.   The true tale of distress is often disbelieved ; but the rogue, because of his skill and cunning, continues to victimise the benevolent.

THE " SAVAGE " DOG DODGE.

IN LONDON'S LESSER CLUB-LAND.

By HENRY LEACH

IT is with considerable hesitation that one enters upon a task of naming and describing a number of London clubs under such a general title as the above, which, however, is certainly the only one that can be adopted in the circumstances. So at the outset it is desirable to indicate clearly what for present purposes is regarded as this lesser Club-land, and the first intimation it seems necessary to make is that we do not necessarily mean that the clubs here are of lesser importance to their own particular spheres. In another article in this work the paramount features of London Club-land in chief have been set forth. The clubs with which the writer most concerned himself were what are usually and simply known as the West-End clubs, including, of course, the greater and more universal political and social ones. They are clubs principally for people with plenty of money and more or less leisure, and as such they, perhaps, in some cases, possess less individuality than many of those which we shall name. The members of the latter may, indeed, be poorer in the world's goods than the former, but they have an abundance for their needs, and they consider themselves many times blessed by their nature and calling, and are happy and contented accordingly. For all the glory of the Carlton and the Athenæum they have no envy. They have each a pride of their own.

In this lesser Club-land, then, there are clubs of practically every conceivable character, and, viewed from the mere outsider's standpoint, of widely differing degrees of importance. There are clubs for the tolerably well-to-do, and clubs for the people of most humble means and circumstances. There are clubs for the professional man, the business man, for the working man. There are clubs for the man who lives laborious days of thought and study, and clubs for him who gets up late and stands most in need of

cheerful company when the night is far spent and most of London has once more sought its bed. And again, there are clubs innumerable for the men who are treading particular paths in life, and for those others whose peculiar tastes and temperaments are regulated to the finest nicety. The Londoner is more gregarious, far more so, than any other class of the human species, and the wonderful, puzzling variety of his clubs tells a vivid story of the universality of the Metropolis.

All things taken into account, consideration should first be given to the literary and Bohemian clubs of London. It is necessary to group them together, for the dividing line between the peculiarly literary and the peculiarly Bohemian is thin. It would be hard to find a literary club—such is the nature of things—that was not in some measure Bohemian, and it would also be difficult to discover an avowedly Bohemian club that had no suspicion of a literary flavour. For clubs of this kind London is indeed famous. Take, for example, that one which is very representative of the class —the Savage Club. The Savage is literary, artistic, musical—everything pertaining to the arts, and everything else that is not commonplace. The cleverest men of many professions may be found chatting together in the smoking-room, and you can observe a Royal Academician and a famous novelist discussing the points of the newest play, when, lo! the playwright himself suddenly swoops down upon them, and the conversation is forthwith switched off to the weather. The members of the club call themselves " brother Savages," and on Saturday nights they are given to feasting together. Above all things, they like a " lion," a brand new " lion," amongst them, and, if there is a great general fresh from a war, an intrepid explorer newly arrived from the Antarctic region, or a famous musician who has just completed a tour of triumph, depend upon it the Savages will do their best to lure him to their dinner, and cheer him when he makes a great speech.

There are other clubs which, to a large extent, are on the Savage Club lines. One

feature in the winter season. At these gatherings some leading light in literature, science, or art is invited to open a "conversation" on a selected topic; after which a pleasant couple of hours are spent

ECCENTRIC CLUB : READY FOR DINNER.

of them is the Yorick, in Bedford Street ; and, though less Bohemian, more purely literary, there is the Authors', in Whitehall Court, to which an aspirant may not hope to gain admission until he has published something. The only "lions" which the Authors recognise are the literary species, and they are never so happy in the true club season as when a great man of letters, the particular guest of the evening, is talking to them over the dinner table about something or other which is more or less near to their hearts and work—publishers and publishing for choice. The Whitefriars Club, which meets at Anderton's Hotel, in the newspaper quarter, is also inclined to letters, and its Friday evening dinners form its special

in discussing or talking round the subject. The rest of the evening is devoted to chat of a more intimate or personal nature. The meetings are well attended by authors, journalists, and members of kindred professions ; and *confrères* from across the Atlantic or elsewhere are frequently present as guests. From a consideration of such clubs as these it is a natural transition to the New Vagabonds, who, in their club capacity, do nothing else, indeed, but dine. Periodically in the season they assemble together, the gentler sex at times included amongst them, and invite into their midst some other lady or gentleman, or both, who have won laurels in the fields of art and literature, and then there are compliments and happy speeches till the home-going time arrives. Next, perhaps, to the Savage there is no club more thoroughly typical of Bohemia than the Press, quartered in one of those old-time courts which run north and south from Fleet Street. It is a club for journalists, and it is in a secluded spot such as is loved in Bohemia. These newspaper workers are necessarily late birds, and thus it happens that the club is only really warming up to its work, so to speak, when the midnight hour has chimed.

There are, again, one or two clubs of the literary sort which specialise in literature, as it were, and most interesting they are. One such is the Johnson Club, the members of which practise the cult of famous old Doctor Johnson and have an absorbing love for all his works. Numbered amongst them are men who are distinguished in the literary and journalistic world, and they meet together in the Old Cheshire Cheese, off

Of much the same style is the Omar Khayyam Club, though the members here are, perhaps, rather more inclined to good spirits. Thus, upon one occasion, when the club held a dinner and those present had the coronation of the King in mind, a Member of Parliament who was in the vice-chair must needs contemplate the possibility of their celebrating that auspicious event as did Edward Fitz-Gerald himself, greatest Omarian of them all, with two of his friends, celebrate the coronation of Queen Victoria. On that memorable morning of a long-gone June the trio wended their way to Leith Hill, and, when the distant guns announced to all that the coronation had taken place, in their exuberance of loyalty and youth they flung themselves into a neighbouring pond and sang "God Save the Queen." And another curious but very select literary club is that which goes by the name of the Odde Volumes, who give themselves strange names

WELCOME CLUB: A SUMMER EVENING SCENE.

Fleet Street, which Johnson is said to have much frequented, and there they dine and read papers and provoke discussions, afterwards publishing, for private circulation only, some account of all that they have said and done.

and surround themselves and their literary deliberations with a spice of mystery.

There is another club in Bohemia which well deserves its name, and it is called the Eccentric. Those who belong to it like to be called the Eccentrics, and they are never

117

so pleased as when they are showing the
ordinary people outside that they are not
at all like them.   They have a great love for
the stage, and therefore they will take over
to themselves for an evening a considerable
portion of a theatre where some popular
favourite is playing, and will convey themselves to the theatre in many vehicles and
with much show.   At home in Shaftesbury
Avenue they exhibit a liking for cosiness
and club comforts, in which their Bohemian
taste is not to be excelled.   Now that the
Eccentric has brought us into the region of
the Club-land of the stage, there are discovered in it many clubs quite different from
any that may be found elsewhere, and each
one usually differing to a marked extent
from its fellows.   To begin with, there are
the Garrick and the Green Room, both of
which, as their names imply, are principally
dramatic, and are frequented, not only by
the people who love the drama and take their
pleasure from it, but by the others who make
it for them and by the actors who present
it.   At the Garrick, which is proud of its fine
collection of pictures, many of the most famous
lights of the present-day stage may be found
of an afternoon chatting together and enjoying a rubber at whist before the time comes
for the early dinner and the call-boy's summons to duty.

Then there are the Playgoers, and the O.P.
clubs, who do the same thing in much the
same way, that is to say, the members go to
the theatre and then meet together to talk
it over.   On Sunday nights they meet in
a great hotel, with friends of the fair sex,
and listen to the words of an actor or actress
who has graciously come amongst them,
or, as an alternative, debate with keenness
some old or new problem of the stage.
It was by a flash of genius that one of
the O.P.'s invented the name for the club.
They were seceders from the Playgoers,
and their title will stand for Old Playgoers, but it is also a stage abbreviation
for " opposite prompt "—one of the entrances
from the wings of the stage—and which
precisely was the more in mind when the
club was named no man knoweth and no O.P.
would venture to guess.   The New Lyric,
at the corner of Coventry Street, with a pretty
interior, also belongs to a series of stage clubs,

and so does the Gallery First Night Club,
the members of which make a speciality of
paying a shilling to see the first performance
of every new play, and ever and anon entertaining a footlight favourite after the manner
of the other clubs whose names have been
mentioned.

Before the arts are quitted, mention should
be made of the clubs which are purely artistic.
There is the Burlington Fine Arts, in Savile
Row, and, away in the King's Road, Chelsea,
in the true artistic quarter, is the Chelsea
Arts, which is a comfortable social club for
professional artists alone, and where, fresh
from their easels and brushes, they foregather
and talk over their ideas in art.   And then
there are the Hogarth, the Langham Sketch-
ing Club, and many others.   The true photographer would resent it if he were not
included in the artist category, and, at the
Camera Club, in Charing Cross Road, which
is the elysium of the sun artist, he can show
many proofs that he is what he claims to be.

Of social sporting clubs we have in London
a great assortment.   At the top there is the
Turf Club in Piccadilly, premier of them
all, and the Badminton, close by, with the
Victoria in Wellington Street, where the
" prices " are largely regulated.   For a
quiet game of whist or bridge with foemen
worthy of the best tempered steel, the
Baldwin Club is pre-eminently the one to
visit, and the Pelican is another club which
is all for the sportsman.   But no sporting
club in London is so much a club by itself
as the famous National Sporting Club in
Covent Garden, where, in a theatre of their
own, the members regularly assemble and
with eager faces and quickened pulses
watch a game tussle, under Queensberry
rules, between two young boxers who have
already won fame in the ring, or are
on the way towards winning it.   Some of
the battles that have been waged in the
National Sporting Club are historic.   Of
course there are specialists in sporting clubs
as well ; that just named is one of them.
Another is the Gun Club which meets at
Notting Hill for pigeon shooting, another
the Alpine Club, the members of which have
an undying fervour for mountaineering, and
there are the Automobile in Piccadilly, and
its sister club the Aero, whose ambition is to

produce flying machines and to fly away in them. Nowhere has the game of chess so many keen votaries as in the Metropolis, in which they have two or three pretentious clubs of their own. There is one in the City, another, the British, at Whitehall, and there is another in the St. James's quarter, which is called the St. George's.

men; but, to go to the other extreme, the workman also has his clubs — hundreds of them — all over London. The workman's club may be called by such an out-of-the-way name as Eleusis, or it may have a political name, or it may make no secret of the matter, but call itself simply a workman's club with the name of

O.P. CLUB: A SUNDAY EVENING DEBATE.

Mention of this City club serves as a reminder that the City possesses many clubs which are peculiarly of itself. The City Carlton, the City Liberal, the Gresham, and the City of London present a beehive kind of scene in the daytime, especially during the luncheon interval when they are thronged with merchants, bankers, stockbrokers, and commercial men generally; in the evening they are deserted or nearly so. These are the clubs of the wealthy business

its district prefixed, but it all amounts to pretty much the same thing at the finish. Here the workman of greater or lesser degree smokes his pipe and drinks his glass of beer in the evening, and discusses the affairs of the Empire, or, as an alternative, those of the London County Council and the increasing rates. He varies the monotony by a game of dominoes, or cards, or billiards, and feels that he can live the club life with the best of us. In the East End may be

ELEUSIS CLUB :
  A DISCUSSION.

found workmen's clubs of a peculiar and pretentious type. There is one, the Netherlands Social and Dramatic, it is called, though it is no longer of the Netherlands only, which in point of size will match with many of the clubs in the West-End, and which has its own theatre, ball-room, and everything else on a grand scale. The workman, too, has his boot clubs, his slate clubs, and many others of the same sort, and in the Hoxton neighbourhood there are the Sunday night clubs. In the east, also, and again in the neighbourhood of Soho, there are clubs for the strangers within the gates of London who belong to foreign nationalities. French, Germans, Italians, all have their own clubs, and the foreign waiters, generally, have a club of their own, where they hold high revel when the table has no need of them. Not only the comparatively impecunious workers, but the even more impecunious boys have their clubs. These latter also are scattered all over the Metropolis. The boys pay their penny a week, or whatever it is, and they are better off reading good books or

playing innocent games than they would be in the streets outside.

All these make up a long list, and it could be made very much longer, for we have as yet by no means exhausted the wonderful variety of our London Clubland. But there may be a tendency to weary, and with a few more specimens, isolated from any particular class, there shall be an end as far as this article is concerned. A good-sized directory could be made of these isolated ones alone. In the fashionable West-End there is the Caledonian, for Scotsmen of recognised position only, and in Holborn there is an Irish club. There is the Bath Club in Dover Street, which is just what its name implies, and there is Prince's Club at Knightsbridge, where often a brilliant gathering of society folk may be seen, come there to watch the skating. The Supper Club, smart as it can be, also describes itself. Once more, there are anglers' clubs for the fishermen, there is a Couriers' Club in Davies Street for messengers who cross continents, and there is a host of others, fashioned according to the pleasures or the occupations of their members.

There is a pretty club scene with which to close. In the exhibition grounds at Earl's Court of a summer evening there is a place apart, which is like a little fairy-land, and glitters with myriads of fairy lights. In the shadows, separated from the passing crowd by an illuminated barrier— shown in the photographic illustration on page 161—men and women in evening attire chat and sip coffee, and listen to the music of the band. It is a feast of contentment. It is the Welcome Club.

And so, season in and season out, this London Club-land goes on its way in a happy, rejoicing frame of mind. There is no indication that the club habit is in any way decreasing in popularity, or that those who practise it feel that it has been overdone in variety and specialisation. Rather is there a tendency to start a new club on the smallest pretext. The simple fact is that this is an age above all others when the principle of there being strength in numbers is most willingly applied to most departments of life, and particularly to that which is most concerned with the proper occupation of leisure time. And those who know London well know that if there is one place in the whole world where the fellow-ship that only a club can afford is a real necessity, that place is the great and the lonely Metropolis.

LADS' CLUB (CRAVEN TERRACE, HYDE PARK): RECREATION ROOM.

COURT CEREMONIES IN LONDON.

By NORMAN WENTWORTH.

ROYAL ARMS.

THE most magnificent, the most dazzling Court in the world in this the twentieth century is the Court over which the King and Queen of England rule when they are in their capital. In days which have not been left very far behind, London, in so far as its higher life was concerned, possessed, rightly or wrongly, a reputation for the cultivation of the dull and sombre, and if in those times you were to talk to the foreigner of the Court ceremonies of London, it was as likely as not that he would betray something of a snigger and bring forward the fierce contrast of France when a Louis sat upon the throne.

But in these later days our Court ceremonies are real things, alive and palpitating, and they are worthy in their splendour of the greatest Empire that the world has ever seen. Nor are signs wanting, to even the meanest subject of his Majesty, as to when these same Court ceremonies are in progress, apart altogether from the glowing accounts of their brilliance which appear in the newspapers of the next morning. In the days of the Victorian era there were only the Drawing Rooms of the afternoon ; but now the Court of the evening is the topmost social event. In the West-End of London the close observer is aware of an indefinable something tingling in the atmosphere. There is a palpable stir amongst the great ones of the land. The King and Queen have come up to town from Windsor, and, with their prancing escort in attendance, have driven through the streets from Paddington to their palace. Carriages with gorgeously liveried attendants are somewhat more numerous than usual, and in those quarters where are the fashionable modistes there is a busy hum, although, of course, these indispensable providers of society ladies' needs have long ago finished the bulk of their work for the Court. He who has heard nothing of the Court will, after one brief look round, be prepared to hazard the gains of a day that this afternoon or evening there will be an event of vaster social importance than usual in the capital, and that, for choice, it will be in the social temple of the Empire, in Buckingham Palace, the London home of the King and Queen.

It is in the spring when nature, even in the dense atmosphere of town, is making her endeavour to enter into a brighter and more joyful life, that Royalty and Society awake in glad agreement with her, and deck themselves in all that is beautiful and costly for the festivals that are to come. In the later hours of evening, when the more humble pleasure seeker first gives a thought to his return to his home, the Court begins, and when it is at the height of its splendour much of London is fast asleep. The invitations were issued two or three weeks ahead, and now, on the great night itself, some thousand or more of the greatest of the land hurry to the Palace, so that they may be there by ten o'clock, which is the hour of beginning. There are some notable ladies of society who have for weeks been planning a great victory for this occasion. With a dress which will be a dream of art and taste, jewels which will dazzle almost to momentary blindness, and a personal beauty which by every device known to woman will have been enticed to the superlative of radiant charm, they will so deck themselves that on their entry to join the glittering throng something in the nature of a mild sensation will be produced, and there will be agreement that never before in all her triumphant social history has My Lady been so fascinating. A thousand pounds will be a cheap bill for such an achievement, fleeting as is the glory, and forgotten as it will be almost by the evening of the next day.

Long in advance a crowd of expectant watchers has gathered outside the Palace, and now swarms round all the approaches, peering eagerly in the uncertain light into every carriage as it comes rolling up. There is a guard of honour on duty in the quadrangle, giving the indispensable military touch to the approach to the Court. Though in the popular belief there is but one entrance to the Palace for occasions of this kind, it may be explained that there are as a matter of fact two of them. There is the great central gateway, known to everybody, which is used by the majority of those attending these Court ceremonies, and there is another situated outside Buckingham Gate, which is strictly reserved for those very high persons who have the privilege of entrée by it, which peculiar privilege is one of the surest indications of the highest distinction and of the descent of the royal favour upon the holder of it.

By ten o'clock, or very soon afterwards, the general assembly is complete, and all is in readiness for the coming of their Majesties, which, however, will not take place at once. Next to the magnificence of the dresses of the ladies, the thing most noticeable, perhaps, is the glitter of the uniforms—uniforms almost of every imaginable variety. There are here mounted the Honourable Corps of the Gentlemen-at-Arms, and the Yeomen of the Guard, and the Sticks and Staves and others are to be seen in their proper places. When the members of the Royal Family, as apart from the King and Queen, arrive at the Garden entrance the White Staves receive them, and conduct them to the Council-room. Thence they proceed to the White Drawing-room, where they join the King and Queen, and here at half-past ten the stately, impressive procession to the Ball-room is formed. Slowly, majestically in the extreme, it wends its way along through the chief State apartments, which now are to be seen in all their splendour. The furniture

AT A COURT : PRESENTED TO THEIR MAJESTIES.

is beautiful, and the hangings and the gilding have an air of freshness which gives an extra scintillation to the life of the scene.   From the White Drawing-room through the Gold Drawing-room, the Blue Drawing-room, and the State Dining-room to the Ball-room the Royal procession passes along. The King is in the uniform of a Field Marshal, and as he escorts the Queen through this most brilliant assembly, homage and marks of loyal respect are tendered at every step, and these his Majesty graciously acknowledges by a slight but graceful bow.   And the Queen, as she passes along, is a picture of true queenly charm, while her grace and her royal courtesy to the wonderful gathering which with an open heart tenders its admiration and its devotion are the subjects of the unspoken thoughts in every mind.   The Queen is very likely attired in the most complete perfection in a gown of creamy satin, which is embroidered in silver and diamonds, and on her long train, carried by little scarlet-coated pages—a pretty innovation in the ceremonies of the Court— there are diamond embroideries also.   A magnificent tiara of brilliants rests upon her head.

In days gone by, what is known as the " passing " ceremony, was, it was freely confessed by all, a somewhat wearisome affair. As it was conducted the whole of the assembly had to be marshalled in order and then had to pass in procession before the throne.   This took up much time and savoured too much of awkward routine to be enjoyable, or even, after the first few minutes, particularly interesting, except to those most intimately concerned.   But now a new and happier order of things has come about, due to the wise instincts of King Edward and his Queen. Certainly among the most important factors in this Court ceremony are the trembling, blushing *débutantes* who will only have one greater day in their lives than this, and that their marriage day, which, as they are now on the threshold of their social careers, will not itself be very far distant.

Sweet indeed in the fresh bloom of youth are these maidens in their 'teens, the fairest flowers of British humanity. They have but left their school-rooms, they are new to all this dazzling world of rank and fashion ; but it is many chances to one that in fewer years than can be counted on the fingers of one's hand some from this gathering of girlhood will be presiding over the most ancient ducal homes and will be developing a claim to lead the society of which they now know so little ; and there is again a very fair prospect that in the lapse of a little time one or other of them will herself be a vice-queen in one of those vast pieces of the Empire which are far away o'er the seas.   So it is fitting that in the dawn of their new lives, when they come to be presented to their King and Queen, they should be honoured above all others.   The " passing " ceremony of old, then, has gone, and when the King and Queen place themselves in front of their respective Throne chairs in the Ball-room, all who come before them are these blushing *débutantes* and those others who have special occasion to be presented. Each of them is accompanied by a sponsor, who, in distinction to all the other ladies in the general assembly, must wear a train. They come forward treading lightly upon the thick, soft, red carpet, and the *débutante*, head high and heart low, having handed an official card with her name upon it to the lord-in-waiting near the door—who in due course hands it to the Lord Chamberlain near the Throne—hears now that name read out loudly and clearly. To the chief participator in the little drama the seconds seem like years ; but it is all over in a wonderfully short space of time.   There is the curtsy, the delicate kiss of the hand, then it is ended, and before the *débutante* is quite aware of it she is curtsying in retiring to the remaining members of the Royal Family, and making a tremendous effort to remember that, fearful as she may be of the safety of her passage, she must on no account turn her back to the throne.

The presentations being complete, their Majesties give their attention now to all those others who have attended the Court. They have been arranged in the various state apartments in such a manner that when the King and Queen pass along they will have these honoured subjects upon

THE KING CONFERRING A KNIGHTHOOD.

AT A LEVEE : A MILITARY PRESENTATION.

Different in a degree, inasmuch as it is "for men only," but not less interesting, is the King's Levee. A Levee will never cease to create a stir in the royal regions of the west. It is announced that his Majesty will hold a Levee at St. James's Palace at noon, and in the sunshine the crowds gather and line the route from Buckingham Palace. There are ringing cheers for the King as he rides along in a State carriage with trappings of scarlet and gold and with a flashing escort of Life Guards before and behind. At St. James's Palace his Majesty is received by the great Officers of State and is conducted to the Throne Room. Outside there are Guards of Honour mounted, and inside his Majesty's bodyguard of the Honourable Corps of Gentlemen-at-Arms and of the Yeomen of the Guard are on duty. Other male members of the Royal Family are present, and in immediate attendance upon the King is a host of the higher dignitaries of the State. The scene is a brilliant one, brilliant in the extreme. There are the Diplomatic Circle and the General Circle, the Ambassadors of almost every civilised country in the world in all their brightest and most distinctive vestments, as well as our own Cabinet Ministers and many other distinguished persons. The foreign Ambassadors have newly-arrived deputies or visitors of official distinction from their own States whom they are anxious to present to the King, and one by one they do so, and the Belgian, the Chilian, the Argentine attaché, and the Naval Commander from Japan—to draw a few instances from this brilliant international medley— file past the King and pay their respects. And then those of our own countrymen who are deemed worthy of so high an honour are likewise presented. The ceremony comes to an end, and amidst more cheers from the crowd the King drives slowly back to Buckingham Palace.

their right. The formation is maintained by the Yeomen of the Guard and the Gentlemen-at-Arms, and as soon as the presentations are over their Majesties leave the Throne chairs and make a tour of these apartments, walking through and round them, everybody rising as they enter and remaining upon their feet until the King and Queen have departed. It might so happen, upon occasion, that their Majesties in this procession would stop for a moment to speak to some one or other of the brilliant crowd—a signal honour which all would notice and which would for ever be remembered. When the Court is over there are buffet refreshments for the general assemblage, and there is supper laid for the members of the Royal Family and specially invited guests. And then it is finished, save for the visit to the fashionable photographer's, which the *débutante* will inevitably pay, and the almost interminable discussion afterwards of the events of the night.

These are the most regular and most formal among the Court Ceremonies in London, but there are others amongst the

number which have their own special importance and their own special interest. For
example there is, now, the investiture of
knighthood, when there are indeed but a
small attendance and a minimum of pageantry
in comparison with such ceremonials as those
we have been considering, but which is a
pretty instance of the survival of an old and
picturesque form. The King is with his

we saw her at the Court, surrounded by all
the bravest and most distinguished men
and all the fairest women, enjoy the sweet
pleasures of dreamy music, while they
converse with their guests and anon take
their part in the specified pleasure of the
evening. And there is the State Concert
when their Majesties bid their guests to an
evening's feast of music at Buckingham Palace;
and there is the
State Dinner when
such a distinguished
gathering assembles
round the Royal
board as seldom, if
ever, can be gathered
at any other. The
King is at the head
of his sumptuous

noble attendants, and there
comes to him, humble, grateful,
and upon his bended knee, the
subject whom a little while
before his Majesty intimated it
would be his pleasure to honour
with knighthood as an expression of his appreciation of services rendered to the State. And
plain Mr. Worthy advances,
bends, and with the sword tap
as the official intimation of his
birth to a new dignity, is
bidden "Arise, Sir John
Worthy." A less formal matter is a Privy
Council, usually held at Buckingham Palace,
with his Majesty presiding over it, which is
convened from time to time as may be
thought desirable.

Strictly speaking, this, too, is one of the
Court Ceremonies of London ; but of a
very different character are three others
which still need mention. There is the
State Ball for one, when the King in his
military uniform, and the Queen, if possible
even more radiant and beautiful than when

THEIR MAJESTIES DRIVING. I. WITH A GUARDS' ESCORT.
II. IN STATE.

table, and discourses pleasantly with all
about him. Fortunate are they who are
so greatly honoured by the hospitality of
their Majesties.

Such are the chief of the Court Ceremonies
of London which, whilst they undoubtedly
excel in these days in brilliancy and splendour, gain again in dignity, so that the
British Court may be held as a pattern
to the world of all that is best and as it
should be in the highest social life of a
mighty Empire.

A ROWTON HOUSE : COURTYARD.

LONDON'S MODEL LODGING-HOUSES.

By T. W. WILKINSON.

FORTUNATE as London is in many things, it is in none more so than its model lodging-houses, which for size and appointments are unrivalled. No doubt the luckless professional man who has only just reached the gutter—the man who has become painfully conscious that there are times when all life's problems are crystallized into one : Where is the biggest penny bun sold ? — is not wholly pleased on making his first acquaintance with even one of the best of the London "models." But that is inevitable, inasmuch as the privacy, the comfort, and the associations to which he has been accustomed are of necessity unobtainable in such a place.

In visiting the superior class of lodging-houses you can begin anywhere. The best starting point, however, is the Victoria Home No. 2, because this hotel for working men belongs to the pioneers in lodging-house reform. Like its progenitor, No. 1, in Wentworth Street,

Whitechapel, it is owned by a trust composed of earnest and philanthropic gentlemen, who neither bestow charity through their houses nor make a dividend from them. The places pay ; but the profits, instead of being divided, go to the extension of the work, which aims at raising men to a higher level, socially and spiritually.

It is a large brick building, the more modern Victoria Home, divided into two blocks. Passing under a big lamp and through a corridor, you catch sight of a sign at the top of a staircase leading to subterranean depths : " Shaving Saloon." Another flight of steps leads you into one of the kitchens, boxed off at the westward end of which is a miniature coffee shop. Glance at its framed price-list, and you can form an idea of how some of the dejected specimens of humanity scattered over the kitchen can live on a shilling a day, lodgings included. A plate of hot roast beef costs 3d. ; a portion of pudding, 1d. ; half-a-pint of tea, ½d. One of the best patronised dinners consists of a basin of soup (1d.) and a hunk of bread (½d.). And all the food sold here, let it be noted, is good and wholesome.

Next we go upstairs and look at the sleeping accommodation. Light, airy, scrupulously clean—these are the first impressions. Here is a room full of sixpenny beds. It is split up into cubicles, the partitions of which are formed of hollow tiles. Inside each hangs a small picture, as well as a looking glass—an unusual luxury. A short walk brings us to the fourpenny quarters, where the beds are mostly four in a room, one in each corner. And, finally, here are the fivepenny cabins. They are practically the same as the sixpenny cubicles, though the partitions are of corrugated zinc.

Descending again, we reach the recreation room, which is open to all the lodgers—a room calculated to shock beyond measure some of those gentry who exploit the homeless. Truly, it is a delightful feature of the house, for it contains, not only a piano, but three bagatelle tables and one for billiards. That this admirable room helps many men temporarily to forget the sorrows and disappointments of the day is clear from the aspect it presents in the evening, when there is always a large gathering in it.

To learn what class of men the Victoria Homes benefit, it is only necessary to descend at night into the kitchen of the Wentworth Street establishment. This is a huge room, broken up by a number of iron pillars, round which is an ample supply of clothes hooks. At one end is a bar, where food is sold at the cheapest possible rate.

The kitchen is now full of lodgers,

some clustered near the huge coke fire, some eating at the tables, some sitting aloof from their congeners, apathetic, dull-eyed, temporarily oblivious of their surroundings. These men are a part of the human wreckage which by some strange under-currents drift into the East-End. But most of the lodgers are palpably labourers and waterside workers. If any proof of that were needed, it would be found in the fact that about 500 men went from the homes to South Africa at the call to arms.

Leaving the east, we may go to the west—to Hammersmith Road, where is situated the fourth of the series of Rowton Houses, those admirable poor men's hotels which, while they return their proprietors five per cent., yet afford the best accommodation procurable in England for sixpence per night. Admission is gained, as at the other "Rowtons," through a turnstile, to many a poor outcast the gate of an earthly paradise. Early in the morning you may sometimes see a sombre figure, haggard, pale, and footsore with wandering about all night, dart through this opening when the coast is clear, whip off his coat and waistcoat to make it appear that he has just come

VICTORIA HOME (WHITECHAPEL) : KITCHEN.

downstairs, and then proceed in a much more leisurely fashion to the lavatory. And thus it is that many poor wretches tide over a highly critical period. At night they have the key of the street; in the morning they slip unobserved into "models," and, not being detected as "deadheads"—for the staff cannot possibly know all the lodgers—wash, rest, and pick up the crumbs that fall from the tables.

present in the morning, when the men flock in to breakfast. The capitalist with a four-figure banking account—a retired business man of Bohemian tastes, or, it may be, a world wanderer who cannot adapt himself to a sybaritic life — chats over a table with a starveling who has not tasted food for twenty-four hours, and knows not whence his next meal will come. Respectability incarnate, habited in a glossy silk hat and a fashionable frock coat, borrows a knife from labour in clayey corduroys. An

A ROWTON HOUSE : DINING ROOM.

On the left of the entrance is the office, where each lodger is given, in exchange for his sixpence, a ticket that is cancelled as he goes upstairs to bed. Beyond lies the main corridor, which is lined with glazed brickwork from floor to ceiling, leading to the smoking room, dining rooms, scullery, etc. All these apartments are uniformly furnished, exceedingly well lighted, and adorned with pictures and art pottery. It is, perhaps, in the dining rooms, which correspond to some extent to the kitchen of a common lodging-house, that most human interest is found.

Endless are the studies and contrasts they

expert "moucher" in his working clothes —he knows better than to go to business in any of the suits he wears after the day's toil is over — discusses the news with a mechanic who has suffered torture rather than ask for a crust.

It is a strange assemblage. Clerks "out of collar," actors whose "resting" more than ever deserves another name, failures in shabby black edged with linen long past redemption, well-dressed "somethings" (what, no man knoweth), mechanics and labourers in steady employment, wrapper writers, billiard sharps, thieves, begging letter writers, blackmailers, commonplace "mouchers" and "tappers" — all these mingle in the dining-rooms.

Here, at Hammersmith, there are also a number of men with small incomes, chiefly pensioners. Among these aristocrats you may find scores who could tell grim life-stories. For one reason or another, they are impossible at home ; so they have been banished, and their relations pay their lodging money monthly or quarterly in advance. If you met them in the street, you would not in your wildest flights of fancy think that their address is Rowton House, Hammersmith Road.

And the difference in the lodgers' modes of living! While many a labouring man purchases a substantial breakfast at the bar —where edibles of all kinds, cooked and uncooked, and of uniformly excellent quality, are obtainable, at very reasonable prices — an immaculately-dressed guest, who from his appearance might be anything from a shopwalker to a South African millionaire, may often be seen toasting a bloater at the fire. He could buy one ready to eat at the bar for a penny ; but then for the same coin he can get two uncooked outside.

Beyond the dining rooms are the barber's, the tailor's, and the shoemaker's workshops, and what the house agent calls the "usual offices," as well as some which are not usual. Included in the first class is the lodgers' wash-house, where every man can be his own laundress, and in the other is a room fitted with deep troughs specially for feet washing— a boon not to be fully appreciated save by him who has tramped all day on London's stones.

The courtyard! It is opposite the dining rooms and runs along the whole of the frontage. Fitted with seats and relieved of bareness by tubs of plants and small rockeries, it is a favourite resort for reading and smoking.

Ascending now one of the three fireproof staircases, we reach a corridor, which presents a long vista of open doors to right and left. These are the sleeping apartments. To see one is to see all. It is a sort of wooden box open at the top, and fitted inside with a shelf and clothes hooks. Besides the bed, it also contains a chair for the use of the occupant, while for ventilating purposes there is a window absolutely under his control. Of these cubicles there are no fewer than eight hundred in this one building.

Altogether, the Hammersmith Road "Rowton" is not comfortable merely, but positively luxurious judged by the "model" standard. All of the series, indeed, situated in various districts of the Metropolis, are splendid institutions and a lasting credit to

A ROWTON HOUSE : ENTRANCE HALL.

their founder, who has his reward in knowing that they are full every night.

The County Council Lodging-house in Parker Street, Drury Lane, next awaits inspection. Pass through the doorway into the wide lobby, cross it, through another doorway, and we are in the kitchen—a fine, light room, with a huge flat-topped stove

L.C.C. LODGING-HOUSE TICKET.

on which half-a-score of kettles are always boiling. Just now the pungent aroma of onions comes from its direction, as some of the lodgers are cooking their evening meal. There is, as in the other " models " we have visited, an ample supply of plates, cups, saucepans, frying-pans, etc.

From the kitchen we might go to the shop, the counter of which is in the main lobby, but let us instead pass the office —where, as in the " Rowtons," the lodger gets a voucher on paying sixpence — and enter the living room. At one end is a platform, used for concerts in the winter; at the other, the library, books from which can be had by lodgers on application to the manager. Near the door are some newspaper stands, at which many lodgers keep themselves abreast with the world's doings—and wants. Opposite us, at a table, several " writers " are bent over their task, the dreariest and most ill-paid of all kinds of clerical labour. The usual rate of remuneration for addressing wrappers is 2s. 6d. per thousand, and he must have rare application and much skill in pen-driving who can get through that number in eight hours. Here and there about the room are other lodgers, most of them laughing and jesting as if the world were using them fairly well. Several—shopmen and clerks, maybe—are arrayed in silk hats and frock coats, but the majority are, unless their dress misleads, mechanics and labourers.

The way to the lavatory, wash-house, etc., lies across a courtyard provided with seats, so that the lodgers may smoke or read in the open air. Wonderful are some of the operations carried on in this municipal laundry. I have seen a man iron his

shirt with a bottle filled with hot water; and a still more ingenious lodger once contrived, after washing and starching his collar, to give it the finishing touches with the bottom of a tin teapot. As he ruefully remarked, his makeshift lacked weight; but for all that he made a surprisingly decent job of the article. It is not every man who is equal to a feat of this kind, or even to doing a little washing. One poor fellow, being wholly ignorant of the niceties of laundry work, struggled long over his collar with a halfpennyworth of stale bread, which he bought especially to clean it, and rubbed at it till he had utilised every crumb. Herein lies another illustration of the worth of a halfpenny. Of course, an immaculate collar, ready to wear, can be obtained for a penny at any laundry, where there is always some unclaimed linen.

Upstairs the Parker Street home differs from most of its class. The dormitories, of which there are three, are on the well system, the cubicles being ranged round landings rising one above another, and consequently they are somewhat suggestive of prison—an impression which is heightened by the cubicle partitions, which are of iron. This arrangement, excellent though it is from a hygienic point of view, has one little drawback. When a certain type of lodger is not used to the place, and does not reach it some morning till London is asleep, he is apt to wonder, at getting up time, what he is " in for " again. The cubicles, however, are not only private, but sufficiently roomy and very comfortable.

Let us apply the practical test. This is the result: The house is always full, and

ROWTON HOUSE TICKET.

applicants have frequently to be turned away. Moreover, a number of men have lodged in it ever since it was opened in 1893.

Of smaller "models"—"models" approximating more closely to the ordinary provincial class—there are so many that to visit them all would be impossible. A great recommendation of some of these houses, such as the "Shaftesbury Chambers," in Macklin Street, Drury Lane, is their nomenclature, which appeals strongly to some men. Not that they are fond of Swivellerism; the reason is of a much more weighty character. If an unemployed clerk or shop assistant makes application for work, and lets it be known that he is stopping at a lodging-house, good-bye,

citizen turns away with a shocked underlip. He looks upon even a "Rowton" as a blot upon the applicant's escutcheon.

Incredible as the thing seems, it is none the less a fact. Here is an actual instance of the prejudice against lodging-houses.

L.C.C. LODGING-HOUSE (PARKER STREET). I. WRAPPER WRITERS AT WORK. II. SITTING ROOM.

A clerk who was staying at the Victoria Home No. 2 gave as his address, in applying for a situation, "77, Whitechapel Road," in place of the name of the institution—77 used to be the number of the house; it is now 177. He was engaged. Instead of then leaving the home, he determined to remain there for a short time, that he might pull himself together. One night a boy engaged at the same office saw him drop off the tramcar and enter the house, and next morning he must needs go and tell his employer what he had witnessed. This was fatal to the wretched clerk's hopes. He was discharged. So difficult is it to rise from the gutter.

in nine cases out of ten, to his chance of success. Everything may go swimmingly till the poor castaway incautiously mentions a house which the employer knows by its name or its reputation to be a common lodging-house. Then negotiations are quickly broken off, and the respectable

That blessed word, " chambers," then, is taken into account by some of the unemployed. Men can, and do, invent fanciful names for well-known "models," but, since the Post Office Directory is at hand in most business establishments, that involves some risk. "Chambers," however, sounds well, and continues to sound well after that bulky tome has been consulted.

If a man is the worse for a sojourn in any of the principal hotels for working men, he alone is to blame. While there are no irksome rules in such houses, cleanliness, order, sobriety, and other cardinal virtues are rightly insisted on in the interests alike of the management and the lodgers generally, and as a result their tendency is to elevate, not degrade.

L.C.C. LODGING-HOUSE (PARKER STREET) : CUBICLES.

UNIFORMED LONDON.

By ALEC ROBERTS.

BEADLE (ROYAL EXCHANGE).

IN London the apparel oft proclaims the man; likewise the woman. The prim little maid also; and the boy, with shining morning or smudged afternoon face. If the uniformed, liveried, and badged tribes of the Metropolis were marshalled in one huge procession, how it would impress us by its magnitude and its strangely varied aspects! Century would jostle century, for in this up-to-date London of ours there are persons garbed exactly like their predecessors in bygone reigns—back to the seventh Henry's. Courtly splendour and military pomp, civic state and panoplied caste — all these and their uniformed opposites would pass before us.

Ideas may differ, however, as to what constitutes uniform. Step from the work-a-day Strand into the mediæval-looking Law Courts, and you will see survivals that make the American visitor utter exclamations of astonishment. For judges and counsel in their degrees are robed and wigged in a manner as fantastic-seeming to him as the Chinese Legation out for a stroll may appear to self-satisfied London. Religion, like justice, is uniformed—Bishops and Clergy, High Church, Low Church, and Church Army, Roman Catholics, English Nonconformists, the Salvation Army, and Jews. The palace and the workhouse are alike governed by inflexible rules concerning uniform. But print and corduroy are not the garb of palaces; nor do the gauds of earthly greatness gleam in workhouses. Royal receptions, however, are a blaze of uniforms—home and foreign. Even ladies attending at Court must conform to dress regulations. Parliamentary officials are uniformed; and when the Faithful Commons attend the Speaker's Levees they must—no matter how lathy or how tubby—wear cutaway coats, knee-breeches, and silk stockings. The satellites of fashion, too, are proclaimed by their livery. You need not be a grandee to secure liveried service in London. Go to a restaurant, hotel, theatre, or music-hall and you may be received with as much deference as if you were a duke by janitors in blue, or green, or brown and gold. If you have driven up with a sister, a cousin, or an aunt—or someone else of the gentle sex—those magnificoes will see to it that

DUKE OF YORK'S BOYS : COLOUR AND ESCORT.

her dress is not soiled by brushing against the wheel of the cab or carriage as she alights. They have for the purpose wicker mudguards which they dexterously fix on the tyre of the wheel. Enter a theatre or music-hall, where you have been received with such distinction, and you may perceive not only young lady programme-sellers of soubrette aspect and page boys, but also attendants in impressive liveries with powdered heads and silken calves. At the Army and Navy Stores you may see soberly arrayed doorkeepers mounting guard over chained pet dogs. Uniformed janitors are also now extensively employed by London shopkeepers.

Quaint costumes in London still? Many and many. Gone may be the Blue Coats, and Grey Coats, the Green Coats and the Red Coats of the schools, but the older time is still with us nevertheless. Are there not the Tower "Beefeaters"—or Yeomen Warders—whose costume has varied little during four centuries? The Yeomen of the Guard, too, who are on duty at royal palaces, are similarly garbed and armed with partisans. They, like the Honourable Corps of Gentlemen-at-Arms—in uniforms of scarlet with blue velvet facings—act as a bodyguard to the Sovereign on great occasions.

Why, even the heraldic costume of the Life Guards' bandsmen is quaint—very different from that of the cuirassed and helmeted troopers who, being scarlet coated, are distinguished from the Horse Guards, otherwise "The Blues." And what think ye of

RESTAURANT ATTENDANT.

the City Beadles? Those of the trade guilds and the wards wear the same style of costumes as their predecessors in office centuries ago. The Beadle at the Royal Exchange perpetuates the cloak and the cocked hat such as were worn by an earlier functionary when good Queen Bess reigned. It is a showy uniform ; but not more so than that worn by janitors in the Bank of England, and less so than that of the red cloaked official on duty at Lloyd's. Other institutions, such as the Baltic—the home of the floating grain trade—have impressively garbed officials. The bank messengers who swarm in the City are of a more modern type. They are generally prim men, clean-shaven, except for side whiskers, and uniformed in dapper style, with a possible concession in respect of aggressive waistcoats. Make way for the Lord Mayor, Aldermen, Sheriffs,

SCHOOL FOR SOLDIERS' DAUGHTERS (HAMPSTEAD) : AT PLAY.

BOY MESSENGER.

Lieutenants, and high officials of the City with their small army of liveried attendants! There's a blaze of uniformed glory for you which does not differ essentially from that of Whittington's Mayoralty. Why, the splendours of London's civic uniforms and liveries are such that the secondhand robes, cocked hats, and insignia have been eagerly desired in the past by

be distinguished by a red band round their caps; the Coldstreams wear a white one; the Scots a die-patterned ribbon, and the Irish Guards a green one. But who are those who stride along so perkily to drumming, cymbal-clashing and fifing? They call themselves "the Sons of the Brave." They are the boys of the Duke of York's School for soldiers' sons. They have their uniforms, their own colour, their guns, and the traditions of the British Army behind them, so let the audacious foreigner beware! There are soldiers' daughters, too, who wear the Army scarlet. Those bright little maids are from the Soldiers' Daughters' Home at Hampstead, and see—there are the girls from the Patriotic Asylum at Wandsworth.

barbaric ambition on the West Coast of Africa. Guildhall Museum and Library attendants are uniformed, but they have not the brilliant red and gold facings of certain British Museum officials.

Passing along the great highways from east

A BOYS' BRIGADE MUSTER (OLD SQUARE, LINCOLN'S INN).

Uniformed boys abound in London. Thousands of them belong to the Boys' and the Lads' Brigades — the product of a very remarkable movement initiated in Glasgow in 1883, but which has since ramified throughout the

to west, what a variety of uniforms you may note! Many of them are feminine. There, for example, is the hospital nurse in blue, with linen collar and cuffs. How she pervades London! She ascends to the 'bus top and she descends to the nether regions of the Twopenny Tube stations. She is everywhere. Then there are the Grey Ladies, Brown Ladies, and Ladies in Black —deaconesses and nursing sisters of religious orders. And who has not seen the "Hallelujah Lasses" of the Salvation Army? Of very different and nun-like aspect are the Roman Catholic Little Sisters of the Poor—devoted to the sweet cause of charity. Soldiers and sailors in the multi-coloured uniforms of Mars afford a vivid contrast. The Grenadier Guards may

BOYS OF THE CHAPEL ROYAL, ST. JAMES'S.

SHOEBLACKS PAYING IN THEIR DAY'S EARNINGS
(SAFFRON HILL).

Empire. It is organised on a military basis for physical and moral training. Boys between the ages of twelve and seventeen are eligible for enrolment. Thirty boys form the minimum of a company. Each company is under the command of a captain, who has at least two subordinate officers as lieutenants. The non-commissioned officers are promoted from the ranks. Six or more companies in any town or district may, with the sanction of the Executive, form themselves into a battalion. Every company must be connected with a church, mission, or other Christian organisation, the aim of the brigade being "to promote habits of obedience, reverence, discipline, self-respect, and all that tends towards a true Christian manliness" by means of military organisation and drill. The boys whose muster our photographic illustration on page 181 shows are those of North London's crack company—the 58th. In the case of the Church Lads' Brigade, the Roman Catholic Boys' Brigade, and the Jewish Lads' Brigade definite religious adherence is required. Quite an army of boys —and not lacking drill either—wear the uniform of the State in London as telegraph messengers, and even such bicycles as are provided for them are painted red, thus being in harmony with the mail-coaches and the pillar letter-boxes. The District Messenger Boys are under, not public, but company control. They are a wonderfully well-organised corps, prepared to go any-

where and do anything at duty's call by day or by night. Sometimes—if Hibernian licence may be permitted— the District Messenger boy is a girl! But not often: nor do the girls occasionally employed when boys are scarce wear uniform. The cable companies, the press agencies, and many private firms have their own boy messengers distinctively garbed. Uniformed boys abound, also, as pages in clubs, hotels, and institutions, as well as in various other capacities. But the paragons of boy splendour in London are the choir boys of the Chapel Royal, St. James's. They have been mistaken by simple-minded visitors for royal princes on the rare occasions when they are seen out of doors. Fine as their every-day dress may be, it is quite eclipsed by their State costume, which is a brilliant creation of scarlet and gold with purple bars, lace ruffles at neck and wrists, and glorified "mortar-boards" brimmed with gold. Each boy's State suit costs £40! At the other end of the boy-uniformed social scale are the shoeblacks —already referred to in "London's Street Industries"—who are red or blue or brown or white jacketted according to the brigade to which they belong. The Central Shoeblacks (red) Brigade originated at the time of the Great Exhibition, and has ever since done wonderful reformatory work as well as public service.

Of all London's uniformed host none are more popular than the Corps of Commissionaires, who have their headquarters off the Strand not far from

PARK KEEPER (L.C.C.
PARKS).

Charing Cross. The institution of the Corps was a really brilliant idea, which ensured civil employment mainly for ex-soldiers and sailors, and supplied a long-felt want by providing handy men—at once trustworthy and responsible — for regular or casual service. They are active men in the prime of life — though some may bear the scars of honourable service. They are not grizzled patriarchs like the uniformed pensioners of Chelsea Hospital, who have found there a pleasant haven of refuge when their campaigning days are long since over. The London police look fit and workmanlike, though more sparing of gleaming white metal on their helmets than, say, the Loamshire County Constabulary. There is an army of variously uniformed railway men. There are the postmen—men of letters, who make a noise in the world with their rat-tat-tat. There are firemen, clothed like sailors—as, indeed, most of them have been —but wearing helmets instead of navy caps when on service fighting the flames.

PARK KEEPER (ROYAL PARKS).

There are the ambulance men of the St. John's Brigade—the modern representatives of the Knights Hospitallers of the Crusades — ready to tend the injured and the ailing on public or other occasions, or even in time of war. There are the park-keepers, prepared to defend at all hazards the flower beds and the duck ponds from juvenile aggression. There are the various out-door employés of the County Council, the Metropolitan Borough Councils, the Gas and the Water Companies—these ranging from tram conductors to tall-hatted turn-cocks, whilst there is quite a formidable army of variously garbed street orderlies and dust-men. But now, though we have not quite exhausted the vast and fascinating theme of "Uniformed London," we must bring our observations to a close, merely claiming in conclusion that even superficial survey justifies the opening proposition concerning the magnitude, the vivid contrasts, and the impressiveness as a whole of London's uniformed multitudes.

A PARADE OF COMMISSIONAIRES : CALLING THE ROLL.

WORKING IN TRENCHES (OXFORD STREET).

LONDON "UP."

By GEO R. SIMS.

LONDON is always more or less "up," but sometimes it is so much "up" that it resembles, so far as its roadways are concerned, a new city in course of making, rather than an old one in the course of repair. Macaulay's New Zealander has of late years lived in comparative retirement. But he occasionally peeps round the corner in one's mental vision when one takes one's walks abroad, and sees thoroughfare after thoroughfare being excavated by an army of labourers, with stones, wood blocks, drain pipes, poles, barrows, huts, rollers, pickaxes, spades, bricks, sacks, and cement lying about in all directions in unpicturesque confusion. The New Zealander was meditative over the ruins of London Bridge. If he came in these years of grace he would be able to meditate on a very near approach to ruin in every part of the Metro-

polis. The buildings stand, but the roadways that lie before them are constantly broken up.

There are some districts even in the heart of fashionable London where the road may be said to be permanently "up." It is taken up for drains and re-made. No sooner have the barriers disappeared than they are replaced in order that the road may be taken

LAYING WOOD PAVING (OUTSIDE THE ALBERT HALL).

up for gas. The gas pipes having disappeared from view for a week, the road is taken up again for the electric light. Peace may then reign for a day or two. But, just as the inhabitants of the neighbourhood have breathed a sigh of relief at the disappearance of the gangs of workmen, the barriers, the blazing fires, the foreman's office, and the builder's yard exhibition in their beloved thoroughfares, the borough council or the County Council makes the discovery that the wood pavement ought to be renewed. Up comes the roadway again. A rampart of wood blocks is erected along the pavements, the swarthy Swiss-Italians, in blue and pink shirts, of the Val de Travers Company are replaced by British workmen, who are accompanied by huge boilers of an evil-smelling liquid which gives off black smoke that penetrates the houses and chokes the inhabitants. The wood pavement is only one remove in the unpleasantness of its public preparation from the old asphalt, the laying of which it was ever the delight of Londoners to watch.

An entirely different form of torture in connection with the breaking up of London's roadways is experienced in districts where the old macadam still holds sway. One fine morning the sleeping householder is aroused from his slumbers by a sound which resembles that of an asthmatic railway engine trying to draw too many trucks up an inclined plane. The householder looks out of his window and discovers that a steam-roller has arrived and is crushing new laid stones down into their places. Perhaps before the roller arrives a gaunt, scraggy engine, built on lines suggesting the first attempt of an early Briton, has put in an appearance. To this is attached

a kind of harrow with formidable iron teeth. This is the scarifier; and as it is dragged along by the engine it tears up the road. Poets contemplating the process have been heard to remark that it suggested a virago with long nails scratching somebody else's face.

The scarifier is the prose of road-making—asthmatic, ill-balanced, ill-regulated prose; the poetry of the process comes in when the steam-roller, preceded by a hydrostatic

TEMPORARY PATH OF PLANKS (SOUTHAMPTON ROW).

van in action, humbly follows the bearer of a red flag, who seems to be attending the funeral of an Anarchist and keeping time to an invisible band playing the Dead March in "Saul." The grim sternness with which the great metal wheels of the steam-roller crush the rebellious flints flat into the bosom of mother earth has attractions not only for unthinking childhood but for philosophic middle age. There is the note of destiny in it. From the moment the roller starts on its journey the fate of every pebble is sealed. All are relentlessly and methodically crushed down into one common flatness.

The Strand is a favourite field of operations for the authorities and the private companies.

I. COLLECTING WOOD BLOCKS (WHITEHALL).   II. STEAM ROLLER AT WORK (THAMES EMBANKMENT).   III. ROAD WORKMEN AT DINNER.

If one part of it is down the other is up. When the up part is finished the down part is taken up again. The pulling up of the Strand we seem to have always with us. If by chance the entire road is in possession of wood blocks which will bear the traffic, that is the psychological moment seized upon by an electric lighting company, or a kindred spirit, to tear it up from end to end.

In the daytime the uppishness of the Strand provokes only protest and objurgation. The pavements are blocked with men and women, who elbow and struggle and push in a fierce attempt to find a passage for themselves. At one part of the Strand during the making of a new street pedestrians had to use a wooden bridge, as shown in our illustration on page 189. The heavy traffic, under ordinary alterations forced into a narrow channel, advances at a snail's pace, and has considerable difficulty in keeping off the pavement and sometimes even out of the shop windows. But late at night, when the last omnibus has crept to its rest, and only a solitary cab glides now and then like a weary spirit along the deserted thoroughfare, the attack upon the Strand has many picturesque features. The men usually work through the hours of sleep. Then great yellow flames flare up against the blackness of the night, flinging a strange and ghastly hue upon the faces of the toilers and of the wayfarers who stand at the pavement's edge and look on in silent rapture.

East and west, north and south, you may wander, and never will you wander far without coming upon an army of labourers, either digging deep trenches in the centre of the road or breaking the surface in order to lay tram lines or laying down new wood blocks or turning the well-worn macadam into a stretch of asphalt.

Occasionally only a narrow path of planks is left for the pedestrian, who, like the time-honoured hen, crosses the road because he wants to get to the other side. You may see this in the photographic reproduction, on page 185, of a scene in Southampton Row.

Now and again you come upon a scene of London "Up" which is really picturesque— a scene which a painter might transfer to his canvas. It is at the dinner hour—

when the men, some sitting in the night-watchman's hut, some making a shelter of an uptilted hand-cart, squat round the red coke fire and smoke their pipes and read last week's—sometimes last year's—news in the torn, greasy bits of newspaper in which some of their provender has been wrapped.

The adjuncts of the meal have generally in themselves a picturesque suggestion. There is the plain white basin tied up in a big red handkerchief; there is the queer-shaped metal bottle which contains the tea—or is it beer? There are the big pocket knives which take the place of table cutlery; and often there is the little girl or the young woman who has come to see father or husband at dinner-time and has thoughtfully brought him "something hot."

The children who gather about the road-makers are not always there for pleasure. There are times when the roadway is a veritable Tom Tiddler's Ground, not for the picking up of gold and silver, but the securing of wood blocks and chips which are of considerable value for domestic purposes. You will see ragged children—it is generally a little girl who carries the biggest burden—staggering along bravely with a sack-load or an apron-load of wood saved from the *débris* of the repairing operations. Occasionally the children are warned off, and the old wood blocks become the property of grown-up men, who take them away on donkey carts and hand-carts. The children are the most interesting "adventurers" to watch. Having secured their wood, they occasionally retire with it to a convenient dead wall, and there they proceed to chop it up into pieces of smaller size.

The tradespeople of the thoroughfares which are the favourites of the road-making operators are long-suffering folk. They endure something which is an unhappy compromise between a siege and a blockade for long periods with despair in their hearts, but the despair only rises to their lips when the state of things is continued until it denudes the thoroughfare of those passers-by on whom they depend for custom. All classes suffer alike. The little ready-money shop loses its cash customer; the big establishments suffer because no cab or carriage can come within several hundred

WATCHMEN.

and naphtha jets. That on foggy nights these open ditches in the centres of the principal thoroughfares do not become filled with bodies of lost wayfarers is one of the mysteries of London.

The wardrobe arrangements of a gang of road-makers are strongly conservative. In a busy thoroughfare they generally manage to put their outer garments into trucks, carts, or empty hand barrows, but in a residential quarter they prefer hanging their coats up in the orthodox fashion—on something that projects. They invariably choose the adjacent area railings ; and so it may come about that you may suddenly enter an aristocratic square and find the railings in front of some of the most magnificent houses given up to jackets and waistcoats which would hardly find hospitality on the clothes pegs of Rag Fair.

London "Up" is not a subject on which you can tell the Londoner much that he does not know. It is part of his daily life. He cannot go out for an hour's walk without coming upon the scene in one form or another. So familiar has he grown with this phase of civilisation that even when he walks along a narrow way and hears the voices of men down in the very bowels of the earth he rarely pauses to lean over the dividing pole and have a look at them. And yet some of the men are down in trenches several feet below the level of the omnibus wheels which frequently passes so close to the edge of the abyss that they collide with the barriers. Sometimes when men are making only a hole in a limited area they simply protect them-

yards of their doors. Sometimes there are public meetings of protest, but, as a rule, the indignation finds a safety valve in letters to the newspapers. Of late years, however, so many parts of London have suffered from the roadways being made impassable by the works in progress on them that Londoners have ceased to "write to the *Times*," and have begun to recognise the grim humour of the thing.

London "Up" presents its romantic side in the winter days when a heavy fog suddenly converts the inhabitants of the capital into a people groping their way through a city over which has been spread the mantle of invisibility. Then does the passage of Ludgate Hill, the crossing of Berkeley Square, the navigation of Holborn become as dangerous as the Alpine trip of the tourist whose proud motto was "Excelsior." Humanity is not dead, even in the heart of the contractors for road repairs, and so, when a black fog comes, fires are lighted and torches hung on posts, and from innumerable pots and skillets a weird red flame makes the surrounding darkness more visible. The ghostly horse in a phantom hansom led by the cabman, who is a voice and a cough and nothing more, appears to be — if you are unfortunate enough to be inside the cab—a shadowy salamander threading its way through a Hampton Court maze of posts and barriers marked out into avenues of red lanterns

READY FOR REMOVAL.

selves by putting a temporary wooden cross-piece at the corners. These are occasionally also collided with and carried along by the wheel of a passing vehicle.

When an extended area is given up to a great army of labourers it is dotted with many quaint and curious structures—wooden huts, a thing that looks like a bathing machine on trolley wheels, but which is labelled "Foreman's Office," huge sheds covered with tarpaulin, circular barriers in sections which enable the operators to cut off portions of the pavement from pedestrians while they, the operators, perform conjuring tricks with a network of wires below; and last, but not least, the deftly rigged up shelter of the watchman who spends the night by a cheerful coke fire smoking his black dhudeen and gossiping occasionally with a loafer to whom the glow of the coke is welcome. This watchman in his Robinson Crusoey hut is envied by all small boys—even by those who have luxurious homes—and often, I have no doubt, by many a grown-up boy in whose nature there still lingers the spirit of romance.

I have been privileged to spend some hours of the night with one of these lonely guardians, and it brought vividly to my mind old stories of the camp fire on the prairies by which the lonely trappers of Mayne Reid so often took their rest and yarned to each other. These men are only on duty at night-time during the week, but on Sundays they have to put in a day as well. Then they have visitors. It is no uncommon sight to see the watchman's wife and daughter seated beside or near him on the Sunday morning, and I have heard of friends of the family dropping in to tea. But this is in the summer, when a turned-up wheelbarrow or an inverted bucket is a pleasant enough resting place, seeing that the blue skies are overhead and the sunshine all around.

These, then, are the principal features of London "Up" as they strike the Londoner. What the people of Continental cities, where a system prevails and the authorities combine to minimise the evils of road disturbing, think is probably "another story." Foreigners who have seen the sights that London presents under its permanent "up" condition elevate their eyebrows in astonishment. But London is the capital of the land in which everybody is free to do as he likes within limits. Whether this freedom is not abused by the various authorities, who have the right of taking the roadway from beneath our feet whenever they choose, it is not for the chronicler of "things as they are" to dilate upon. That enters more legitimately into the sphere of the writer on "things as they ought to be."

A BRIDGE IN THE STRAND.

MOTORING LONDON.

By H. O TYMAN

THE cult of the automobile, which since the great Paris-Bordeaux race of 1895 has been adopted with enthusiasm almost amounting to passion by the inhabitants of the French capital, enjoys a continually increasing following in the Metropolis. It really dates from the month of November, 1896, for it was then that, by the passing of the Light Locomotives Act of 1896, it became possible for Londoners to use self-propelled carriages in the streets of their city. Notwithstanding the legal disabilities in the matter of speed under which automobilists at first laboured, the use of mechanically propelled vehicles employed for pleasure-driving, for goods transport, and for passenger traffic has increased to such an extent that the passage of a motor car through the crowded streets of the town or the comparatively lonely roads of our huge suburbs, now scarcely provokes remark or tempts a passer-by to turn his head in curiosity.

Slowly, but very surely, the horseless vehicle, devoid of nerves, muscles and sinews liable to shock and pain, has effected a revolution in the traffic of our London streets. The time is not far distant when all utilitarian vehicles as opposed to carriages used by London Society for pleasure and ostentation will take the form of road machines depending upon a mechanical economy for their propulsion.

It is chiefly for pleasure that the Metropolis motors and automobilists, from a variety of causes, form but a small and not too favourably regarded section of the London vehicular public. Prejudice, deep-rooted and obstinate, will harass them and the growth of the movement for years to come. A retrospective glance over the locomotive changes of the past conclusively proves that automobilism is fighting against the same conservative, non-progressive spirit which for so many years oppressed the cyclist and caused him to be regarded as an Ishmael amongst his fellow users of the road. Prejudice against any novel form of street traffic dies hard, particularly with our friends the omnibus driver, cabby, and the carman. These honest folk, who for ages past have esteemed themselves the very salt of the roadway, naturally resent the coming of the new form of travel just as keenly and as bitterly as did the whips and guards of the old stage coaches. But in such opposition they do but re-enact the part of Mrs. Partington with her mop ; and their ill-judged and ill-tempered opposition can no more set back the period when a horse-drawn vehicle will be as infrequent a sight on our London streets as a motor car formerly was, than could the old lady above referred to stem the oncoming tide with her useful household implement.

Serious opposition and injustice such as automobilists have suffered from have had just the effect that the opposition of a non-progressive majority to a progressive minority invariably entails. It has caused that minority to combine for their mutual protection and for the advancement of the cause they have at heart and the objects they have in view. The concrete result of that combination is the Automobile Club of Great Britain and Ireland, which is the headquarters of Motoring London. To this club, now an influential and potential body, every automobilist of good social standing considers it a duty to his cult to belong. From very small beginnings, in comparatively humble premises in Whitehall Court, it has advanced in an incredibly short space of time to the dignity of a powerful, well-equipped and luxuriously appointed West-End club, with a noble habitat overlooking the Green Park, at No. 119, Piccadilly. To this establishment rally all men of light and leading in London who favour and who have adopted that form of road locomotion which depends for propulsion upon steam, or petroleum spirit, or electricity ; and to-day the Automobile Club, with its vigorously

AT AN AUTOMOBILE EXHIBITION (AGRICULTURAL HALL).

urged progaganda, its comforts and conveniences, stands forth and is recognised as a power and an influence to be reckoned with.

During its existence the Club has performed wonders in introducing automobilism to the country generally, and the London public in particular. It has held exhibitions, organised trials, arranged runs and tours, fought legal cases *à outrance* in the interests of the movement, and continues and will continue in these good works for many a day to come. Within the Club are discussed all the subjects at the moment on the *tapis* with the world of automobilism. There the latest home or Continental news, of great trials or events, new inventions and introductions which may or may not revolutionise the outward appearance or the internal economy of automobiles are discussed from every point of view. But foremost of its aims is the watchful safeguarding of such liberties of the streets and highways as it has already secured, and in this regard and in still further advancing the cause a mountain of labour stands always before it.

Apart from the buzzing, hissing, droning presence and passage of automobiles amidst the London traffic, that which most impresses the permanency of the latest form of locomotion upon the observant citizen is the appearance of what for lack of an adequate English word are termed " Motor-Garages." These are becoming plentifully sprinkled about the more fashionable parts of London, and have even invaded the precincts of the City

INTERIOR OF A GARAGE (QUEEN STREET, E.C.).

itself. These establishments stand in the same relation to the automobile as do livery and bait stables to horses and carriages, for therein automobiles may be safely housed by the day, week, or hour, and while so housed are tended by skilled assistants, cleaned, furbished, and fed with water or petrol, or, be they electro-mobiles, attached by carefully insulated wires to brass studded and handled slate slabs affixed to the wall, in order that the particular form of aliment they require, so that they can roam the streets, may be conveyed to them from the electric mains. To the uninitiated the interiors of these garages present a curious appearance. They boast no stalls, no loose boxes, no mangers, their floor spaces are clear and

MOTOR TRAILER.

scenes of much animation and bustle. On the one side are cars ready to take the road, with their engines in motion and snorting as explosion engines do when running light, and as though eager and impatient to be gone into the outer air. On the other are, perhaps, steam cars, silent but for the mild roar of their burners by which steam has been raised and retained to the necessary pressure in their boilers. Then the electro-mobile, which for the whole period of its sojourn in the garage has been noiselessly absorbing power through the insulated cables already mentioned, takes its departure with quietude and dignity, and in marked contrast to the impatient snorting of the petrol car and the fretting fussiness of the steam-propelled vehicle preceding it. In corners of these establishments stand cars undergoing repair, and to the novice, strange, nay, almost un-

marked only by what suggests the familiar cellar flap of the public-house. These are the covers of sinkings in the floor technically termed "pits," into which the skilled leather-clad automobile mechanic descends beneath a car for the purpose of more conveniently effecting such repairs and making such adjustments as the carriage in hand may at the moment require.

STEAM LORRY.

canny, is the spectacle they present, as with motor bonnet or entire body removed they bare their ungainly mechanical details to the light of day. But for the wheels which link them to the traffic of modern times they might be well esteemed by the un-initiated as weird fossils upheaved from the nether slime.

Above or below in the best appointed garages are well-equipped engineering workshops amply provided with lathes, drilling machines, benches, vices, brazing hearths, smiths' fires and anvils, by the aid of which repairs, however heavy, can be effected to the more or less complicated mechanism of the cars. Provision in the shape of a bricked and isolated cavern is made for storage of that high distillate of petroleum known in this country as " petrol." Many of these establishments rejoice in more than one floor, so that when business is brisk and automobilists driving into the West-End or the City from the outlying districts of our brick and mortar labyrinth crowd the place with their vehicles, these are borne slowly aloft on huge lifts to remain in the regions above until again required by their home-returning owners.

In the busy season these garages are the

But apart from all hitherto touched upon, Motoring London is most apparent to the average Londoner in the evidences of auto-

Photo: Ar,ent Archer, Kensington, W.
ABOUT TO START.

mobilism that confront him day after day in the streets of his city. In the early days breakdowns in the public thoroughfares were frequent enough, and the spectacle of an unhappy automobilist prone on his back on the road beneath his vehicle struggling with some obstinate adjustment was too frequent for the chauffeur's comfort or self-respect. But improvement and betterment have advanced with the passing years, and so sad a sight is

season is at its height. The London doctor hies him on his humane rounds in a well-ordered car particularly designed for his use, and is able to get through his work in half the time at half the cost and with no anxiety as to waiting and overworked horseflesh.

The wealthy sportsman, keen on polo at Rane-lagh, pigeon "potting" at Hurlingham, or golf yet further afield, drives where he may find his pleasure on the swift car,

I. A TEMPORARY BREAKDOWN.   II. INTERIOR OF A GARAGE (SOUTH KENSINGTON).

seldom if ever seen in these happier days. Motoring London takes the shape of the frequent appearance of automobiles of many and divers shapes and systems of cars, running in and out, through and by, the long lines of traffic on our arterial thoroughfares. Skilfully handled vehicles thread their way through the press of horse-drawn conveyances, comparing in carriage work, upholstery, and general turn-out with the most sumptuous of the smart vehicles they overhaul and pass with such apparent ease.

The Society lady, on "calls" or "shopping" bent, uses her automobile with more frequency than her carriage, and even at times invades therewith the Lady's Mile when the London

eschewing trains and cabs and saving his own horses. The public who affect "the sport of kings" at Sandown, Kempton, or Hurst Park largely betake themselves thither by automobile. The London commercial traveller, hitherto doing his business with an apology for a brougham, and therein hedged to suffocation with piled boxes of his samples, has adopted motor cars suited to his particular needs, and in consequence effects a great saving of time and money. The great catering and provision supplying establishments have also recognised the capabilities of motor transport, and automobiles, for carrying goods, are frequent features in our streets and at our doors. The Postal Department too has profited by the example of the big traders, for now and again the monotones of the traffic lines are accentuated by the bright red of a self-propelled Post Office van.

But to see Motoring London at its best, one must take one's stand on certain of the great traffic conduits leading outwards from the metropolis, when on high days, holidays, and at week ends, all Londoners who possess engines and gear over four wheels, whirl and skir, trumpet and hoot, country-wards and sea-wards to escape the city for a little space. It is then, and only then, when every minute sees the passage of a car bearing its freight of cloaked and head-shrouded women and heavily coated and goggled men to pure air and open heath, along the pleasant roads of the home counties, that the wholesale manner in which motoring has popularised itself can be fully realised. From the spitting, fast-flitting motor-bicycle, with its rigid rider, up through the gamut of motor-tricycle — carrying a single passenger or hauling a light trailer with family loads — motor-quad, voiturette, light car and heavily engined automobile, roofed and hooded and screened, all sorts and conditions of the self-propelled proffer themselves in an incredibly short space of time. Motoring London makes then all haste it can to get out of London and leave the town behind it. Vehicles worth thousands of pounds surge by in one short hour, and from morn to dewy eve and late into the night the dwellers along suburban roads are never free of the roar of the passing cars.

By good fortune the observer may even be able to catch sight of the King in one of his roomy cars hastening down to Windsor. At night, too, the electric car or cab, silent but for an internal hum which suggests the labour of some huge imprisoned insect, and brilliantly lit without and within, is seen gliding through the traffic as it conveys its passengers to theatre, concert, restaurant or dance. So brilliant and attractive an appearance do these vehicles then present that they might almost be described as the meteors or comets of the London streets. When the weather of our English climate is altogether too bad for pleasure motoring, the sight-loving citizen can obtain full evidence of its vitality by paying a visit to one of the annual motor exhibitions held at the Agricultural Hall or the Crystal Palace.

Automobilism has very truly been said to be the special pastime of the fairly well-to-do, but London possesses several public motor services, and will in time own more, and in the vehicles employed the poor man may taste some of the pleasures of the self-propelled carriage. So we find that every class of wheeled conveyance in the London streets has been invaded by the horseless vehicle. And with the continual growth of that invasion our pleasure and convenience are increasingly served, while we are spared to a greater and greater degree the sight of over-worked animals, and our streets are the cleaner and sweeter for the diminution of horse-drawn traffic.

THE KING READY FOR A DRIVE.

SUNDAY EVENING EAST AND WEST.

By A. ST. IOHN ADCOCK

THERE is many a little country town where on this evening some ivied parish church shakes its silvery chimes into the quiet air while the townsfolk, in their sober Sunday best, are straying leisurely through the sleepy echoing streets, church-wards or chapelwards. Later, returning, in neighbourly converse, they will find their ways home by the glimmerings of sparse gas-lamps, or by moonlight only if the moon be at the full. They will pass hobbledehoys speeding the dull hours with gossip at the corners ; there will be sweethearts lingering in the dimness and coolness of leafy green lanes ; there will be loafers late at some of the public-houses ; but the evening offers no other distractions, and by ten o'clock lights will be fading from upper windows and the whole town getting to bed.

No wonder strangers, fresh from the deep tranquillity of a place of such unvaried, primitive observances, find the breadth and strenuousness and religious and secular variety of our London Sunday evenings bedazzling and bewildering.

Here, this summer evening, before the bells start and the streets are alive with all sorts and conditions of men and women streaming to their multifarious places of worship, trams and 'buses and trains in the suburbs are beginning to pick up passengers who are travelling in to some famous City church, to Sunday League concerts at Queen's Hall or the Alhambra, or merely to hear the band in Hyde Park ; and in the heart of the comparatively deserted City itself long rows of towering, matter-of-fact ware-houses and offices are roused from dreams of the week's work by a clash and thrill of music, and from all their business windows see the commonplace thoroughfare below strangely transfigured by a passing procession.

It is a procession of surpliced choristers and musicians headed by a white-stoled leader uplifting a cros . Earlier or later in the year some in this white procession carry ships' lanterns flashing at the tops of poles, but now lanterns are needless. The lifted cross leads the way eastwards through the twilight, drawing stragglers from the highways and byways after it, and the whole body swings round Eastcheap, down St. Mary-at-Hill, to the grey old church there that is rapidly filling, and in up the aisle, sending the triumphant crying of its sounding brasses echoing into answering hollows of the roof.

This is the Church Army, or a section of it, and here are its headquarters.

In the church itself (which justifies its methods by being packed upstairs and down, in contrast with the emptiness of most of the neighbouring churches) a suspended sheet is unrolled and shuts the orchestra out of sight, lights are lowered, a huge lantern reared in the gallery flings a great moon on the sheet, and presently pictures illustrating some sacred or secular topic—mostly some topic of the moment— are flitting across that magic moon-circle, while from the darkness the lecturer's voice rises to "adorn the tale " and point an occasional moral. If the lecturer be the good Vicar himself, then, when the lights are turned up again and there is music, you may see him in the pulpit enthusiastic-ally adding to the general harmony with the aid of a trombone ; and, later, you may listen while an address by some absent but famous preacher or speaker is reproduced through the large megaphone—shown in our photo-graphic illustration on page 198.

Meanwhile, there are forlorn and broken human creatures gathering in a lengthening line down the narrow, dark lane behind the church, waiting patiently to be admitted to the free supper given to them here at the close of the more orthodox service that follows the lantern lecture.

IN HYDE PARK.

AN EAST-END SALVATION ARMY SERVICE.

AT ST. MARY-AT-HILL CHURCH.

round them: there are slatternly women and unwashed men in it, dockers and decent artisans in their working clothes, a sprinkling of dapper shop assistants, a soldier or two, bronzed seamen of many nationalities ; with here and there, peering grotesquely beside pallid Cockney faces, black visages of negroes, brown visages of lascars, yellow visages of wondering Chinamen, astray from ships in the docks.

An increasing and motley crowd, but respectful and fairly attentive, most of the male portion of it sucking ruminatively at pipes or cigarettes ; and even the aliens who can make nothing of the preaching can enjoy the music and the singing, and translate their appreciation into pennies when the cheery, pleasant-featured " lassie " passes persuasively among them with a tambourine for a collection plate.

The last hymn is scarcely ended when one of the wearers of red jerseys—a wan, eager young man—bares his head, and stepping to the centre of the ring shouts an impassioned prayer with his face turned heavenward ; then, beseeching the bystanders to go with them to their " citadel," he makes a sign at which his comrades promptly fall into marching order, and with the flag fluttering, drums thumping, and brasses braying, away they sweep, keeping step, up the road, accompanied by a small salvage of their audience—up the road and in at their " citadel " doorway, which is pinched rather tightly between a couple of shops.

By this the bells all over London have finished their clangour, and every church and chapel and little meeting-house and

But we do not wait for all this. Indeed, before the moon on the sheet is flushed with its first picture we have gone up Eastcheap, through the Minories into Aldgate, and from Aldgate away down Commercial Road East, past dingy coffee-rooms where Jews and Christians, Britishers and aliens, sit at bare wooden tables in clouds of tobacco smoke, reading, meditating, sipping their drinks, or beguiling the time with dominoes ; past Jewish, Russian, Italian, and many other shabby or shabby-genteel foreign restaurants, all busy, but not so busy as they will be later; past numerous public-houses, where men and women are sociably regaling themselves ; past large and small sweet-stuff and pastry shops, wherein juvenile Don Juans of the district are lolling gloriously at the counters treating themselves and their " donahs " to ices and ginger-beer.

Farther east we come upon a group of Salvationists holding a perfervid meeting. Half of them are there to speak or sing only, the other half blow or beat lustily at musical instruments, even two of the women, in their neat blue uniform dresses and scoop bonnets, playing cornets.

A large and increasing crowd is clustering

meeting-room has its gathering of worshippers. In the west the fashionable world inclines to go to church on Sunday mornings or afternoons and sends its servants in the evenings, but there are not a few exceptions in this respect. The middle and lower classes, east and west, perhaps for reasons which are not unconnected with working late on Saturday nights and with the preparation of Sunday afternoon dinners, have a preference for evening services; wherefore this evening many churches and chapels are fuller almost than they can hold.

And while westward the services are commencing in such churches as St. Paul's with solemn rollings of the organ and chantings of the choir, and in such as the Brompton Oratory with organ and choir music and a swinging and smoking of censers; here, at the other extreme, they are commencing in bare little seamen's missions scattered about Poplar and the waterside parishes with wheezy groanings of small harmoniums and the hearty bass of voices that may this time next week be uplifted aboard ship far out under the stars on lonely wastes of sea.

Electric or gas lamps are shining now along every line of roadway; and in Commercial Road and Whitechapel Road, and the tangle of streets that intersect them, the many shops, mostly Jewish, that are open have lighted up their windows and made those that are shut look deader than ever by contrast. Here and there, in main road or byway, a big warehouse is open, clerks can be seen at work within, and carts backed against the kerb before it are loading or unloading.

Here and there, at corners, as you may find them now and for the next two hours at corners of the West-End also, open-air evangelists are preaching by the light of street lamps or of lanterns carried by their supporters. Sideshow shops liberally furnished with automatic picture machines are flaring wide open, with a constant flow of customers pushing in and out; here and there, in shops or private houses that have been converted from their original purposes or in small halls of their own, working men's clubs are debating set subjects of social or political moment over pipes and glasses, or, like less utilitarian Jewish clubs in the neighbourhood, are recreating themselves with smoking concerts.

Diverging up Osborn Street, Whitechapel, just about the time that carriages are driving to some of the fashionable West-End churches to fetch their owners home, and hansoms are hovering about most of them on the chance of capturing fares, and just a little before the organ recital begins at the People's Palace, in the Mile End Road, we come upon

OUTSIDE A WEST-END CHURCH (ST. PETER'S, VERE STREET).

waggons standing by the roadside, some horseless and with their shafts up, others already horsed, with drivers lighting their lamps and climbing to their seats. Not far off the gates of a contractor's yard are yawning, and more vans are getting ready inside : one after the other they move rumbling away, and vanish in the direction of the docks or towards railway termini, and in the very small hours of the morning they will be toiling heavy laden into London's markets.

In all the back streets and alleys hereabouts people are leaning from their windows, sitting on their doorsteps, obstructing the pavements, or strolling in the roads, taking the air, with a tendency to gravitate towards corners and stop there. Nearly every corner here and throughout Spitalfields has its knot of cosmopolitan babblers of both sexes ; some have lounged as far as the garden - churchyard opposite the Market to sit down, but most prefer to remain standing about the familiar streets.

As you retrace your steps along Aldgate, look into Middlesex Street (the Petticoat Lane of the past), which until after noon was a seething, roaring fair through which one had almost to fight a passage. Although it is only a little after eight, the last stall has been spirited way, and the " Lane " is so utterly deserted that the few children playing at leapfrog over its littered stones look lost in it.

From an early hour of the evening one side of Aldgate and one side of Whitechapel Road have been promenaded from end to end by an apparently interminable crowd of boys and girls, youths and maidens, men and women, shabby and respectable, elegant and super - elegant, chattering, laughing, jostling, perambulating as happily as if the barren pavement were an enchanted sea-front and the muddy road a breezy ocean under an evil spell, and they were momentarily expecting the spell to break and the very trams and 'buses to burst into white sails, or into funnels and paddles, and be afloat on shining, surging waters.

But such promenades are a regular Sunday evening feature of the west, and for that matter of north and south London also, as well as of the east. Unaristocratic swarms from east and west mingle in the Strand and traverse its pavements all the evening ; while similar multitudes are likewise engaged up and down Oxford Street, Edgware Road, Upper Street, Islington, and up and down broad, electrically-lighted

IN A RESTAURANT (FRASCATI'S).

thoroughfares round Clapham Junction, at Hackney, at Harlesden, and a score of other suburbs, near and remote.

Yet all the evening, too, there are retiring Londoners who have withdrawn into the reading-rooms of free libraries; there are Arcadian strollers, singly, in pairs, and in family parties, on all the commons, in all the garden spaces, in all the parks

AN OPEN-AIR SERVICE
(HYDE PARK).

where there are no bands, and especially in all the parks where there *are* bands.

Most of these bands subside on "God Save the King" at eight o'clock, and at many places, as at Hampstead Heath and in Regent's Park, immediately the players have blown the last notes out of their instruments an evangelist will take the bandstand for a pulpit and will promptly address the immense congregation that has thus been brought together before it can dwindle away.

The Sunday evening band in Hyde Park, however, starting later than the others, does not finish until half-past nine, and it draws a vaster, a livelier, and perhaps more miscellaneous, crowd than any of its rivals. The seats in the large enclosure immediately round the bandstand soon fill, and steadily emptying from time to time fill again as steadily, and a ring of economical enthusiasts barnacle the outer railings of the enclosure from the opening of the programme to the close. The garden seats strewn about the grass are so liberally patronised that the lynx-eyed collector has never done collecting his pennies; and over grass and gravelled pathway, round and round the bandstand, a dense, far-stretching crowd revolves and eddies, and occasionally bubbles and roars into such a tumult that it drowns all sound of the music from those who are struggling in its currents.

Out beyond the radius of this circling mass is a larger, less concentrated, throng sitting, and standing, and pacing to and fro: coquettish housemaids with their chosen soldiers; sedate parents with their children; shopmen and shopgirls; young City clerks of both sexes; office boys in gorgeous raiment consorting together as in despair at finding themselves isolated among the vulgar; persons of fairly high position, of fairly low position, and no position at all; and with so much talking and giggling and whispering and flirting to be transacted between them that some of them hardly know when the music is going and when it is stopped.

Since the first tune was played the warmth of sunset has withered from the sky, the air has darkened, the stars have become visible, and gas and electric lights have been set twinkling and glowing in every direction across the Park. The outlines of the bandstand have been gradually obscured by the darkness till the red-coated bandsmen sitting in it under their circular roof, high among the trees, and thrown into sharp prominence by the gloom of the night beyond them and the brilliance of the half-dozen lamps shining down on their scores, might be swinging in a mammoth cage from the branches for all we can see to the contrary

Leaving the band to the crowd, and a stone's throw from it an evangelist still preaching under the trees to his limited audience, we return to the streets again.

Quiet people in the suburbs, who have spent the day between church and home, are sitting reading in their own parlours or have gone out to supper with friends as quiet as themselves. Suburban people who are not so quiet are giving and receiving other suppers that are not so quiet either. Sunday evening " at homes " are still in progress in Bohemian quarters of the town; small but special dinner parties around Mayfair and Belgravia are just in the dessert stage; pianos innumerable are rippling and voices singing, alike in aristocratic and plebeian drawing-rooms, and the songs are various.

All the time the clubs in and about Pall Mall and elsewhere are not left desolate; public-houses and tobacconists are still doing brisk trades; oyster bars and the principal hotels and restaurants are at their busiest. The Playgoers' Club is in the heat of a crowded lecture and discussion at the Hotel Cecil, or the O. P. Club is in the middle of an equally crowded smoking concert at the Criterion. Gay but decorous and more or less affluent revellers of all ages are refreshing themselves to piano and violin accompaniments in ornate halls scattered about the west; snug, secret gambling clubs of Soho are just becoming animated; and there is a select dance going on at a very exclusive waiters' club in the same locality.

But the slowest vergers have done with shutting up their churches; the Sunday League concerts, which began at church time, are all over; donkey-carts, heavy with tired but vocal passengers, are homing from Epping Forest in the east; and east and west thousands are turning to tramp or ride home by road or rail. The season is yet young; nevertheless, a char-a-banc or two may be seen near Trafalgar Square with excursionists from Hampton Court; smart coaches and smart private barouches are bringing smarter people back from outings to Richmond and other Thames-side pleasure resorts; steamers are returning crowded from places below-bridge; boating parties higher up the river are thinking of pulling shorewards; motorists and cyclists—the latter singly, in pairs, and in droves—are converging upon home by every glimmering, starlit highway that leads to London; for Sunday evening is past, and this is Sunday night.

COMMENCING WORK (OSBORN STREET, WHITECHAPEL).

WAITING FOR
PARCELS OF FOOD
(CHEAPSIDE).

CHARITABLE AND BENEVOLENT LONDON.

By DESMOND YOUNG.

STONY-HEARTED London! They who call her so libel her grievously, for of a truth the stream of charity in the Metropolis is wonderfully deep and wide. It may not be obvious or easily accessible to some who thirst for it; but it exists all the same, and its healing and reforming influence is world-wide. While it flows steadily all the year round into thousands of channels, it increases enormously in volume at Christmas, the season of good-will, when the blessed spirit of benevolence is supreme.

The useful handbook of the Charity Organisation Society—a society which seeks to give a definite aim to the benevolent force at work in England and particularly in London, and to direct it into the most effectual courses—is a sufficient answer to those who fling the oft-repeated epithet at London, since within its covers is a long catalogue of thousands of metropolitan charitable agencies. Perhaps, however, it is meant that there is little promiscuous almsgiving in London. In that case appeal may be made to the Mendicity

Society, whose annals and museum tell a very different tale. Every night thousands of outcasts are sent to bed by the pennies harvested in the streets.

Nearly all classes of society contribute in greater or lesser measure to the stream of London charity, sometimes in special ways and at others in common accord. If we visit Westminster Abbey on Maundy Thursday, we can see the King's particular share distributed. For centuries the scene has been the same. The choristers and clergy are in their places; the dean, canons, and minor canons occupy their respective stalls; and the Lord High Almoner and the Sub-Almoner sit in the sacrarium. At the foot of the steps leading to that part of the sacred building stands a table on which rests a gilt dish containing the alms. Seated in their appointed places are those who have been selected to receive the King's bounty, the number of men and of women corresponding with the age of his Majesty. A touch of colour is imparted to the assembly by the presence of some Beefeaters, whose quaint mediæval garb stands out vividly against the blacks and whites.

And now the service begins. After the second anthem, the little purses in the dish are distributed by the Lord High Almoner. They are, like the coins, specially made for the occasion, and are of two colours, white and red. The former contain £2 10s. in gold, the latter as many pence as the King is years of age, given in silver pennies, two-

A GOOD FRIDAY MORNING CUSTOM (ST. BARTHOLOMEW'S CHURCH).

pences, threepences, and fourpences. Then the service is resumed, and with the Benediction the ceremony ends.

Now take, by way of contrast, a glimpse of the working man's charity. We are in the City at lunch time. From a small factory door comes a toiler, who, walking straight across the road, places a mysterious paper parcel between some railings. That package contains the remains of his dinner, and by-and-by some poor homeless wanderer will pounce on them and eat them ravenously. It is peculiar to London, this custom of placing leavings where the first comer who is hungry can see them, and it materially helps to keep the man in the street—the real man,

not the imaginary figure of editors and orators—from starving.

Another distinctive form of class charity often comes under the notice of him who rambles in the highways and byways of Babylon. It is the shopkeeper's, and consists of the daily distribution of tons of stale food, customers' leavings, and other "waste." Transport yourself to Cheapside at 5.30 a.m. Ranged in front of Sweeting's even at this early hour are half a dozen children with bags. As the great city awakes others arrive from all points of the compass, till at last there are fifty or sixty youngsters drawn up in a *queue*, which needs the strong arm of the law, personified by a policeman, to regulate it. Seven o'clock! While the sound of the last stroke still lingers in the ear the door opens, and a shopman comes out with a basket and hands a parcel of bread and pieces to each of the little ones, whereupon the children instantly separate and scamper away. And how often does their haste suggest that the family breakfast is impossible till they reach home!

Of the charity of all classes of Londoners, from royalty to sweated white slaves, there is no more striking illustration than the success of the Mansion House funds. Whenever a great disaster befalls mankind in this or any other country, the victims look to the Lord Mayor's official residence for relief, and never do they look in vain, no matter what their creed or nationality. For the greatest philanthropic agency in the world is at once set to work, with the result that there is invariably a generous response from the public. Five or six funds have sometimes been opened simultaneously, and all have been subscribed to with great liberality. The rich have sent in their cheques; the poor have dropped their mites into the box which is usually outside the Mansion House—a box from which as much as £50 worth of copper has been taken.

Seasonal benevolence largely helps to swell the stream of London charity. In the summer months you see one delightful result of it at the great railway termini. Some day the platform is monopolised by a crowd of

AT THE GUILDHALL: READY TO DISTRIBUTE THE REMAINS OF THE BANQUET.

PRESENTING MAUNDY MONEY IN WESTMINSTER
ABBEY.

ness, the delighted recipients are each made happy with a substantial basketful of the capital fare. Some, you notice, get besides a portion of the world-famed turtle soup. These have invalids at home. But this epicurean delicacy is not always appreciated. The taste for it, like that for olives or tomatoes, must be acquired, and so the semi-liquid part of the gift sometimes descends hastily to the cat or dog

Now let us drop in at the Shoreditch Town Hall. It wants but a few days to Christmas, and all over London seasonable benevolence is bringing joy and thankfulness into thousands of homes. Here at Shoreditch, from a fund raised by public subscription, about 600 of the respectable local poor are each to receive a parcel containing tea, flour, sugar, raisins, etc., while in addition every one of the old men and women has had, or will have, 1 cwt. of coals delivered at his or her house. During the evening the beneficiaries go to the platform and receive their gifts, some with a beaming face, some shyly, but all with evident gratitude. Let us hope that their Christmas will be merry.

Much London charity, also, springs from endowments or filters through institutions. Of late years the Charity Commissioners have diverted many ancient bequests into new channels; but numbers are still distributed in accordance with the directions of pious benefactors. Marriage portions, loans to young tradespeople and others, rewards for faithfulness and fidelity on the part of domestic servants—these are a few samples of the unusual objects to which the revenue from endowments is devoted. Many doles of bread and money, moreover, are made annually, generally at Christmas, and some of them subject to the repair of the donors' tombs or the observance of a ceremony in connection with them.

A quaint custom which appears to have originated in a bequest of this character is to be witnessed every Easter in the churchyard of St. Bartholomew, Smithfield. Let us see it with the mind's eye. Good Friday morning.

children, vociferous, pushing, eager to be off, each labelled like a parcel. They are going into the country for a day or a week. And think what that means to some who never see a field! "What is this green, soft stuff I'm walking on?" asked a girl of about twelve with much curiosity. "This green, soft stuff" was grass!

No less pleasing a picture, but one of a very different character, is to be seen in the Guildhall on the 10th of November. Scattered about the historic building are a number of tables, laden with pies, joints, and other good things left from the Lord Mayor's banquet on the previous evening. The remains of the feast have previously been divided by the pantrymen into as many portions as there are members of the committee which carries out the arrangements, usually twelve, and these gentlemen, duly aproned for the occasion, are now carving the pies and joints according to the number of the tickets they have given away. All being in readi-

Round a horizontal gravestone, coated with the grime of ages and broken in three places, a small crowd is gathered, the greater part consisting of twenty-one very old and very feeble widows. Presently a churchwarden places a new sixpence on the stone, whereupon one of the old ladies approaches, kneels on the slab, and picks up the coin. A gentleman then hands her a hot-cross bun, while another member of the company assists her to walk over the stone—an important part of the custom. The rest is mere repetition, each of the other ladies doing likewise in turn. According to tradition, the ceremony, which has for centuries been carried out practically as it is at the present time, began through the terms of a bequest by a widow whose remains lie under the stone. Nowadays, however, each old lady who fulfils the conditions is presented with half-a-crown in addition to the sixpence and hot-cross bun.

Well-nigh endless seem the benevolent and charitable societies and institutions of the world's capital. All our invaders—as the Jews, the French, the Germans—have their own charities, while for aliens generally there is the Society of Friends of Foreigners in Distress. Even the county societies—the Lancastrians, the Devonians, and the like —relieve such of their countrymen as fall on evil days in London. Nor must we lose sight of the fact that much charity is distributed quietly and unostentatiously by the Freemasons, Oddfellows, etc., to such members of their several orders as stand in need of help. On the other hand, pecuniary assistance is given from many sources without respect to race, creed, or the bonds of fellowship. One will occur to everybody who knows anything of the seamy side of London life — the police-court poor box.

Class constitutes the main ground of eligibility for the benefits of other charities. The Shipwrecked Mariners' Society

is a case in point. So is the Asylum of the Good Shepherd, at Hammersmith — a well-known refuge for fallen women. And among other societies of this kind are those for the reclamation of thieves and gaol birds generally.

We have, too, large numbers of charitable agencies which, while they recognise neither race nor creed, give relief only in one particular form. First and foremost among these are our magnificent hospitals, homes for incurables, and similar institutions—the most glorious feature of Charitable London. Next, perhaps, may be placed the societies whose object is the alleviation of pain and the removal of physical disabilities by means of surgical and other instruments, as the Spectacle Mission Society and the Provident Surgical Appliance Society. Then we have such admirable charities as the Southwark "Pinch of Poverty" Relief Fund, from which the deserving are helped to redeem tools and clothing, to pay rent, to tide over illnesses, and to emigrate. Finally, there are the soup kitchens, of which those in Euston Road, Ham Yard, and Gray's Yard may be taken as types.

Gray's Yard is a favourite dining-place

GIVING AWAY CHRISTMAS PARCELS (SHOREDITCH).

OUTSIDE THE SOUP KITCHEN, GRAY'S YARD, W.

of the poorest of the poor, because of the variety of food which can be obtained there under cost price. Turn any week-day about noon from Oxford Street into James Street, and you will, by following the string of nondescripts in front of you, be guided to the well-known ragged church and school. Outside the entrance scores of poor wretches are assembled, drawn here by the cheapness of the edibles and the superintendent's culinary skill. In the kitchen—a large room on the ground floor, well supplied with forms and tables—you find a number of unfortunates of both sexes enjoying a warm, nourishing, palatable meal. The food supplied has two good qualities: it is nutritious and it is cheap. If a man has only a halfpenny, he can get a basin of soup; if he can rake together twopence, he can dine satisfactorily off a plate of excellent stew. There are many less deserving charities than those which thus minister cheaply or gratuitously to man's natural needs.

Let us now glance at the trade and professional benevolent institutions, which do so much to ameliorate the lot of the orphans, the widows, the aged, and those incapacitated from earning a living by disease. And to see something of the inner aspect of the working of such charities

we cannot do better than be present at a typical election at the Cannon Street Hotel, one of the principal places where courts of governors are held.

Picture, then, a large room, with tables on each side and down the middle. Seated at these are the anxious candidates and their representatives. At the official table, which is situate at the end of the room, are the chairman and board of management of the Commercial Travellers' Benevolent Institution. The poll has now been open about an hour, and the friends of the candidates, of whom there are about thirty for eighteen vacancies, have handed bundle after bundle of voting papers, duly filled up by the subscribers, to the president, who has passed them on to the scrutineers in an adjoining room.

Another hour drags slowly on amid much bustle and movement and effervescence; and as the crucial moment approaches the anxiety of the candidates becomes painful in its intensity. You wish yourself miles away. Two o'clock at last. The poll is closed. And now all wait, many with quivering nerves, for the result of the ballot. After a short interval, the chief scrutineer returns to the room with a paper in his hand. Then there is a moment of silence and tense excitement such as comes in a court of law when the jury in a trial for murder return to their box, and not a sound can be heard as the poll is declared save that of an occasional sob or gasp and of a movement indicative of joy or despair.

No need to ask which of the candidates are successful: you read their fate on their faces. Mark, for instance, that aged widow. A flush of colour has just come into her cheeks and a joyous light into her eyes, while her lips move in thankfulness as she turns round to her friends, whose countenances reflect her pleasure and gratitude. She has been elected. And now look at the other side of the shield. Sitting at the next table but one is an old greybeard whose head droops lower and lower as the names are read out, and who at last fumbles for his pocket-handkerchief. Our heart goes out to him, and yet we can but pity

and wish him better fortune when he applies again.

Such is a typical election. Though the system is not always alike, and though the chief actors differ in social status—licensed victuallers here, poor clergy there; now distressed ladies, then poor governesses; sometimes the parents of cripples, at others the friends of orphans—the drama is always essentially the same. The elements are invariable. An election has its pathos; but uppermost, perhaps, is a feeling of satisfaction engendered by the content and gratitude of the successful candidates.

No; London is not stony-hearted. This is merely a cursory survey of her charitable and benevolent side, and yet, inadequate as it necessarily is, it shows that she is doing her duty in caring for the hungry, the fallen, the ailing, the afflicted, the fatherless, and all who stand in need of help. Rather is she the City of Charity.

OFF TO THE COUNTRY.

123

GOLF (RANELAGH).

LONDON'S FASHIONABLE AMUSEMENTS.

By GILBERT BURGESS

THE average foreigner who visits London must indeed be of opinion that we take our pleasures sadly. The loneliness which a chance traveller must almost inevitably experience in a great city is proverbial; but if a foreigner be duly armed with letters of introduction to members of fashionable Society he will speedily discover that the pursuit of the business of pleasure is waged more industriously in London than in any other European capital.

He will find every kind of sport ready to his hand. If he is fond of polo, there are clubs where the game is played at Hurlingham, Ranelagh, and Roehampton. The most beautiful grounds are those of the Club House—an early Georgian building—at Ranelagh. The house itself is surrounded by magnificent old trees. From the back a perfectly kept lawn sweeps down to a lake whereon are boats. Although you are still in London, and only half an hour's drive from Piccadilly Circus, you may readily imagine that you are in the heart of the country. There are also golf links and a racecourse. A summer afternoon spent on the polo ground is delightful. The match about to be played, we will say,

is an International. Dainty muslin dresses abound among the fairer portion of the spectators, some of whom occupy the stands others are seated in carriages or on coaches. The King and Queen may haply drive into the ground, taking their places in a specially constructed private box. The players enter the field, salute their Majesties, and without further delay the ball is thrown and the game commences. The ponies, as keen on the game as the men who ride them, dart hither and thither with movements only comparable to the swift gyrations of a dragon-fly. In itself polo is the most picturesque sport in the world, but when it is played before a background of pretty frocks and faces it becomes a spectacle of surpassing charm.

At Ranelagh, too, there are driving competitions for ladies, horse and dog shows, balloon ascents, meets of stage coaches, and motor-car races. Automobile gymkhanas are arranged, and a band of one of the Guards regiments makes music merry or sentimental the while. Then, if you have no engagement for dinner, or are not obliged to put in an appearance at Covent Garden Opera House, you may dine in the club's new dining-room, and smoke your cigarette on the lawn afterwards what time the daylight gives place to the mysterious shadows and fragrances of an English twilight.

Here, of an afternoon, on the golf links a learned judge may happen to be going round the " holes " in animated conflict with a noted and fashionable physician. His lordship, when occasion demands, may be heard to give vent to mild expletives which would not appear seemly in a court of law. There are also facilities for the alleged sport of pigeon shooting. Whether this be sport or not is a matter of individual opinion.

At Hurlingham the game of croquet flourishes exceedingly. But croquet has become an exact science—almost a duty, instead of a diversion. Yet it is a boon to the occupants of many London houses which have attached to them small gardens. A gardener who will construct a good lawn is never far to seek.

Another form of amusement, this time ostensibly for the benefit of children, is the sailing of model yachts upon the water of the Round Pond in Kensington Gardens. Embryo challengers for the America Cup direct their mimic yachts with considerable skill, although the fathers—many of them sea-dogs who have retired from the Service—stand by to assist in cases of emergency. On a fine Sunday morning, when the clouds fly high and there is a brisk breeze blowing, there will be found a crowd of spectators admiring the expert manner in which the smartly dressed children adjust the rudders and sails of their toys so that when the craft is once adrift it shall eventually find a harbour in some part of the pond.

In trying to make a general biograph, as it were, of the diversions which a large class of Society employs as pastimes one must inevitably fly off at tangents.

Private theatricals have not at present the vogue which they enjoyed at the end of the nineteenth century. This is because the tendency of the age is all for specialisation, and unless an amateur actor can *really* act people do not want to be bothered by sitting through a performance which is not efficient. Nevertheless, from time to time entertainments are arranged in private houses by leaders of Society which are often of astonishing excellence. Sometimes a theatrical manager is present, and finds talent of such calibre that he is emboldened to make an offer of a professional engagement. This in many cases has been accepted with successful results. The old-fashioned

SKATING (PRINCE'S).

prejudice against acting or singing as a profession no longer exists. For sweet Charity's
sake tableaux vivants are also arranged, and
various funds in connection with the wants of
the widows and orphans who have to suffer
for the benefit of the Empire have been
materially helped by those who have made a
fashionable amusement a means of well-doing
for others.

During the winter months Prince's Skating
Rink is a favourite rendezvous at tea-time or
thereabouts. The artificially manufactured
ice on the rink is invariably crowded by
skaters; those members who prefer to watch
and wait are accommodated with chairs and

MODEL YACHTING (KENSINGTON GARDENS).

tables on raised platforms which flank either
side of the interior of the building. You may
see experts from Canada, the United States,
or from Scandinavia, mingling with a crowd
of graceful English girls. Children, too, who
have not reached the first decade of their
earthly existence glide backwards and for-
wards on the ice with a precision and *insou-
ciance* which are pretty to witness. A Hungarian
band in a gallery plays waltzes and mazurkas
throughout the afternoon. The sport appears
to give a healthy glow to the faces of the
skaters, though doctors are divided in opinion
as to the hygienic value of the exercise.

The cult of the motor-car has had a belated
growth in London. The writers who foresaw
that, apart from utilitarian reasons, steam or
electric traction on the King's highway was a
potential amusement were for a time as voices

crying vainly in the wilderness. But London
has become converted, and even in Hyde
Park the drivers of the automobiles speed
merrily on the macadam road which skirts
the Row that is sacred to equestrians. Many
ladies drive their own machines, whether these
latter be of English, French, or American
make.

As an amusement "motoring" is incom-
parable; the mechanism nowadays is so
exact that complete control is almost absolutely assured to the driver. But the horse
is still with us, despite the prophecies of the
quidnuncs, and, although the equipages and
horses in Hyde Park cannot compare favourably with those to be seen in the
Bois de Boulogne in Paris on a
fashionable afternoon, there is a
certain quality of solid magnificence
which is always impressive.

In the early morning, in Rotten
Row on a June day, you may see
a Prince of the Royal blood cantering
side by side in earnest converse with
a Cabinet Minister. Passing them
comes a popular actor or a King's
Counsel; a young stockbroker gallops
along at full speed, hoping that he
shall ride off the effects of a late
supper at one of the Society or
sporting clubs which he has left but
a few hours previously.

In Regent's Park the game of
hockey is very popular. There are
several ladies' clubs, and pupils from fashionable boarding schools and colleges for girls
can be seen playing the game with a zest
only comparable with that with which a
Rugby boy plays football. The sport of
archery, which was almost the sole outdoor
amusement indulged in by ladies towards
the middle of the nineteenth century, is
not so popular as it used to be. Nevertheless, the Royal Toxopholite Society holds
meetings from time to time in the Royal
Botanic Gardens in Regent's Park, and it is a
very picturesque sight on a ladies' day to
watch the fair, up-to-date Amazons drawing
the bow, not at a venture, but with nice and
exact precision. Some of the shooting is of
exceptional merit; the colours of the targets
themselves have an Imperial note, which is
only fitting when one remembers what a great

CROQUET (HURLINGHAM).

Photo Bowden Buckingham Palace Road.

ARCHERY (REGENT'S PARK).

BILLIARDS.

part the English bow has taken in the formation of our "rough island story."

Tennis—real tennis, the Royal game, as opposed to lawn tennis and its variants—still has its vogue among those who are able to afford the luxury of membership in the pleasant club, the Queen's, which is situated in Kensington. Here, watching from the gallery of the building, spectators, guarded from the fearsome effect of blows from the hard ball used by the players by an iron net, may see this glorious game played by enthusiasts in the great spacious court below. Tennis is a perfect form of exercise, bringing as it does every muscle in the body into play harmoniously; and at Queen's some of the *habitués* who have passed middle age seem to be as alert and active as they were when, as boys at one or other of the public schools, they played the game with the zest and verve which are perhaps the most fascinating attributes of budding manhood. At Queen's, too, members may play rackets—cousin-german of real tennis—if they be so inclined. Both these games, from the expensive environment which the rules demand, are solely available for the well-to-do strata of Society. Still, they form two facets in the elaborately cut diamond which may be symbolised as London's fashionable amusements.

Lawn tennis is played in the gardens of houses of the more outlying districts, and wherever space permits. In some of the private squares in the central districts enthusiasts may also sometimes be seen playing croquet, which has now almost attained the dignity of chess. No longer may the *dilettante* laugh when he misses a hoop, or fails to hit the ball of an opponent, or is impotent to execute some far-seeing series of manœuvres.

Of indoor games billiards still must be accorded a certain standard of authority. Most large houses contain a billiard room, and nearly all clubs. Fashionable Londoners are whimsical in their adherence to any particular game, and for the moment billiards is somewhat neglected. Nevertheless, every evening you shall see hotly contested games in club or mansion. The *jeune fille* does not despise the fascination of billiards, and sometimes this exacting young lady is a remarkably good player. A very pretty after-dinner picture is that of a well-appointed billiard room, simply furnished, and with only a few sporting prints hung upon the walls. Some girls are playing a "foursome"; the green shades which shield the light from their eyes give an air of coolness to the room. The mere men who are relations or fellow-guests smoke their cigarettes while seated on settees which are arranged on raised platforms around the room. Gracefully the lassies wield the cue in this pretty pastime. I fear our grandmothers would have lifted their hands heavenwards in holy horror, but the modern maiden does not see why she should be excluded from amusements, perfectly harmless in themselves, which were once the prerogative of her father or her brothers.

In a few houses the billiard table has been sacrificed to a game which bears the sufficiently inane title of "ping-pong." This is practically lawn tennis played upon a table with a wooden or parchment racket and celluloid balls. It was invented by an Army officer who thought it would be an amusing toy; but the toy soon became a tyrant. "Ping-pong" took the suburbs by storm, and finally even laid successful siege to Belgravia. But the wild enthusiasm with which the game was first greeted cooled after a time, for—as you will notice if you are interested in games—over-proficiency of the few destroys the zeal of the average or amateur many.

Lastly, we come to the all-pervading tyranny of "bridge." This game, which is a form of whist, has (to use a dear old journalistic phrase) shaken Society to its very foundations. Man, who plays it, cannot resist its fascinations; but Heaven knows the havoc it

has wrought among us! This is the average day in the life of a Society woman. At noon a few friends arrive for luncheon—ostensibly. Select parties play bridge until two o'clock, when luncheon is actually served. Bridge again from four to six. Then a drive in the Park, followed by dinner, and—bridge until the small hours of the morning. As a natural corollary—since games of cards are rarely played unless the element of gambling in actual specie enters into the matter—the results of this mania will be apparent to everybody. At clubs the card rooms are filled with quartettes of gamblers; nominal points are exacted by the committees, but this is a matter which is easily evaded by very obvious subterfuge.

For the rest, fashionable London has concerts, theatres, cricket matches, balls and cotillons, and many other of the raree shows of civilisation. The restless, soul-harassing pursuit of pleasure goes merrily apace— or tragically, which you will. The matter is interesting when one realises how limited fashionable amusements were a hundred years ago. Who shall say what they will be a hundred years hence?

BRIDGE.

BILL-POSTERS AT WORK.

SOME FAMILIAR THINGS IN LONDON.

By GEORGE R. SIMS.

DINNERS.

"TAKE me for a walk and tell me things," says the foreign friend who, having done London with his red guide book under his arm, wants to understand something more of the living side of the great city than the guide book tells him.

You know exactly what your friend means. He has seen the brick and mortar side of London, he has visited its "chief sights," wandered through its museums, gazed at its monuments, and sampled its entertainments. Now he wants to take the people as they come, and to have certain features of their daily life pointed out that he might not notice himself, or which, if he noticed, he would not quite understand.

A definite programme under these circumstances is impossible. You cannot arrange a series of episodes beforehand. The episodes arrange themselves. The only way, therefore, is to stroll through the streets quietly with your foreign friend, and explain to him the various "phases" and peculiarities of London life as you come across them.

The first thing to attract your foreign companion's attention may be a huge London hoarding, on which the staff of the advertising contractor are busily engaged in fixing the posters, plain and pictorial, artistic and the reverse, which are such a feature of the capital.

Here you have an opportunity to make an interesting little discourse on London's methods of advertising. You explain that we have firms who do an immense business in designing picture posters for theatrical managers, patent medicine vendors, magazines and periodicals, and the proprietors of soaps, sauces, beef extracts, baking powders, cordials, infants' foods, cigarettes, cocoas, jams, etc. You tell him that many firms spend thousands of pounds annually in this form of advertisement alone, and that some of the best designs are the work of men who hold high rank in the world of art.

You tell him that a wet season means an enormous loss to these hoarding advertisers, for all over London the bills soak off or assume an utterly disreputable appearance, and have to be renewed on the

being capsized. You tell him that when the day's work is done some of the men assemble in Ham Yard and receive the price of their promenade.

You explain that the night side of advertising offers a strong contrast to the devices of the day. You mention the men who wear a lighted lamp in the place of a hat. You point to certain little lamps

SANDWICHMEN IN HAM
YARD: WAITING TO
BE PAID.

first fine day. Then you may describe to him London's other methods of out-of-door advertising. You can take him into a railway station and show him the walls so covered with trade announcements that on some of them the stranger may easily be forgiven for failing to find the name of the station at which he wishes to alight.

You tell him of the sandwich men who walk the gutters of the principal thoroughfares from morning to night with their boards high above their heads, secured to their shoulders by iron clips and a strap. You tell him of the weird picture these men present when a violent gust of wind sweeps suddenly down a broad thoroughfare, and compels them to hold on to pillars and lamp-posts to save themselves from

fixed in the form of letters high up on tall houses, and you explain that at night these will light up letter by letter until the word—the name of the article advertised —is complete, and that from dusk till midnight these specialities will spread themselves out in letters of light about every half minute. Harking back to day advertisements you will, probably, be able to show him a magnificent coach drawn by piebald horses, driven by a man in livery and having behind two elegantly attired footmen, and you explain that this is the advertisement of a certain perfume. You will also explain that the police law with regard to vehicular advertisement is very strict. Cabs are not allowed to adorn themselves in the interests of the advertiser, although

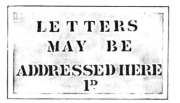

LETTERS MAY BE ADDRESSED HERE 1ᴰ

EXHIBITED IN SHOPS.

prints his name, or that of his article of commerce, on the presented headgear.

The omnibuses of London—the foreigner will have noticed for himself—are now so closely covered outside and in with theatrical or trade advertisements that it is difficult for anyone but a Londoner to know which portion of the printing refers to places on their line of route, and which does not.

He will also have noticed that many London streets are adorned with advertising boards standing outside a certain class of shop, and that in the windows of these shops hang or lie in picturesque confusion "window bills" of the various entertainments of London. You will explain to him that for showing these bills there is no payment, but a list of persons displaying them is kept by the bill inspector of the places of amusement, and this official is empowered at certain times to give orders for free admission to his particular establishment in return for the courtesy. There exists in London a curious club, whose meetings are held in a coffee house in the West-End. It is called the Wanglers' Club, and its members are the theatrical bill inspectors of London. They meet once a week, and for their mutual convenience exchange orders or passes. In this way an inspector is able frequently to oblige his customers not only with an order for his own theatre, but for others. "Bill orders" are not, of course, given during the early days of a success. It is towards the end of a run that they are distributed, and then generally only for Friday night, which in most places of amusement is the slackest of the week.

It is possible that your foreign friend may ask you to translate a mysterious notice which he will have frequently observed on certain walls—"Bill stickers will be prosecuted." You tell him that this notice is rendered necessary by the fact

in the summer heat waves the generous donor of sunbonnets to the horses occasionally

that there is a system of advertising which is known as "fly posting." You send a man out with your bills and a pastepot, and he sticks them up, wherever he finds a chance of doing so, on any wall or hoarding that is not labelled as the property of such and such a firm of advertising contractors.

As you stroll through the town, if it should happen to be between one and two in the afternoon, or between five and six in the evening, your foreign friend will probably be struck by the number of lads flying about with trays covered with a cloth, or with piles of plates with tin covers over them. You will then be able to inform him that a large number of clerks and warehousemen, frequently employers themselves, have their meals sent in a rough-and-ready fashion from small restaurants, public-houses, and coffee-shops, and eat them on their business premises. In the City and in Newspaper London the sending-out trade is one of the principal items in the business of many refreshment houses. You may frequently meet small boys in their shirt sleeves steering their way along the crowded pavements with a pyramid of plates balanced as deftly as the Japanese jugglers balance their pyramid of boxes. The beer-boy is another curiosity worth pointing out. This young gentleman carries a dozen cans of beer at a time to thirsty workers at the "beer hour" by the arrangement shown in our photographic illustration on the opposite page.

Sending out the "evening tea" is largely a coffee-shop trade, but if your foreign friend asks you about our London coffee-shops you will have to tell him that their glory has considerably departed. One by one the dear old places with the high-backed boxes have been driven out of existence by the foreign restaurateur, and the establishment in every direction

A POLICE WARNING.

of "tea rooms" run upon the marble table, female attendant, no gratuities, and "pay at the desk, please" system. There are a few coffee-shops of the superior sort left, which are still frequented by students, journalists, and men who want to read the papers and periodicals quietly over their coffee and muffin, but, as a rule, the coffee-shop caters principally for the cab-drivers, carmen, and working folk who in their working clothes do not care for the marble tables and general air of superiority of the "tea rooms."

As you pass along, the attention of your foreign friend will, possibly, be attracted to the police notice stuck about in certain districts, requesting that the public will assist in preventing orange peel, banana, and other fruit skins from being thrown on the pavement. When you have informed your friend that the London boy and girl take their dessert al fresco, and constantly make a plate of the pavement, you can further explain the necessity for these police warnings by telling him that during the orange and banana seasons quite a large number of cases of fractured limbs, which are all the result of slipping upon the cast-off outer covering of these favourite fruits, are treated at the hospitals.

BEER.

As you walk through the by-streets in order that he may see something of the swarms of children who make the roadway their playground after school hours, your friend may mention that in several shops he has seen a printed or a written notice to the effect that " Letters may be addressed here." This is an industry which adds considerably to the income of many a small shopkeeper. There are a large number of people in London who are not certain of a permanent address ; there are others who do not want their letters to be dropped into the family letter box ; there are people who wish to insert advertisements without giving their own address ; and there are some who choose this method of receiving their

correspondence from motives which would not bear close investigation. The charge for receiving correspondence is generally a penny per letter.

Out in the high road again you may come suddenly upon a procession of vehicles crowded with boys and girls in their Sunday finery. The boys will be shouting in a shrill treble and waving flags ; the little girls will be exercising their vocal powers with greater restraint and waving their flags with less vigour. Accompanying the children will be a few grown-up people, and probably a clergyman. You will explain to your friend that this is a great feature of the summer and autumn seasons— a Sunday school treat The children have been out for the day to some green spot on the outskirts — perhaps Richmond, perhaps Barnet, it may even be to Epping Forest. They have had games on the grass and a picnic, and are now returning to their homes. It is doubtful if any part of the entertainment has caused them greater pleasure than the drive through the streets of the Metropolis. That has given them the opportunity of making a public demonstration of their joy.

The public demonstrations in which the adult population indulge are not, as a rule, of a joyful character. The Londoner's favourite amusement in this line, you will explain to your companion, is an indignation meeting. If your friend wants to see something of the sort you may make an appointment with him for the following Sunday (there will probably be a demonstration of some sort in the Park) and take him first to Oxford Street, where he will see the various trade Friendly Societies, with their banners and their bands, marching in more or less solemn procession towards the Marble Arch through which they will pass with some confusion in order to make their way to the space set apart in Hyde Park for demonstrations. Here, surrounded by a vast crowd, who have mostly come to look on, orators will stand up in waggons and make speeches of more or less coherency, and eventually a "resolution" will be moved and carried amid wild cheering from thousands of people who have not heard a word of it.

Then the crowd will gradually disperse, and the procession, the bands and the banner-bearers, will find their way out, some to the nearest public-house, others to their

skinned, would consider blasphemous. The good sense of Londoners has long ago seen that prosecution would give the ignorant ranter a widespread renown, and probably lift a bumptious nonentity into temporary popularity.

If your foreign friend asks if our London demonstrations always take place on a Sunday, you can tell him that they do so as a rule, because the Trade Societies find

A DEMONSTRATION: FORMING UP ON THE THAMES EMBANKMENT.

homes. The speeches and the resolution will probably be forgotten in a couple of days, but the "meeting" will have expressed its indignation. The free speech allowed to Englishmen is a great safety valve. The foreigner rarely understands its value to the authorities; if he did he would cease to wonder why men are allowed to say in this country things which in any other would bring them into immediate acquaintance with the police and the public prosecutor.

A man may talk as much treason as he likes in our parks and public places if he is addressing a crowd. In certain parts of the park he may even give forth views on religion which a good many people, not too thin-

it difficult to get home to the outlying districts, wash, dress, unfurl banners, and form up, say, on the Thames Embankment—as shown in the photographic picture above—on a Saturday afternoon.

Your foreign friend will be impressed with the good order that prevails, even at mass meetings, where the authorities or employers, or the capitalists, or the Government are denounced in the most violent terms. You can explain to him that our London police are taught and trained to avoid any interference likely to provoke hostilities. Their instructions are to preserve order, not to provoke disorder. If an anarchist who had denounced them as miscreants were attacked by the bystanders, they would protect the anarchist and call upon the bystanders to disperse. The perfect coolness of the London police under the most trying circumstances is a point which you can proudly impress upon your foreign friend.

If you take your friend to a district where a large number of operatives are employed in some great works it is possible that you may be able to show him another phase of the friction between capital and labour. You will come suddenly upon groups of working men talking excitedly together. Near to the gates of the works or the factory you will discover men hanging about in twos and threes and eagerly scrutinising every person who passes.

You will explain to your friend that a great strike is on, and that the works are picketed. Any worker attempting to go in and offer his services to the firm is instantly surrounded by the men on picket duty, who endeavour to dissuade him. During great strikes all the centres of a trade are picketed, and the progress of the negotiations between the masters and the men is followed with interest by everyone. But the strikes which the general public discusses most eagerly are those which interfere with its personal comfort and convenience, to wit, coal strikes, tram and omnibus strikes, gas workers' strikes, and strikes connected with the railway system.

These things will not require much explanation. From whatever country your friend hails he will have had experience of them. They are familiar to the other capitals of the world as well as to Living London.

A SUNDAY SCHOOL TREAT : STARTING OFF.

SOME LONDON SHOWS.

By CHARLES DUDLEY.

LONDON would hardly be London without those shows which run through their course in a year. We have become so habituated to their regular appearance that the disappearance of one of the more important would leave a sensible void. It would be missed, and not in London alone, either, for the country cousin is a great patron of the exhibition connected with his trade or profession; and what else would serve him so well as an excuse for a run up to town? "Really necessary to see what is going on," he explains to his wife. "Besides, look at the people you meet. It's folly to throw chances away." And, having thus arranged matters satisfactorily, he hies him to London town—to look in at the show occasionally, and to spend the rest of his time at the West-End.

The exhibition year opens with Cruft's Dog Show—one of several annual gatherings at which more or less domestic pets are apotheosised. No sooner has the Agricultural Hall, Islington, been cleared up than it is transformed into stables, with a ring in the middle of the floor. Three horse shows succeed one another in quick succession, the exhibits appearing on a gradually diminishing scale. One week the hall is monopolised by the massive shire, the next by the pounding hackney, the third by the graceful, spirited thoroughbred, the useful hunter, the lively polo pony, and the smaller members of the equine race.

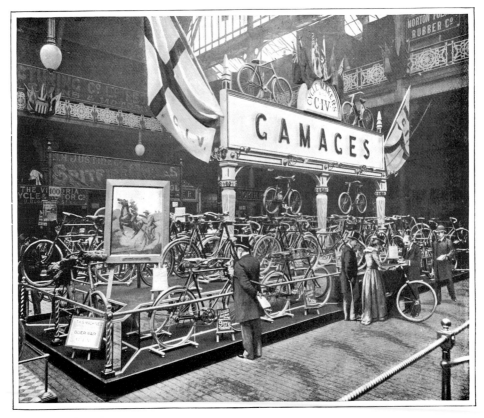

A CORNER OF A CYCLE SHOW.

All these shows have certain characteristics in common. If you enter one when the judging is in progress, you find round the ring a crowd of visitors from all over the country, many of them of a type common in small market towns. Ruddy-cheeked, heavily shod, habited in serviceable tweed, they are more used to striding over stubble and furrow than London stones. As a

PREPARING FOR A TRADE SHOW.

horse is run round the ring they are quick to recognise its good points, and when one shows exceptional merit their admiration finds vent in deep-chested cheers. Still more appreciative and enthusiastic are they during the tussle for the championship. Then the British love of horseflesh is roused within them to the highest degree, and they become ebullient, incoherent, wild with excitement and delight.

From a strictly business point of view—an aspect disregarded by the casual visitor—these shows are yearly becoming more important. They are now horse marts, at which very many sales are effected. Among the exhibitors' best customers are foreigners, who attend the Agricultural Hall in force and snap up the best horses they can obtain without overmuch regard to price.

After the horse shows we enter upon a long series of trade exhibitions. The first is the "Salon Culinaire," at the Royal Albert Hall. This is an exposition of international cookery, and it is as instructive as it is interesting. To ramble through it is to realise that the chef is indeed an artist. Dishes of all kinds, from *foie gras* to plain preparations that the dyspeptic can look at with toleration; large wedding cakes of ornate design, "creations" alluring enough to stimulate the marriage

rate; statues, railway engines, and other objects in sugar white as snow, with every detail accurately represented—such are the exhibits that meet the visitor at every turn. In addition, the main confectionery section contains a similarly endless variety of sweets and cakes. Two admirable features of the show are a number of demonstrations in cookery given by experts, and a competition in table-laying.

But the home of trade shows is the Agricultural Hall, a building that plays many parts. From March to December, with the exception of a brief interval in May, it is given up to such exhibitions. The last of one show is no sooner swept away than another begins to come on the scene. Then the interior is chaos—a wilderness strewn with packing cases, engines, machinery, timber, odds and ends innumerable, and swarming with carpenters, fitters, labourers, and silk-hatted superintendents; then, everything having by superhuman efforts been reduced to order, the public flocks in by the thousand; then chaos again; and so on, till the World's Fair opens at Christmas.

The Automobile Club's Exhibition, which succeeds the Furnishing Trades' Exhibition and is the second of the trade shows at Islington, is miles away from the horse shows.

GUN DRILL AT THE ROYAL
MILITARY TOURNAMENT.

Grocery, and the Shoe and Leather Exhibitions have a spectacular as well as an educational and a business value; but the most popular of the trade displays at the Agricultural Hall after the Laundry Exhibition are, perhaps, the Dairy, the Brewers', and the Stanley Cycle Shows. The Dairy Show, held annually for more than a quarter of a century by the British Dairy Farmers' Association with the object of improving dairy farming, brings jaded Londoners a grateful whiff of the country, and conjures up mental pictures of sylvan meadows and lowing herds, picturesque farmyards, and ponds wherein cattle stand knee-deep, lashing flies from their flanks continuously. It is, indeed, *rus in urbe*—with a little " make believe."

In the hall you find excellent specimens of cattle, which cast their mild eyes slowly around, as if a little puzzled at their strange environment. Scores of goats are penned in a corner, isolated from the rest of the live stock, which includes poultry and pigeons in endless number and infinite variety. The whole show, in fact, is remarkably comprehensive. All sorts of products connected, however remotely, with dairy farming, from mangel wurzels and oilcake to honey and eggs, are profusely represented in the building. And as for the exhibitors, they are little less varied, ranging as they do from royalty to rural cottagers.

But the keynote of the show is practicality. Butter-making competitions, in which the most expert dairymaids in the country engage and the latest and best churns are employed, are going on from morning till night. In one part of the building the visitor is shown how to rear chickens on the most scientific system, in another he is taught how to kill and prepare them for the market.

Gone the stalls; gone the aroma of the stable; gone the beefy Britons from the country and the horsey London visitors. Instead of the neigh of the steed there is the continuous rattle and grind—the steady, interminable ger-er-er—of the throbbing, panting motor car, while the air is charged with the too-familiar petrol. Mechanics take the place of grooms; and the visitors are mostly fashionable people and business men.

Very interesting, also, is the Laundry Exhibition, notwithstanding that its atmosphere is suggestive of soapsuds. The many labour-saving inventions—the glorified washtubs, the ingenious centrifugal driers, the machines for " getting-up," lineal descendants of the common or domestic flat-iron, though the relationship is not at all obvious—are very impressive singly, and much more so in the mass. For the show contains machinery, working and still, weighing nearly 1,000 tons and worth about £50,000. And this is representative of the industry of the wash-tub! A couple of decades back all the apparatus of a complete laundry could easily be put into that rabbit-hutch which the London builder, with fine hyperbole, calls a scullery or wash-house; now many a metropolitan washing factory contains from £20,000 to £30,000 worth of machinery.

The Ironmongery, the Confectionery, the

The Brewing Exhibition is mainly noteworthy for competitions having a direct personal interest for nearly the whole population of the three kingdoms. For, if a man is not affected by the one for the national beverage, beer, the chances are that he is by that for non-intoxicating drinks. The mineral water trade, moreover, makes a fine display, and there are all manner of substitutes and preparations used in the manufacture of drinks, alcoholic and "temperance."

Taking the trade exhibitions as a whole, they are interesting and valuable alike to business men and the public. At them travellers meet customers, firms display their newest products and machinery, and technical skill is stimulated and rewarded, to the great gain of British industry. Recognising what an educational force a trade show is, many a struggling business man in the provinces goes to the expense of regularly sending his manager or some subordinate *employé* to it. The cost is not so small that he can always afford to consider it as a mere drop in the bucket ; but it comes back to him sooner or later, with liberal interest added. On the other hand, many of the competitions—as, for instance, that for bread-making at the Confectioners' Exhibition—are a benefit to the community, which profits in obtaining improved articles of daily consumption.

In the trade exhibitions at Islington the Military Tournament forms a delightful break. Though not a show in the ordinary sense, it may be styled such, inasmuch as it is a display of military feats and evolutions, in connection with which prizes are awarded as at the recognised shows. But, call it what you will, a more generally attractive event—an event in which all classes and all ages are more interested—is not included in the Londoner's calendar.

Its popularity is not surprising. That is explained by the skill and alertness of the combatants in the purely military items, such as "sword *v.* sword" and "lance, mounted, *v.* bayonet, dismounted" ; the dash and brilliancy of the picturesque Indian soldiers at tent pegging—a sport at which they have no equals ; the smart performances of the Royal Marines and the Army Service Corps ; the superb rush with which the Artillery bring up the guns ; the famous musical rides, with their elaborate movements ; the mimic warfare, which gives the audience a sniff of powder and a thrill of excitement ; and the many admirable "side shows." These features, moreover, make the display a potent recruiting agency. In the London district nothing brings more men to the colour than the Military Tournament. No; not excluding fickle love itself !

Besides benefiting the Service by adding

OUTSIDE THE TEMPLE ROSE SHOW.

to its strength, the show is the means of distributing a good deal of money in directions where it is needed. About £1,000 is given in prizes for all ranks, while every penny of profit is devoted to benevolent purposes.

Another attractive summer gathering is the Temple Rose Show, held, of course, in June— the month of our national flower—and due to the enthusiasm of the National Rose Society. To ardent rosarians it is the event

Royal Horticultural Society, which has the management of the exhibition, arranges the classes so that every fruit grower in the kingdom, whether a humble cottager or a peer's gardener commanding all the resources of wealth and science, an enthusiastic amateur or the owner of a fruit farm, has the same chance of distinction. Moreover, it gives special prizes for new and improved methods of packing, thereby showing that it is conscious of one of the British fruit grower's weak points.

Photo: Russell & Sons,
Crystal Palace, S.E.   AT A BIRD SHOW (CRYSTAL PALACE).

Still later in the year the London Ornithological Society holds its exhibition at the Crystal Palace, where about a hundred classes of birds are shelved in a large space curtained off in the central transept. If this show is not so intensely British as the fruit exhibition, none the less does it make for a better appreciation of our native feathered pets. For, though canaries are easily first in point of numbers, and foreign birds deafen

of the year, and the champion trophy is the Blue Ribbon of Rosedom. He who misses the show is not up to date in the cult of the rose, since at it the new varieties are introduced ; nor does he know the possibilities of the bloom in table decoration. To the general public it is a charming spectacle and an occasion for social intercourse, especially in the afternoon, when tea in the gardens is a very popular feature.

In the autumn, after most of the flower shows are over, comes the Crystal Palace Fruit Exhibition—the principal annual display of British fruit. Two or three hundred varieties are, as a rule, on view, mostly hardy, though among them are luscious pines, fine hot-house peaches, and grapes with a rare bloom. It is, however, mainly a show of apples and pears. The

the visitor with their perpetual din, many English birds—linnets, redpoles, larks, thrushes, and others—have a place on the benches. Why, to one class that perky, impudent little freebooter, the London sparrow, sends representatives ! An admirable section of the show is that devoted to stuffed birds, some specimens of which reveal much taste and skill in taxidermy.

It is at the back end of the year, too, that the wheelman has his innings, for then the cycle shows are held, at which manufacturers bring forward their designs and improvements for the coming season, and these the wise cyclist studies before ordering his new mount. At them, too, a number of " freak " inventions are always gravely paraded—wildly outrageous mechanical monstrosities that stagger even the tyro, sublime as is his faith in novelties.

AT THE SMITHFIELD CLUB CATTLE SHOW.

Last of all in the yearly round of exhibitions is the Smithfield Club Cattle Show, which takes place in December. Again does the Agricultural Hall undergo a transformation. To anybody who knows it merely as it is while it houses a trade show it is almost unrecognisable during Cattle Show week. If you visit it then, you fancy that all the over-fed animals in the kingdom are assembled within its walls. Massive bullocks, sheep of overpowering dimensions, and pigs of marvellous rotundity, are ranged in long lines according to class. Fat is everywhere. The whole show is a carnival of it.

And yet how the average visitor glories in the grossness! A massive, plethoric steer is to him the supreme achievement of nature and science combined, and he prods it here and strokes it there with an air of much satisfaction. Nothing else, however, could be expected, since he is a farmer, to whom bulk represents money.

Agriculturists, in fact, loom large at the Cattle Show. Ramble round the hall, and you catch snatches of every rural dialect in England—broad Yorkshire one minute, Somerset the next, then an East Anglian locution, then a fragment of the Staffordshire *patois*. All parts of the country are represented, for the show is one of those events which appeal to the great agricultural community in general.

With the removal of the fat stock from Islington the exhibition year ends. Interspersed with the annual shows of long standing are many of a special or sporadic character. Some are held biennially, some triennially, some with longer intervals between, some in connection with centenary celebrations. We have military shows, naval shows, cookery shows, shows of all kinds. Seldom is London without some attraction of this nature. But these are quite apart from the yearly shows.

AT A SHIRE HORSE SHOW.

FRENCH PROTESTANT CHURCH, SOHO : DISTRIBUTING DOLES TO POOR PEOPLE.

SOME FOREIGN PLACES OF WORSHIP IN LONDON.

By F. M. HOLMES.

FROM the flashing sunlight of a bright spring day we turn into the crowded church of St. Sophia, Moscow Road, Bayswater. The large congregation has risen to its feet. Priests, gorgeously arrayed, advance from the richly painted altar-screen toward an open space under the dome. One, the Archimandrite, bears a lighted candle in his hand, while a sonorous voice proclaims in modern Greek, a sentence which may be thus interpreted :

"All come and take the light that never sets, and embrace Christ, Who has risen from the dead."

The second priest, and the lay-reader after him, light their candles at that of the Archimandrite, repeating the sonorous proclamation, and then persons from the congregation move forward, not in a hurried, disorderly rush, but quietly, one or two at a time, and light the tapers which they hold in their hands, at the larger candles borne by the priests. These individuals among the congregation in their turn allow their neighbours to do likewise, and thus the light is passed round the church to nearly everyone in the large and beautiful building.

It is the service of the Resurrection, celebrated on Easter Sunday in the Greek Church. The lighting of the candles is symbolic, and is said to represent the new light which came into the world with Christ—the new teaching of the Gospel.

The service proceeds. The choir sings superbly. The sonorous voice sounds frequently.

The crowded congregation—or by far the greater number—remains standing throughout, though the service lasts for nearly two hours. The dark southern faces appear very attentive, and the worshippers make the sign of the cross at frequent intervals. Some who might be Greek sailors, though dressed in their best, are here ; others evidently are prosperous merchants. It is a festival service, the church is light and bright and ornate, the gleam of hundreds of candles shines on rich marbles, and during the morning the priest proclaims :

"If any be pious and a lover of God, let him enjoy this beautiful and bright festal gathering."

At the close, when the last notes of the choir have died away and the sonorous

voices are heard no more, the priests make
their way through the throng to tables by the
main entrances, and there they distribute
gaily coloured genuine Easter eggs to the
crowds of worshippers according to ancient
custom and as a sign of rejoicing.

At the same time a similar service, but
in the Russian language, has been celebrated
at the little Russian Embassy Chapel, in
Welbeck Street, a building almost like a

DUTCH CHURCH,
AUSTIN FRIARS : COM-
MUNION SERVICE.

large private room, and containing from sixty
to a hundred persons.

Numerous nationalities have their places
of worship in London. The Dutch occupy
an ancient and historic building situated
in Austin Friars, in the heart of the City,
given them by Edward VI. They belong
to the Dutch Reformed Church, and the
communion is celebrated four times a year.

On these occasions the long table at
the eastern end is covered with a white
cloth, and silver beakers are placed upon it for
the wine, and silver plates for the bread.
Toward the close of the usual service the
minister leaves the pulpit and takes his place
at the centre of the table, and those about
to partake leave their seats in the church and
walk reverently to the table, the men sitting
on the one side, and the women on the other
side of the minister. There is no distinction
between rich and poor — all intermingle.
The minister commences the service by offering a short prayer ; then he delivers a brief

address, dwelling on the meaning of the
Supper. The bread has been cut into
"fingers," and he takes these and breaks
them, and hands the plates, one on either
side of him, to the communicants ; after which
he hands round the beakers in a similar
manner. Another prayer is offered, and the
communicants return to their pews and the
final hymn is sung. The idea is to render
the simple ceremony as nearly as possible an
exact copy of the Last Supper as celebrated
by Christ.

From the Dutch church we may go to the
Swedish. It is situated
farther east, in Princes
Square, St. George's —
Princes Square being a
pleasant and retired spot
in that neighbourhood.
We find a square-shaped
but not unhandsome
building, dating from
1728, with a small square
tower rising from the roof
in front. It is surrounded
by splendid lime trees
and by its own — now
disused — graveyard,
which is well kept with
flowers. The beautiful
music, the stately service, the dignified interior,
form a striking contrast to the squalor of
some of its surroundings, and the noise of
East-End Sunday markets.

The denomination is that of the Swedish
National Church, the Lutheran ; and members
of the Swedish Embassy attend here, as
well as sailors — 7,000 Swedish sailors, it
is said, pass through the port of London
yearly ; substantial Swedish merchants ;
agents and clerks in City offices, Swedish
tailors from the neighbourhood of Soho and
Golden Squares in the West-End—where
some six or seven hundred have settled down
—and Swedish domestic servants from various
parts of London and the suburbs. All these
help to form the congregation. On festival
occasions the church proves too small for the
thronging assembly.

The minister preaches his sermon from the
pulpit, which is richly carved and ornamented,
but the Liturgy is read from the front of
the altar, before the railings of which stands

GREEK CHURCH, BAYSWATER: EASTER SUNDAY SERVICE.

the baptismal font; while the altar screen behind the table has a beautiful painting of Christ and His disciples at the Last Supper.

Soho Square contains a handsome foreign place of worship. This is the French Protestant Church of London, of Huguenot origin, to which King Edward VI. gave a charter in 1550. Perhaps no religious body has a more romantic history than that of Notre Dame de France in Leicester Square, and of the tiny chapel of the French Embassy near Portman Square; while in "Italy in London" the great Italian church in Hatton Garden has been alluded to; but the French have also a Reformed Evangelical Church in Bayswater, founded in 1861. The church is Presbyterian in government, and it has in operation a number of agencies, including schools, for the benefit of French-speaking foreigners in London. There is also a French Protestant Episcopal Church in the Metropolis. It is situated at the top of Shaftesbury Avenue, and is the only church in London in which divine service is celebrated in French according to the Liturgy of the Church of England.

SWEDISH CHURCH, PRINCES SQUARE, E.: PREACHING THE SERMON.

the Huguenots, and this beautiful edifice in orange terra-cotta—the first example of church architecture in that material—is not unworthy of their interesting past.

The service is partly Liturgical — the Liturgie de la Sainte Céne being used—and at the celebration of the Lord's Supper the participants stand round the table. Several French professors and governesses attend here, also families established in London, and people of the working classes. At the close of the service an interesting little ceremony takes place, when doles are given to the poor. Those Huguenots who became rich did not forget their less fortunate brethren, as many legacies to the Huguenot poor abundantly testify.

Mention is made elsewhere in the article on "French London" of the church of The Swiss Protestants have a substantial church in Endell Street, Long Acre, where services are held in French in the morning, and in the evening by German Wesleyans, who have a mission in Soho. But the Swiss also hold services for girls in French on Sunday, twice a month, at Swiss House, in Mecklenburgh Square. The Swiss Minister attends the church in Endell Street, and is, in fact, a member of the *consistoire* or governing body. At the communion service the participants stand round the table, which is under the pulpit, and the pastor hands them the bread and wine.

In King Street, Poplar, stands the Danish church, chiefly attended by sailors and their families, while, at the West-End, Marlborough House Chapel, St. James's Palace, is also used for Danish services, and is attended by the Danish Ambassador and his suite and Danish

DANISH SERVICE, MARL-
BOROUGH HOUSE CHAPEL,
ST. JAMES'S PALACE :
READING THE LESSON FROM THE ALTAR RAILS.

"For our Danish Church in London.—Alexandra."

German Lutherans possessed at one time a church in the Savoy Palace, but when the Victoria Embankment was constructed it was removed to Cleveland Street, Fitzroy Square, and the present building was erected by Queen Victoria as Duchess of Lancaster in 1877. German merchants attend here from Hampstead and Regent's Park, Cavendish Square and Bayswater, and German-speaking Swiss would probably be found among them. In the year 1894 the children of the schools presented a pretty little window to the building. It is a Lutheran church, and at the celebration of the Lord's Supper the communicants step forward and kneel at the altar rail — a custom different from that of the Dutch in Austin Friars, or the Huguenots and Swiss Protestants in Soho Square and Endell Street.

Another German Lutheran Church may be found in Little Alie Street, St. George's-in-the-East ; but here a curious custom obtains. While the pastor reads the Scripture and

residents. The building, which is not lavishly decorated, will hold about 200 persons. The same pastor is the minister of both churches, holding service in the morning at Poplar and in the afternoon at Marlborough House Chapel. The service is that of the Danish Lutheran Church, the National Church of Denmark, and bravely the Danish sailors roll out their hymns. At the communion service the participants move forward to the altar, where the pastor, clad in the ruffle and black gown of Queen Elizabeth's time, reads a short exhortation before the words of consecration are chanted.

In front of the altar at the Poplar Church hangs a model ship, which was made by an old captain in Denmark. It was exhibited in Copenhagen in 1888, and given to this church. No special significance attaches to it, except that the Church is generally compared to a ship, and in Denmark a vessel is to be found in many churches. Before the service commences many of the sailors step forward to examine the little craft. The service books were presented to the church by the Queen—then Princess of Wales —in 1875, and bear inscriptions in her Majesty's own handwriting:

OUTSIDE THE FINNISH CHURCH. ROTHERHITHE.

offers prayer before the sermon, standing inside the rails of the altar, a beadle in duly dignified apparel of blue cloth and bearing a handsome silver mace, stands outside the rails. The pastor himself does not know the origin of the custom, which was, perhaps, intended to awe into silence fidgety children whose restless feet, not yet tired by the pathway of life, wanted to be more actively engaged. This church was founded in 1762 by some of the German sugar refiners living in the neighbourhood; English employers also took a keen interest in it, because so many Germans worked for them. The church, which will accommodate some 600 persons, is attended largely by German tradespeople, such as tailors and bakers, coming from various districts as widely apart as Stockwell and Covent Garden, Stamford Hill and Camberwell, while the day schools contain over 200 children.

But a German Hamburg Church, near the German Hospital at Dalston, is, as a society, older than either of these, for it was originally founded in 1669 by the Hansa League merchants living in the City. There are several other German churches in London, four describing themselves as Evangelical Union, and being, perhaps, more Calvinistic

than Lutheran; and there is also a German Wesleyan Church in Commercial Road, and a German Catholic in Whitechapel.

Norway and even Finland are represented. Far away down in the south-east our wandering feet will bring us to the neatly built little Norwegian Lutheran church, with its reading-room and its manse; and also the Finnish church, constructed of iron, with its seats painted a light bluish green, and its services much resembling those of its Norwegian neighbour. It also boasts its reading-room for Finnish sailors. Though some little distance apart, both these churches are planted on the borders of the extensive Surrey Commercial Docks. Yet Norwegian residents make their way to this place of worship from Blackheath and the north of London to sit with the Norwegian sailors, who chiefly attend it, at the Norwegian Lutheran service.

And here, at this remote corner, our pilgrimage ends. From the splendid Greek church, at Bayswater, to the Finnish church by the great Surrey Docks, we have travelled far. Great is the variety. Lutheran and Calvinist, Greek and Roman, Jew and Gentile—all find their temples in mighty London, and together they form a remarkable and, perhaps, a little-known feature of its wonderful life.

DANISH CHURCH, POPLAR: ASSEMBLED FOR COMMUNION.

INSPECTING LONDON.

By WILLIAM MOYLE.

As government becomes more paternal— we will not say grandmotherly—the task of Inspecting London, long since a many-sided and most important operation, becomes vaster and more complicated. The law now provides that from the cradle to the grave, afloat or ashore, at work or at play, at home and in public, man shall be subject to inspection, and that his food and his drink, his horses and his cattle, his environment and well-nigh everything that is his, shall undergo the same process. And, as a consequence, an army of inspectors daily pass London in review.

To understand something of the work of these officials, let us begin at the chief doorway of the Metropolis, the Thames. Guarding this entrance to the great city is the port sanitary authority—the City Corporation— one of the chief duties of which is the inspection of incoming ships, that infectious disease may not be introduced into London from other ports. When vessels are about to depart, the Board of Trade sees that they are fit for sea, besides looking to the health of emigrants, if any are carried.

At night we can witness another and a very different aspect of Thames-side inspection. Along the dark river steals a mysterious boat, in which are seated three silent figures. Now it dodges among barges, now it explores creeks, now it stops at a wharf, dry dock, or some other of the thousands of premises that line the greatest waterway in the world. Occasionally the crew go ashore, though they soon return and continue their journey.

No piratical craft, bent on plunder, is this. It belongs to the County Council, and its occupants are inspectors—licensed watermen —charged with the duty of ascertaining that all openings, mostly used for trade purposes,

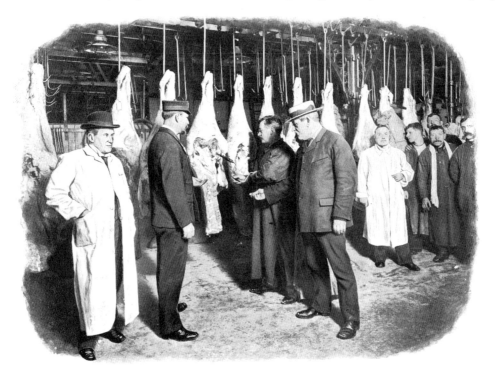

INSPECTING MEAT AT SMITHFIELD.

CHECKING THE WEIGHT OF COAL.

are closed. But for their vigilance, a good slice of London might be startled out of its sleep by serious floods, for many miles of streets, particularly in Rotherhithe, North Lambeth, Battersea, Poplar, and Westminster, are below the high-water level, and, if gates were not closed and boards placed in position, big tracts of thickly populated districts would be inundated.

Not that it is the work of the inspectors to attend to these things. To do that a score or two of men would be required, for within the County Council's area there are some sixteen hundred wharves, at which are more than one thousand tidal boards and gates. The responsibility for closing these lies at the doors of those who occupy the premises on which they are situated. What the inspectors do is to look for cases of neglect, which is punishable by a heavy penalty.

As food is brought into the City it also is inspected. Fish, both at Billingsgate and Smithfield, comes under survey by the officers of the Fishmongers' Company, who have, in addition, certain powers with regard to unclean salmon, etc., while the City Corporation inspectors examine not only the live beasts at the Islington and Deptford cattle markets, but the carcasses of animals killed at the slaughter-houses connected with them, as well as keep a careful watch on the meat and poultry at Smithfield and Leadenhall.

Finsbury and other of the metropolitan boroughs also have meat inspectors; but for the soundness of its flesh food London is mainly dependent on the City Corporation.

Nearly any day you may see the process of meat inspection at Smithfield. It is early morning, when London is rubbing its eyes. A salesman is looking dubiously at a consignment he has received. Perhaps it has been damaged in transit or by exceptional climatic conditions. Possibly it is diseased; but this is unlikely, because very little meat in that condition enters the market. To the stall come two of the inspectors, all of whom, it should be noted, are practical butchers. A brief examination of the doubtful lot, and the dealer's suspicions are confirmed, and the meat is straightway condemned accordingly. Upon this it is seized and immersed in an antiseptic solution, from which it emerges a vivid blue—a dyeing process which makes its sale impossible. By and by it will be removed to the works, where it will be boiled down, and ultimately the fat will be used for greasing purposes and the bone and muscle for manure.

Inspection under the Food and Drugs Act —which applies to all edibles from *foie gras* to the plebeian saveloy and to medicines innumerable—is carried out by the metropolitan boroughs. That innocent fluid, milk, probably receives most attention, especially when vended from barrows, which are often stopped in the streets by the inspectors. Magnificent catches have been made in some districts on a Sunday morning, when the wily adulterator is exposed to great temptation. Not only is there more demand for milk then than at any other part of the week, but the field is usually clear, for, of course, only the sternest sense of duty can keep the inspectors from church. So the iron cow is worked harder than ever on the day of rest. On some occasions, however, the enemy has appeared in the streets on the Sabbath and produced consternation in the milk trade.

The great difficulty in obtaining samples of other commodities lies in the fact that the inspectors are known. Moreover, if they succeed in making one purchase in legal form without the dealer smelling a rat, the whole neighbourhood is instantly on guard. For these reasons agents are commonly employed, and, though they are sometimes outwitted, they bring about the conviction of many food "fakers."

That we get correct weight and measure is, outside the City, which looks after itself in this and some other particulars, one of the many cares of the County Council; and admirably, beyond all question, does it discharge this duty. Occasionally its officers spring a surprise on a suspect. You may, for instance, be idly watching a vanman delivering coal, when round the corner of a sudden there comes a vehicle like a commercial traveller's turn-out. It stops, two men jump from the seat, the back of the trap opens, and, lo! nestled snugly in the interior are strong scales and some "fifty-sixers." To try the bags of coal in the balance does not take long. They are, however, not often found wanting nowadays, though at times the officers catch a man at the old game of pilfering from a number of sacks in order to make up a separate hundredweight.

Let us now pay a visit to the Weights and Measures Office at Newington, and see another phase of inspecting—the testing and stamping of glasses. This work is carried on in a large room having a bench running round its sides. Picking a glass out of a crate, an inspector fills the standard — a half-pint brass measure — with water, passes a strike over the top,

and empties the contents into the vessel to be tested. It holds all the water, and yet is not quite full. Good. The County Council will allow a man to get more than his half-pint of beer (two drachms in excess is the limit), but not a drop less.

The next glass also is satisfactory, the third is too small, and so on. Very variable are the results. Out of one crate not two dozen glasses will be rejected; out of another not two dozen will be passed. Those which satisfy requirements are stamped by the sand blast, while the others are sent back unmarked. They cannot be used by publicans, but are sold for the mineral water trade, household purposes, etc.

Before leaving the office its interesting museum is worth inspection. The fraudulent scales in it are a revelation, while its " iron-clads "—weights hollowed out and filled with cork, a set of which can be hired for a small sum (not from the Council, though)—do not increase one's faith in human nature.

Besides keeping a watchful eye on weights and measures, the County Council does an enormous amount of other inspecting. Everything from the feeding of babies to looking after dynamite and other explosives comes within its scope. It tests the veracity of gas-meters, having an elaborate plant at Newington for this purpose; it inspects buildings, dangerous structures, theatres and music-halls, common lodging-houses; it employs

TAKING A SAMPLE
OF MILK.

surgeons to examine animals supposed to be suffering from contagious disease ; and, among a host of other duties, it enforces the provisions of the Shop Hours and Seats Act.

Not the least valuable service it performs is the inspection of houses where infants are kept for profit—a comparatively new branch of that supervision which aims at protecting the helpless, and which is most strikingly exemplified, perhaps, in the duties of the Commissioners in Lunacy and the Lord Chancellor's Visitors, who jointly keep

belongs to somebody else, and that it has been penned up in the " farm " continuously for weeks, the woman not daring to take it out, lest she should be seen with it.

Sanitary inspection is included in the work of the borough councils, and nobody can profess that it is done as satisfactorily, on the whole, as in the provinces. This is due partly to the people themselves and partly to the remissness of those municipal

TESTING AND ENGRAVING GLASSES (L.C.C. OFFICE, UNION ROAD, NEWINGTON, S.E.).

watch over the whole of the insane. After accompanying one of the Council's lady inspectors on her rounds, you more than ever appreciate the importance of looking closely to baby " farms." A knock at a door in a squalid, depressing neighbourhood brings from somewhere in the interior a slatternly female, who smiles ingratiatingly as soon as she recognises her visitor. How many babies has she? The woman hesitates. Four, but (volubly) one of them is her brother-in-law's ; she didn't register it because she thought it wasn't necessary ; and so on, by the yard. The address of that relation? It is forthcoming instantly, whereupon the patient inspector journeys thither, with the expected result—unknown. More inquiries, and then it becomes clear that the poor little bantling

bodies, whose failings, however, lean to virtue's side. When, as sometimes happens, a landlord threatens that if he catches any sanitary inspectors about his property he will " put a shilling on the rent," the tenants' poverty compels them to bear many evils without complaint. For the same reason outsiders are loth to interfere except in very gross cases. If improvements are made, the cost falls upon the occupiers, who have to pay dearly for them in the form of increased rents. It is charity to them, therefore, not to be more exacting than is absolutely necessary. As to overcrowding, it is practically impossible strictly to enforce the provisions of the law respecting this form of insanitation. What would become of the people ejected?

Ramble about the streets, and you get.

R.S.P.C.C. INSPECTOR DELIVERING A SUMMONS.

glimpses of many other aspects of Inspecting London. A familiar figure in the slums is the officer of the Royal Society for the Prevention of Cruelty to Children. Day after day he threads his way through greasy labyrinths, dropping into houses here and there to see if the improvement has been maintained in cases where cautionary notices have been given, and occasionally delivering a summons to an unnatural mother who persists in neglecting or ill-treating her offspring.

In the roadway the inspector of another humane organisation—the Royal Society for the Prevention of Cruelty to Animals—helps to enforce kindness to God's creatures. As a team is plodding through the street, his practised eye detects that one of the animals is in pain. At his signal the horses are stopped, and on pulling the harness aside he soon discovers a large sore. Then, but not till then, the driver begins to make excuse. Yet he will be prosecuted, nevertheless, and, let us hope, convicted.

One more street scene—a scene with a delightful touch of comedy. In the middle of a small square stands a School Board officer with uplifted forefinger before a wild urchin—a youthful De Wet of the slums— who has been cornered at last. The "kid-catcher" is "administering interrogatories," as the lawyers say, and the youngster is at-

tempting to turn them harmlessly aside. No indication of the marvellous rapidity with which his little brain is working can be seen reflected in his face. In it candour, submission, and modified sorrow are beautifully blended.

The happy hunting grounds of School Board inspectors, however, lie about the great markets, which have an irresistible attraction for truants. Smithfield sometimes swarms with "fat rats"—youngsters who prowl about with roving eyes till they see a lump of fat thrown under a block, when they make an eagle-like swoop for it, and, despite the efforts of the salesmen, bear it off in triumph.

Last of all we come to factory inspection, which we can see both in the west and in the east. Fashionable milliners, in the busy season —from March to July—are, perhaps, the chief offenders in the one part of London and Jewish tailors in the other. Madame gives notice that her girls will work one night a week. Behold, on some other night, the lady inspector arrives. More by force or habit than anything else, she takes a glance at the windows. All are in darkness; not a glimmer of light is visible anywhere. Immediately the door is opened, she walks in and goes straight to a private room. Never mind why her steps are directed thither. It may be, for aught we know, that

SCHOOL BOARD OFFICER QUESTIONING
A TRUANT.

she has received an anonymous letter. Indeed, that is very likely. Reaching the room, she suddenly opens the door herself, and then—a surprise! At one comprehensive glance she sees a dozen tired heads bent over work.

In the East-End you may sometimes meet a factory inspector taking a stroll on Sunday. Going to a house he rings the bell. The servant appears, turns instantly, and, with a cry of alarm, darts upstairs. So quickly does she ascend that the caller, who has followed instantly, has difficulty in keeping close behind her. But he is at her heels when she throws open the door of a room. He is, however, only just in time. Several girls, alarmed by the servant's warning, are leaving the apartment by another door, one of them with a garment in her hand. The Hebrew employer, as he himself afterwards admits — in private — is fairly caught this time. Waistcoats are strewn about the floor, there are bits of cotton on the girls' dresses, and unmistakable evidence exists that the machines have been used recently. That is more than enough to secure a conviction. Would that a case were always so complete!

R.S.P.C.A. INSPECTOR EXAMINING A HORSE.

BOYS' PRIVATE SCHOOL : OFF TO CRICKET.

SCENES FROM SCHOLASTIC LONDON.

By A. E. JOHNSON.

BLUECOAT BOYS IN
LONDON.

AS London is the capital of the British Empire, and consequently its chief seat of government, so is she, the Metropolis, the principal seat of learning and centre of education. And though other cities may set up rival claims, and point with pride to their Universities and ancient associations with deep learning, London remains unrivalled as an educational rendezvous : a vast scholastic repository, wherein may be sought and found all sorts and varieties of education.

It is with this aspect of Living London that we purpose to deal in the present article, or rather to present a few of the more notable " scenes " which are characteristic of " Scholastic London," while taking care not to trench upon " Board School London," which is dealt with elsewhere in this work.

Unique, and perhaps of chief interest, in Scholastic London stands Westminster School, or, more fully, St. Peter's College, Westminster. In the varied pageant of London life to-day the College plays a picturesque part : witness, for example, the striking contrasts produced by the existence of modern public school life amid such antique surroundings. Let the curious visit Little Dean's Yard just before the hour when morning school is over. Entering, he passes beneath a vaulted archway that dates from the monkish days of the fourteenth century. Within, to the left of the flagged and gravelled space, is Ashburnham House, one of the most beautiful buildings in London, and a lasting memorial to the genius of the great Inigo Jones ; while in front is the massive gateway, scored deep with the graven names of old Westminsters, that leads to the big schoolroom (" Up School " as Westminsters call it), ancient and majestic, where stand, beneath the bust of Busby, greatest of pedagogues, and backed by the panelled walls blazoned with the arms of distinguished " old boys," the august seats of the monitorial council.

127

Even as the visitor pauses at the entrance to the school yard, the clock strikes, and forth there streams an ever-increasing crowd of boys in Eton jackets or tail coats. Quickly they disperse in different directions—some, perhaps, to the gymnasium, situate under the groined roof of a crypt-like chamber next to the Chapel of the Pyx; but should the spectator wait a little longer, he will see the majority of them assemble again, this time for dinner, which will be eaten in the old Abbot's refectory, beside the Jerusalem Chamber, which serves

Greeze" (a "greeze" meaning a crowd or mob) on Shrove Tuesday, when the school cook flings a pancake from his pan over the bar which divides "Up School," to be scrambled for by a number of boys who respectively represent the different forms. Then there is the Latin Play performed in College Dormitory every year, with its prologue and epilogue, the latter a skit in "dog-Latin" upon current events of the day. Of privileges enjoyed by the school through its connection with the Abbey, two most jealously prized are the

Photo W. & A. H. Fry, Brighton.

WESTMINSTER SCHOOL : TOSSING THE PANCAKE.

now as College Hall, upon tables that are made—at least so says tradition—of wreckage from the Spanish Armada.

Not far from the Abbey lies Vincent Square, in which are the school playing fields. A curious feature of London life is this centre of healthy athletic vigour set in the midst of Pimlico's dreary wilderness of bricks and mortar; and the casual passer-by may be pardoned his surprise at meeting in the neighbourhood of Victoria Street, as often he will, a knot of lusty youths, dirt-bespattered but vigorous, returning schoolwards from the muddy fray.

Into Westminster's ancient customs and ceremonials it is impossible to enter fully here. There is first of all the "Pancake

rights possessed by the boys to attend when attired in academic cap and gown, debates in either House of Parliament, and at the coronation of the Sovereign, not only to be present in the Abbey, but to be the first with loyal shout to acclaim the monarch when he enters the choir.

Of even older foundation than Westminster is St. Paul's School, which owes its existence to the piety of Dean Colet, who fixed the number of pupils (which still holds good in regard to the Foundation Scholars, who wear a badge in the shape of a silver fish) at 153, the number of the Miraculous Draught of Fishes. Only since the year 1884 has the school been domiciled in its imposing home at West

Kensington, having been previously in St. Paul's Churchyard, close to its patron cathedral. Memorials of antiquity, however, are not wanting, nor are the traditions of an honourable past forgotten. The ground passage of the school is panelled with stone tablets, on each of which is the name of a High Master, and underneath a list of notable Paulines who served their time, as it were, under him. Two of these names are inscribed in letters of gold—those of John Milton and John Churchill.

Social life at St. Paul's differs little from that of other public schools, though day-boys greatly preponderate. To the keenness of the school on things athletic, those who have met the Rugby team in the field can testify: to its capacity for bookwork, the astonishing list of academic successes gained year after year bears ample witness. Few schools are so thorough in practice as well as in theory; and our photographic reproduction on this page, showing an art class at work, may serve as an illustration of the completeness with which every branch of the educational

Photo: Russell & Sons, Baker Street, W.

ST. PAUL'S SCHOOL : AN ART CLASS.

curriculum is carried out. A word should be given to the St. Paul's Volunteer Corps, perhaps the most notable school corps in London, with the exception of those of Dulwich College and Highgate School — neither of which schools, from their positions on the fringe of London, comes strictly within the scope of this article.

A kindred school, in general respects, to St. Paul's is Merchant Taylors', governed by the great City company whose name it bears, just as St. Paul's is ruled, to a great though not complete extent, by the Mercers' Company. As with St. Paul's, the present quarters of the school are different from those which it originally occupied, but, more fortunate, " M. T. S.' has an environment quite in keeping with its traditions. Few can fail to be impressed by the associations of the Charterhouse, and it was a happy day for the Merchant Taylors when the

A HIGH SCHOOL (HAMPSTEAD) : FIVES.

removal of the Carthusians, once prominent figures in the throng of London's schoolboys, to Godalming enabled them to exchange their premises in Suffolk Lane for Charterhouse Square.

Perhaps the most characteristic scene in life at Merchant Taylors' is found in Charterhouse Square during " the hour " —the period between morning school and the mid-day meal. 'Tis there and then that the whole school, it may be said, assembles together for social purposes, and the air resounds with the cries of boys thronging the cricket nets, fives courts, and gymnasium, or disporting themselves, at infinite cost to their knees and garments, upon the asphalt. The grounds at Bellingham, which helped a Merchant Taylor, in the first year of the twentieth century, to make a record score in public school cricket, are also kept busy twice a week.

Of the City of London School, in its handsome home upon the Victoria Embankment, and of University College School, in its less imposing premises beside University College in Gower Street, it is unnecessary to speak at length. They represent the two principal London public schools of more recent establishment—though the City of London School, the large hall of which, with its mural tablets bearing the names of distinguished scholars, may be seen in our illustration on the opposite page, was originally endowed by John Carpenter, Town Clerk of London, so long ago as 1442—and consists almost entirely of day boys.

Of schools designed for the provision of a sound education, on public school lines, at moderate fees, the name is legion. Especially prominent is the ancient foundation of the Mercers' School, in Barnard's Inn, Holborn, close to Fetter Lane. Then there is Owen's School at Islington, another ancient foundation, with which is coupled a companion school for girls; while in Southwark there is the Grammar School of St. Olave and St. Saviour, with special facilities for the education of the sons of parishioners.

And supplementing the schools that exist for London's own children mention must be made of those which minister to the educational needs of the foreigners in our midst. In Noel Street, Soho, are the French

Protestant Schools, to which are admitted, at nominal fees, the children of members of any London Protestant Church where the service is conducted in French, or those whose parents speak French as the mother tongue. Cosmopolitan and intensely interesting little communities these are, where the small aliens of French, Swiss, Belgian, or Flemish birth meet on the common ground of the schoolroom bench, bound by the close tie of school-fellowship. Hard by Fitzroy Square, too, is the German Lutheran School, while in various parts of London are institutions, such as the great Jews' Free School in Spitalfields, and the Jewish Schools in Harrow Road, where the youthful tribes of Israel are trained up in the way they should go.

Let us now turn to the subject of the education of the nation's future wives and mothers. Great have been the educational changes of the last few decades: but it may be doubted if in any direction have alterations more radical been made than in the general system of education for girls. To Frances Mary Buss undoubtedly belongs the honour due to the pioneer; and what she so well began in the middle of the nineteenth century the " High Schools " have well carried on. The doom of the old-fashioned girls' private school with its trivial aims is sealed; and to-day our schoolgirls may be seen on a summer's afternoon strolling, racket in hand, to the tennis courts, or wending their way, alert of step, to the swimming bath — in some cases even to the cricket field, there to learn how to face a fast yorker unflinchingly. In winter time, too, there are fives and hockey to teach the value of unselfishness and co-operation in games as in everything else, and the part which exercise and *esprit de corps* play in health and happiness.

Similar remarks apply to the Colleges for Women. London has now her Bedford College, Queen's College, Westfield College, and so on, which stand in much the same relation to London University as do their fellows of Oxford and Cambridge to those Universities. And though, of course, in a woman's college, less freedom and independence is possible than in a man's, yet the social life is planned on similar, if modified,

CITY OF LONDON SCHOOL : AN EXAMINATION.

lines. There are the same lectures, the same — up to a certain point — athletic exercises, the same social intercourse, all helping to weld that indefinable bond of mutual sympathy and fellowship, "which nothing in life can sever," and which is one of the best results of school and college life.

Then there are the smaller private schools, where the bashful young damsel receives her first lesson in maidenly deportment, and the "prep." where her young brother is primed for his public school career. Never failing sources of amusement are these. Who can resist the unconscious humour of the demure girls' school walking out, two and two, in "crocodile" fashion, and the sidelong glances as the group of boys from the school round the corner passes? And that boys' school: what could be more delightful than to see the youngsters sallying forth on a half-holiday, shepherded by an athletic master, armed with all the paraphernalia of the cricket pitch, and learned already in the lore of lobs and long hops, breaks and bump-balls, drives and —though they admit it not—duck's-eggs? One step lower in the juvenile scale, and we come to the kindergarten, where the infantile mind is first taught to use its awakening powers of reason. This latter is, perhaps, the most interesting phase of educational life. since here the material in the teacher's hands is in its most plastic form : witness, in our photographic picture on the opposite page, the children tending the doves and canary—a simple occupation, not remarkable in itself, but rich in the opportunities it affords for the inculcation of good habits.

A passing reference has already been made to London University. Formerly the university represented merely an examining body, with headquarters at Burlington House, possessed of powers, analogous, on a major scale, to those which enable the College of Preceptors to dispense diplomas to teachers, to grant degrees, which in

ments, with the result that large numbers of boys and girls in all parts of the country enter for the January and June examinations held each year. Our picture on this page shows a group of students up for "matric." outside the examination rooms at the Imperial Institute.

Of college life, indeed, in the usual acceptance of the term, there is practically none in London. The statement, however, takes no account of the theological training colleges. Of these there are several, such as St. Mark's, at Chelsea, and the London School of Divinity at Highbury, where the pale student is trained for the Anglican pulpit, Hackney College and New College at Hampstead, both Congregational in tendency, the Baptist College in Regent's Park, and the Jews' College in Guilford Street, for the training of rabbis, ministers, readers, and other officers of the synagogue.

In the foregoing pages an attempt has been made to take a rapid survey of Scholastic London, to give the reader a bird's-eye view, as it were, of

OUTSIDE LONDON UNIVERSITY : EXAMINATION DAY.

certain faculties (notably that of medicine) carried a world-wide reputation. By an Act of 1900, however, the scope of the university was enlarged, and teaching as well as examining work was undertaken. The principal colleges of the university, which now has its headquarters at the Imperial Institute in South Kensington, are University College and King's College, which afford every facility for instruction, but are non-residential, the students, of either sex, meeting generally only at lectures and examinations. Special reference ought to be made to the matriculation of London University, the preliminary examination which is the first step to higher honours. Success in " matric." absolves from entrance examination at most educational establish-

London's educational centres. It has been necessary, however, to leave much unsaid. Thus, no allusion has been made to the Royal Military Academy at Woolwich, and the Royal Naval College at Greenwich, where many of the future officers of the Army and Navy receive their training. Nor has there been space to deal at length with London's numerous technical schools, headed by those of the London County Council, and including the colleges of the City and Guilds of London Institute at Gresham College, and the various schools attached to the many "polytechnics," which offer to the worker in every station of life the means of instruction in every practical art, from engineering to cookery, lithography to wood-carving, needlework to carriage - building.

GIRLS' PRIVATE SCHOOL : OUT FOR A WALK.

work is something more than a mere euphemism for pleasure or pastime can obtain the best tuition at a nominal cost.

There remains but to bid farewell to this phase of Living London. Though with the removal of Christ's Hospital from Newgate Street to the country, and the consequent passing of the Bluecoat boy, whose once familiar figure we now see only when he visits us in holiday time, the last link was severed that bound us to the quaint and picturesque past, and naught but the prosaic surroundings of modern life are left, Scholastic London will still continue to have its fascination for the philosophic observer. Has it not the charm which ever attaches to the contemplation of the growing mind of youth?

Some of these, however, and such institutions as the Duke of York's Military School, and the Soldiers' Daughters' Homes, are touched upon elsewhere in the present work, as are also the Music and Art Schools, though perhaps we ought here to give a special word of mention to the central "Arts and Crafts" school of the L.C.C. in Regent Street, where those who can produce evidence that with them

A KINDERGARTEN CLASS.

RACING AT HERNE HILL.

CYCLING LONDON.

By C. DUNCAN LUCAS.

OLD-FASHIONED.

TO no small proportion of the inhabitants of London the bicycle as a means of locomotion has become indispensable. The snail-like pace of the omnibuses, consequent upon the congested state of the traffic, and the inadequate train service, render it possibly the most highly prized boon within the reach of the working population. To-day we are about to acquaint ourselves with the part that the bicycle plays in the life of the teeming millions of the great city, and for this purpose we are awakened somewhat earlier than usual. Seven o'clock is our hour for starting, for by 7.30 or thereabouts, the weather being fine, thousands of wage-earners will be awheel.

Hammersmith is a useful point from which to observe the drama, so we steer for that busy suburb. Piccadilly is deserted, and Constitution Hill and Knightsbridge, save for the barracks, are also slumbering, but as we approach the Broadway the hum of wheels is heard. The daily exchange of workers is in progress, London giving to the suburbs and the suburbs giving to London. The triumph of the cycle is apparent at once. Look at that man with the pale drawn cheeks and tired eyes. He is a shopwalker in an establishment in Tottenham Court Road, and lives at Kew because the rents are cheap. He has an ailing wife and six children, and money is so scarce with him that he is obliged to travel to and fro on his bicycle. Be it wet or fine he never dreams of journeying by train.

Contrast him with the bronzed youth who is tearing along at the rate of fifteen miles an hour. He is a carpenter by trade, and has a job at Hounslow. His bicycle—

it cost him second-hand only four pounds ten —enables him to accept employment within a radius of fifteen miles, and gives him health and strength into the bargain. The two young fellows whom he almost runs down out of sheer devilment are badly-paid clerks who spend their days in underground offices.

We are confronted with as many types of bicycles as we are with types of humanity. For example, note that man on the squeaking tricycle who is palpably in fear of

FOR BUSINESS PURPOSES.

the motor-bicycle behind him. The machine has done duty these twenty seasons. Red with the rust of years, there is not a particle of enamel on it, the solid tyres are worn and scarcely visible, the utmost pace that can be got out of it is four miles an hour. Compared with the silvery king of his lordship in Berkeley Square it seems, poor hack, fit only for the scrap heap ; but do not smile at it. To one little household it brings bread and meat and other necessaries. It would perhaps be impossible for its hard-working rider to trudge on foot the three miles which separate his home from the builder's yard in which he works. But he can cycle the distance, and punctually at 7.15 a.m. every week-day the ancient crock, with a can of cold tea and a red handkerchief containing its owner's food hanging beneath the saddle, is hoisted up from the area and despatched on its mission.

London is waking up, and bicycles are pouring in. A corps of military

128

cyclists flashes by : a telegraph messenger on his bright red machine is pursued by a butcher's apprentice anxious to cuff him. The maiden who alarms us with her bell is, judging from the parcel of books which she is carrying, a schoolmistress. If she had no bicycle, train fares would exhaust a large portion of her salary. The two over there—the young man with the billycock hat poised on the left side of his head and the little lady with nut-brown hair — who have just saluted each other meet at this spot every morning, weather permitting. The former is an hosier's assistant, the latter a cashier in a tea-shop. One evening, when they were strangers to each other, the cashier sustained a nasty fall, and the hosier, scorching by, stopped, and gallantly lifted her from the mud. They rode together as far as Chiswick and met—strange coincidence—the next evening and the next ; the friendship ripened, they fell in love, and one day the hosier proposed from the saddle of his bicycle and was accepted.

As we linger hundreds of cycles pass us, and if we could keep an account of every one who will be awheel to-day we should probably have to count up to a quarter of a million.

" WRONG SIDE, MISS."

But another picture awaits us—Hyde Park —and we must hurry back. Stand by the railing for a minute and inspect the parade of rank and fashion. Ladies of title — men are scarce of a morning—seem to rule the road. The cycles here are very different from those in the work-a-day world. Glistening in the sun, not a speck of dust is visible on any one of them. They are the leisured steeds of fortune's favourites, as well studied and admired—for the time being—as their owners' horses of flesh and blood.

ing. Dodging in and out of the mass of cabs and carts she is once again on the wrong side. A constable, ever watchful for beauty in distress, lifts a hand in admonition, but he might as well talk to the man in the moon for all the heed that will be paid to his warning. Our Amazon is as reckless as that sturdy fellow with the bundle of evening papers on his back who is manoeuvring his bicycle across Piccadilly Circus. He has come from Fleet Street in quick time, serving street vendors on his way without dismounting.

Turn where we will in this vast London there is some kind of cycle

START FOR THE CENTURY CUP (HERNE HILL).

Come now to Piccadilly and thence to Holborn, the cyclists' Mecca. Experienced cabmen are not entirely free from nervousness when steering their vehicles through the labyrinth of traffic, but the cyclist has no qualms whatever. Follow that young Amazon with the auburn hair and nicely - fitting costume. She is on the wrong side of the road, and a mineral water cart is sweeping madly down the incline, but she is totally unconscious of the danger that faces her. Just when we think there will be a frightful accident she calmly crosses to the left, shaving the horses' heads. Her sangfroid is astound-

in sight. *En route* to Holborn we encounter seven tradesmen's tricycles, each one in charge of a boy. The weight of these contrivances is considerable, yet little legs propel them from morn till night.

In Holborn a study of the human emotions is presented. The frock - coated man in front of us is darting from window to window. He has promised to buy his sweetheart a bicycle, and is at a loss to know which particular make to select. The youth in the seedy clothes with his nose flattened against the glass would buy a machine if he had the money. He is sighing for better days. Just now he is

It so happens that the great race for the Century Cup is to come off this afternoon, so we proceed to Herne Hill. The huge crowd is bubbling over with excitement, and the neighbourhood of the starting-point is black with humanity. The contest is about to commence. The starter, the judges, the timekeeper, watch in hand, have taken up their positions, the competitors are ready, and presently the order to mount is given. The pushers-off grip their machines and in a second the men are in the saddle. " Are you ready ? " shouts the starter, and everything being in order the pistol is fired and the struggle begins. It is to be a fierce fight, for the cracks are fairly evenly matched. With set faces and straining every muscle round and round they go, first one leading and then the other. The crowd roars itself hoarse, handkerchiefs and hats are waved, and presently the favourite forges ahead, challenged, however, by a youngster so small and thin that we wonder how he is able to hold out. But he has been admirably trained, and on his tiny frame there is not an ounce of superfluous flesh. What flesh there is is as hard as nails. The race is only half done, but the two speed on and on, never relaxing their efforts for an instant. To the spectator it is weary waiting perhaps, but in the last five minutes we get our reward. The youngster has crept up and side by side the two Englishmen race. No one can guess the winner. It is a magnificent

LEARNING TO RIDE AT A CYCLING SCHOOL.

out of a berth. The noisy couple outside the next shop are man and wife. Having tried persuasion and every other artifice— was she not promised a new " bike " at the Stanley Show and also at the National ?— the lady is fast losing her temper. Her machine is horribly out of date, she declares, stamping her tiny foot, and she must have another. She will succeed presently.

How many dealers in cycles there are in London it is impossible to say, but if we estimate the capital that is invested in the cycle and cycling in the Metropolis, without reckoning the annual expenditure on repairs, &c., at eight million pounds sterling we shall probably not be wide of the mark. The industry affords employment to thousands; every neighbourhood has its repairing shop; cyclists' outfitters reap an abundant harvest; while the numerous papers devoted to the wheel circulate throughout the length and breadth of the land.

START OF A LADIES' RACE (QUEEN'S CLUB).

spectacle of nerve and endurance. Yet the final mile tells its tale. The pace is too hot for the new hand, and the old stager, spurting for all he is worth, gradually outdistances his opponent and passes the winning-post a hundred yards ahead.

Another day we can visit Herne Hill and witness the Six Hours' race which is depicted on page 248. The illustration shows the event in full swing. Tandems are making the pace, and the competitors, as fresh as paint, though they have been pedalling their machines for four hours, are moving at a speed that would rival many a train.

At the Crystal Palace and at Wood Green, where there are also magnificent tracks, equally exciting tussles may be seen, while, if we feel inclined, we can be present at a ladies' race—such as the one at the Queen's Club illustrated on the previous page. And here we have ample demonstration of the splendid stuff of which the British girl is made. Her pluck is no less surprising than that of her athletic brother.

Before leaving the subject of racing, mention of the National Cyclists' Union must be made. The N.C.U. is the great ruling body of the cycling world. Amateurs as well as professionals have to be licensed before they can take part in races at recognised meetings, and it is to the N.C.U. that they apply for their licences. This rule, of course, does not apply to ladies.

Now to a riding school. Red, perspiring, fagged out, the three brawny fellows in the centre of the floor are regaining their breath. Six pupils are undergoing tuition—a dapper little gentleman of sixty, a very bulky matron who, if her size does not mislead us, must turn the scale at fourteen stone, two small girls, and a young woman evidently

of the domestic class. Presently operations are resumed. The lady whose avoirdupois has attracted our attention mounts first, heavily and painfully. Laboriously the man in charge pushes his burden. Of a sudden a catastrophe occurs. The massive one leaning to the left loses her balance and falls, carrying the unfortunate instructor with her. She has had enough for to-day,

STORING CYCLES (PADDINGTON STATION).

CYCLE AND TRAILER.

we hear her remark, and will come again to-morrow. The two tiny girls make excellent progress, as also does the domestic lady, who turns out to be a housemaid. Another lesson or two and they will be accomplished riders. The gentleman of sixty, however, is but an indifferent scholar. Nervously he clutches the professor by the arm and sees himself in his mind's eye careering in and out of the traffic of Bond Street. He has had ten lessons at half-a-crown apiece, and is no more advanced than he was at the beginning.

Scenes similar to those we have just witnessed are by no means uncommon. They are enacted not only at riding schools, but in the squares, in the streets, and in several of the parks. Battersea Park is no longer a fashionable rendezvous for cyclists. Regent's

Park, however, has lost none of its popularity as a resort for lovers of the wheel. Here in the Inner Circle, when the elements permit, the practised cyclist and the beginner disport themselves to their hearts' content.

A great world is the cycle world of London. Go to Birdcage Walk on a Sunday morning and watch the parties of lads and lassies setting forth to snatch a breath of fresh air in the country lanes and you will realise the enormous value of the cycle to the inhabitants of the capital. Or visit Paddington Station on a summer morning for proof that the Cockney when on pleasure bent seldom travels without his enamelled steed. An express is leaving for the West, and so plentiful are the bicycles that a special van with padded sides and a device for holding the machines securely in position is provided for them. The two-wheeled roadsters are run up: the guard hauls them in and, placing a canvas pad against each one, stows it away in a place where no harm can befall it. Most of these machines, no doubt, belong to members of the Cyclists' Touring Club—that vast organisation which has done so much to improve the conditions under which cyclists travel from place to place. The C.T.C. has its headquarters in London; publishes a monthly organ, and maintains a fatherly interest in tens of thousands of wheelmen and wheelwomen.

Finally let us stroll, when the sun has set, through some of the leafy squares. The overworked clerk, the shop boy, the tired seamstress, the daring housemaid, out for an hour without leave, the little governess —dozens of them are taking the air on all sorts and conditions of bicycles. London smells fresh and clean to-night, and it is good to be out. The thoroughfares are paved, and every wheel runs smoothly. A gentleman passes us on a bicycle to which a trailing car is attached. Very comfortable looks the lady seated therein, and, judging by appearances, both she and her companion are having a pleasant spin. Another car passes. The rider has been at his desk all day, poor fellow, but he has an invalid wife, and there she sits in the hired trailer, pale and fragile, enjoying the only outing that her husband's humble purse can afford. Let us hope that these evening rides behind the poor man's horse will be the means of restoring her to health.

IN BIRDCAGE WALK.

LONDON BELOW BRIDGE.

By R. AUSTIN FREEMAN.

THE traveller who makes his way from the more western parts of the town to the region that lies east of London Bridge soon realises that he has entered an entirely new and unfamiliar district of which the historic fabric forms the boundary. The transition is the more sudden if he travels by water, for then in place of the barges and lighters seen on the upper river, he is immediately confronted by ocean-going ships that jam their sterns against the very piers of the bridge and rear their masts within a few feet of the parapet. On land the change is more insidious, but is still evident. In the great thoroughfares ship-brokers and teachers of navigation expose their plates; shipping companies display enormous portraits of their vessels; outfitters' windows blossom out into oilskin suits and ready stocked sea-chests; while in the Minories, hard by, the original wooden midshipman continues to "shoot the sun," as he has done year in and year out since the days of Solomon Gills and Captain Cuttle.

But that we may the

better resist the temptation to indiscriminate and discursive rambling, we had better conduct our explorations in a systematic manner, and, to begin with, we will see what is going on on the river itself. With this end in view we make our way to the Old Swan Pier, just above London Bridge, and while we are considering the best method of achieving our object a voice hails us from the shore gangway:

"Want a boat, mister?"

The speaker is a seedy-looking individual of a semi-nautical cut, with an inflamed countenance surmounted by a blue peaked cap, and as we look up he points to a pair of watermen's skiffs that lie alongside the pier, with their painters hitched on to a stanchion, and repeats the question.

And now we come to think of it, a

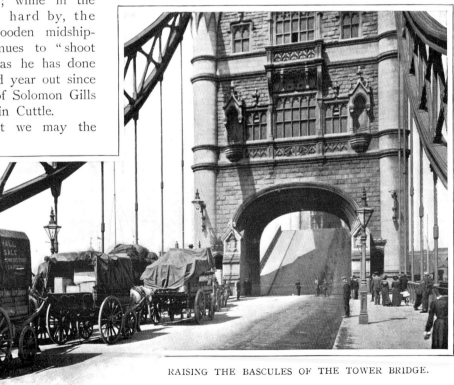

RAISING THE BASCULES OF THE TOWER BRIDGE.

THE POOL.

boat is just what we do want, and we reply to that effect, whereupon our friend comes shambling down the gangway, and, swiftly unhitching the painter of one of the skiffs, gruffly invites us to "git aboard."

The first of the ebb tide is creeping down sluggishly as we push out into the stream and paddle slowly through the northern arch of London Bridge. Above us a great stream of traffic rumbles over the historic highway, while before us, framed by the arch, lies the Upper Pool, closed in at its farther end by the lofty Tower Bridge —London's great watergate.

Close on our left as we pass through the bridge is Fresh Wharf, that famous rendezvous of the London trippers, and the pier barges are even now gay with their somewhat bizarre costumes, for a couple of steamers lie alongside bound respectively for Ramsgate and Walton-on-the-Naze. As we watch, the warning bell from the outer boat begins to ring furiously, occasioning a general stampede on the pier. Flannel-trousered youths in nautical peaked caps, accompanied by young women in white dresses, with shoes and stockings to match, bustle on board, and presently, finding that they

are in the wrong boat, bustle back again: stout, red-faced women drag protesting children up and down the pier, and a belated musician, encumbered with a harp, gets jammed in the gangway and has to be extricated by an attendant fiddler. Then the bell stops; the rattling steam capstans wind in the shore ropes, the whistle emits an exultant war whoop, and the vessel glides away amidst a cloud of black smoke and a burst of harmony from the musicians on the saloon deck.

The whole extent of the Upper Pool is now before us, and a busy place it is when the tide is beginning to run down. On our right the great blocks of warehouses backing on Tooley Street line the river from London Bridge to the Tower Bridge. Battalions of lighters crowd the shore below them, and numerous small cargo steamers, with gaudily painted funnels, snuggle confidentially beside the tall buildings, from the upper storeys of which projecting cranes angle with long lines for the hidden freight and hoist their "catches" —bundles of bales or cases—into yawning openings near the roof.

On our left is Billingsgate, with its two fish-surmounted domes, surrounded by a disorderly mob of lighters, piled high with stacks of empty fish boxes, from which a Grimsby fish carrier is trying to extricate herself. Business is over for the day by this time, but as we paddle by we pass a row of Dutch sloops which supply the London market with eels, as they have done since the days of good Queen Bess; and so unchanging is the type of the Dutch sloop that these vessels, with their massive, mediæval build and antique rig, might have been taken bodily from one of old Van der Velde's pictures.

The ebb tide is beginning to run strong now, and the downward traffic becomes brisk. Down the middle of the fairway a big "dumb barge" or lighter comes sidling broadside on with a freight of empty casks as high as a hayrick and a single figure on her half-deck tugging frantically at a long, supple sweep. Sailing barges with their masts lowered on deck come gliding down with white lug sails hoisted on jury masts, the skipper standing motionless at the wheel and the inevitable dog yapping over the bows at passing vessels. Now and again a tug, towing a long string of lighters, races by with foaming bows and a seething wake and a fleeting vision of grimy faces peering over the bulwark. The fish carrier has just emerged from the jumble of

lighters, and, with a dismal toot of her whistle, hoists the ball at her masthead as a signal to the officials on the Tower Bridge and steams slowly down the Pool. As she approaches the bridge the ponderous bascules slowly rise and she sweeps through into the open river, whither, after a glance at the grim old Tower, with its crowds of loiterers and lounging soldiers, we follow her.

Here, with the whole length of the Pool before us, we are in the very heart of the Port of London. Over the gaunt, unlovely warehouses on our left we see the forest of lofty masts that marks the position of St. Katherine's and the London Docks, while on our right the more slender masts of the Baltic ships in the Surrey Commercial Docks rise above the houses of Rotherhithe as far as the eye can range. The river itself is full of shipping from the great ocean steamer to the " billy-boy " or coasting ketch. On either side long tiers of steamers lie at moorings, leaving a comparatively narrow fairway in mid-stream for vessels under way. Business is even more brisk here than above the Tower Bridge. The line of lighters drifting down stream continues and the destination of many of them appears in the steamers moored in the tiers. Here is a big steamer, for instance, discharging bales of moss litter by means of a forest of derricks into a fleet of lighters that huddle round her like a brood of ducklings round their mother. Near her is another discharging broken granite through large shoots, and as each cataract of stones descends with a roar into the craft along-side, we tremble for the trimmers who dance about, shovel in hand, upon the mounds below.

Some of the sailing barges that we saw

RIVETTERS AT WORK (UNION DOCK, LIMEHOUSE).

AN IRONCLAD ENTERING DOCK (THAMES
IRON WORKS).

drifting down with lowered masts have dropped their anchors while they hoist the masts up, and we may see the entire crew of two men and a boy working the windlass round as they wind in the forestay tackle, until the prostrate bundle of spars has risen into a tall and shapely mast with its spritsail all ready for sea. A few minutes more and the main sheet is hooked to the traveller, the foresail and topsail are hoisted, and the skipper takes his place at the wheel as the mate and boy get in the anchor with much clinking of the windlass pawl, and away she glides with red sails all "asleep," as handsome a freight craft as may be seen on any waterway in the world. As we pass the Shadwell entrance to the docks we see a great wool ship, the very antithesis of the agile, handy barge, creeping out with the aid of three tugs, helpless and gigantic, modern in every rivet from her lean, wall-sided hull of girder and steel plate to her lofty masts and spars of steel tube and her standing rigging of steel wire.

We have noticed for some time a rowing boat some distance ahead sauntering down stream in the same leisurely fashion as our own. She is occupied by three men in peaked caps and blue uniforms, of whom two are pulling and one steering, and as they proceed they gaze about at the boats and shipping around with somewhat languid curiosity. Suddenly the man in the stern stands up and all three stare fixedly at what appears to be a submerged basket floating down in mid-stream ; then the rowers resume their oars and pull smartly towards the object, whatever it may be. As they reach it the coxswain takes a length of thin rope and seizes the floating object, and for an instant a human head appears above the surface. Then the boat starts off again, and we see that the line has been made fast to the derelict, now towed astern and rolling over and over at the end of the cord with a horrid semblance to life. We realise that the mysterious boat belongs to the Thames police, and that presently another poster bearing the words "Found Drowned" will appear among the collection of bills which decorate the door of the riverside mortuary.

Still downstream we continue our way, past Limehouse, where on the shore men with buckets of pitch and long-handled brushes are "paying" the seams of stranded barges, and the clang of the rivetters' hammers comes across the water from the Union Dry Dock ; down Limehouse Reach, past Deptford, where a huge cattle steamer discharges her bellowing freight into the Foreign Cattle

129

DISEMBARKING CATTLE AT DEPTFORD.

Market, and where lighters innumerable are being loaded at the quay of the Royal Victualling Yard ; past Greenwich, up Blackwall Reach, where, on the eastern shore of the Isle of Dogs, the skeleton forms of half-built torpedo boats stand in grim ranks in Messrs. Yarrow's yard, and queer-looking little war vessels, built by that celebrated firm for foreign governments, lie moored in the river. At the head of Blackwall Reach a large emigrant steamer lies at anchor, the steam roaring from her escape pipe and her decks filled with a motley crowd of men and women and children, mostly of the working class, while on shore, where formerly stood the jovial " Brunswick " tavern, famous for its whitebait dinners, is one of the great emigration depôts.

Passing the East India Docks we sweep round into Bugsby's Reach, where we observe a group of men on the Trinity Buoy Wharf hoisting a huge gas buoy on board the smart tender alongside, and a gang of painters smartening up a lightship, on whose red sides is painted in enormous white letters, " Galloper "—the name of a dangerous sand-bank in the North Sea. By the side of the Trinity Wharf, Bow Creek, the mouth of the river Lea, opens into the Thames, and as we pass it we can see on the shore some distance up the creek a mass of scaffolding enclosing a " dim gigantic shape "—an iron-clad in course of construction in the yard of the Thames Iron Works. Presently her enormous hull will glide down the " ways," and the great empty shell will be towed into dock to be " fitted." In Woolwich Reach the river seems busier than ever. On shore huge cranes, lofty chimneys, and vistas of masts from the Victoria and Albert Docks make up the landscape around Silvertown and the great telegraph cable works of Messrs. Siemens ; on the river are unending processions of barges, coasters, and steamers of all sizes passing down the fairway, and grim rows of floating coal derricks and fleets of handsome telegraph cable ships in the anchorage ; and above all is an atmosphere charged with the din and smoke of factory and steamer, and the stench of chemical works. Such is London Below Bridge from the water.

We must now turn our attention to the shore district ; and hastening past Billingsgate (which is described elsewhere in " Living London ") take a hasty glance at the more distant below bridge districts — Wapping, Shadwell, Ratcliff, Stepney, Limehouse, and Blackwall on the north, and Bermondsey, Rotherhithe, Deptford and Greenwich on the south. Broadly speaking, the waterside neighbourhoods are much alike, although there are characteristics peculiar to particular localities which may be noticed in passing. In general the streets are narrow and mean, the houses ill kept and sordid, and the shops unsavoury. But it is not the squalor and poverty which specially impress the visitor, for these are not peculiar to the district. It is rather a certain salt flavour in the air of the place and the appearance of its inhabitants that make riverside East London so different from the rest of the Metropolis. This nautical savour is universal. Each narrow side street has its vista closed in by tall masts rising above the houses, and in the little parlour windows the familiar wedding cake ornament, or pot of musk or family Bible, is replaced by a square glass case containing the model of a brig or full-rigged ship or a steamer vomiting forth clouds of cotton wool from her funnel. In the slop shops tarpaulins and sou'-westers take the place of billycocks and "all wool tweeds," and the pawnbroker's window is filled with strange idols, opium pipes, telescopes, and curious knives. On the pavements swarthy shrunken coolies and solemn Chinamen jostle boisterous negro seamen, and blue-eyed Scandinavians look out from the windows of "Norsk" boarding-houses. Even the public buildings maintain the local character. On one we read, "Home for Asiatic Seamen"; on another, "Passmore Edwards' Sailors' Palace"; on another, "Sailors' Home"; on yet another, the "Victoria Seamen's Rest"; and thus we learn that the reign of the crimp is drawing to a close, and that merchant Jack is at last remembered by the country that he serves.

There is a curious attractiveness about these riverside neighbourhoods notwithstanding their squalor—a charm that was keenly felt by Dickens, who pictured them with a graphic force that has never been surpassed. But the riverside of Dickens' day is rapidly passing away, and will soon be as extinct as the old quarter-galleried Indiamen that were wont to moor in the crowded Pool, and the "light horsemen" who crept stealthily in among them by night, when the riding light burned dim in the fog and the anchor watch was dozing.

ON BOARD A LIGHTER.

SOME LONDON CONTESTS.

By GEORGE R. SIMS.

THE spirit of emulation which distinguishes Londoners is keen, whether in their work or their play, their business or their sport. But so far as this article is concerned we shall see London engaged only in such struggles for victory as come legitimately under the meaning of the word "contests." The political contests of London are at their height at a time of General Election. Then the walls and windows, the hoardings and the streets, are ablaze with the addresses of the rival candidates, with posters of patriotic appeal, with party sneers, with political cartoons, and sometimes with doggerel verse. In almost every street one comes upon a building pasted from top to bottom with electioneering printing and announced in bold letters as "Mr. So-and-So's Committee Room." The town during the weeks of a General Election gives itself up to political strife. Addresses are delivered nightly in halls and assembly-rooms. Sometimes, especially on the Surrey side, a theatre is taken, and the dramatic performance is cancelled in order that one of the leading politicians of the day may address the electors.

The results of the contests that are taking place all over the kingdom are announced by various devices. The position of parties is marked in the windows of illustrated journals by the varying position of the Government and the Opposition Leader on ladders placed side by side. At the theatres and music-halls the results as they come in are given from the stage. Huge crowds gather nightly in front of the newspaper offices and certain political clubs to see the returns that arrive after midnight flung on a large sheet, to be greeted with mingled cheers and groans by the partisans of the winning and the losing side.

During election times private carriages appear in the London streets curiously decorated. Tied on to them behind, at the sides, and sometimes in front, are placards urging all whom it may concern to vote for Jones or Smith, as the case may be. These carriages, which range from the gig to the four-in-hand, drive about to pick up voters at their houses and convey them to the polling stations.

Political organisations play a large part in these contests. The Primrose League with its habitations, its knights, and its dames, is one of the most famous and influential. The Liberal party has an organisation which, if it does not attain so much publicity as its great rival, yet accomplishes an equal amount of hard work. Conservative, Liberal, and Radical associations have their headquarters in London, and they have branches all over the Metropolis. From these is issued the literature, plain and pictorial, which is so much in evidence at periods of political contest.

The election fever is at its highest during the General Election, when the swinging of the pendulum is in doubt. It is at medium temperature during the School Board and London County Council elections, and at its lowest during the election of Borough Councillors and Guardians.

After politics, the contests in which Londoners are most interested are those in which some popular form of sport is concerned. During the winter the great football contests literally hold the field; in summer the flannelled hero of the wicket takes the place of the muddied hero of the goal posts. Both football and cricket have their due share of attention elsewhere in "Living London."

Horse-racing is not now carried on inside London proper, the Alexandra Park meeting being the nearest to the Metropolis, but equine contests appeal to a large public, and the cry of "All the Winners" is familiar in our ears as household words. There are still a few trotting meetings held within

BOXING ("WONDERLAND")

PING-PONG.

the radius we have assigned to the London of which we treat, but the interest in trotting contests is confined to a small class which is not a very representative one. Many efforts have been made to lift the sport into a more aristocratic atmosphere, but none have been very successful. Athletic contests are dealt with in "Athletic London," and boxing contests have also received attention.

Ping-pong has risen so rapidly in favour that its contests, or tournaments, are now held not only in places of ordinary resort, but at that noble abode of "the Heavenly Maid," the Queen's Hall. It is even possible to find ping-pong contests in progress in the business-like City after four o'clock.

Billiard contests take place continually, east and west and north and south. In certain halls you may see a fashionable and attentive crowd sitting in spellbound silence while the great professionals of the cue make marvellous breaks in matches of ten thousand up. Applause is frequently given at the proper time, but the general atmosphere of a billiard room during an interesting match is that of a scientific lecture—with "smoking allowed."

For the humbler folk of the south and the East-End, where billiard saloons are not so plentiful as at the north and west,

the bagatelle board has a special fascination, and matches are constantly played which excite considerable local interest.

Pigeon-shooting matches at the gun clubs in different parts of London were at one time fertile sources of protest from the humane, who objected to the element of cruelty in the sport. The clay pigeon has done much to remove the prejudice against this form of contest. A match at one of the leading gun clubs draws a fashionable audience not only of sportsmen but of sportswomen. At Ranelagh and Hurlingham the fairest in the land assist at the contests arranged during the season, and fashionable London flocks in such numbers to polo matches that the resources of the "tea tents" are strained to their utmost. Here also take place many contests in which the fair themselves may engage—driving contests, bicycle contests, gymkhanas, and the like.

At the lawn tennis tournaments there is always a great crowd, for everybody plays lawn tennis to-day and talks of it learnedly. The game holds its own in spite of the immense attraction which golf has become to the man of middle age who finds himself past certain other forms of sport which delighted him in his lighter and nimbler youth. Golf clubs are now established all over the outer ring of the Metropolis. Golf has more than one organ of its own, and the Londoner with his golfing impedimenta is a familiar spectacle on the railway platforms of the Metropolis.

During May the great military contests held at the Agricultural Hall draw two huge audiences afternoon and evening. The earlier bouts of the fencing contests—"Sword v. Bayonet," etc.—are brought off in the morning before the audience assemble, so that only the finals may be left to delay the showier parts of the great Military Tournament. But the tug-of-war, physical drill, artillery trotting and galloping, riding and leaping contests are all fought out before the huge assemblage, and, in spite of the vast expense of the show, many thousands of pounds are annually earned for the military charities by the brilliant performances of Messrs. Tommy Atkins and Jack Tar.

Wrestling contests, which at one time were a great feature of Good Friday and drew the great men of the Dales to London, are now principally confined to the Palaces of Variety, where much-advertised champions meet on the stage and wrestle in various styles — the Græco-Roman, catch-as-catch-can, etc.—as part of the performance. Walking contests have lost something of the glory that was theirs in the days of the Six Day Trials of Endurance at the Agricultural Hall, though now and again famous pedestrians match themselves against each other in the sporting papers, but bicycle racing has ousted the old heel and toe champion from his vantage ground.

Gymnastic contests are mainly confined to institutes and schools, but the members of the German Gymnastic Society give every year a great show at their hall in St. Pancras Road, and the contests are largely followed by a crowd of members and their friends and the public fortunate enough to obtain admission. It is at the German Gymnasium

that a big boxing competition takes place annually, just before Christmas, under the rules of the Amateur Boxing Association. This association has its own annual competition, which generally takes place at St. James's Hall. The audience on these occasions form a strange contrast to the regular *habitués*. The great international boxing competitions take place at the National Sporting Club, whose premises are in King Street, Covent Garden. Boxing contests also form an important item on the programme of the famous "Wonderland," in Whitchapel, illustrated on page 261.

Swimming contests, both for ladies and gentlemen, are constantly held in London swimming baths. Some of those for ladies are almost society functions. The most peculiar of the swimming contests is the Christmas Morning Handicap, which takes place at an early hour in the icy cold waters of the Serpentine.

There is one interesting contest which takes place at the Crystal Palace and brings thousands of burly bandsmen from all parts of the provinces. The brass band contest is a spectacle to see, a performance to listen to with admiration mixed with awe. Some forty bands perform the same selection one after the other. Late in the evening the massed bands meet and perform together

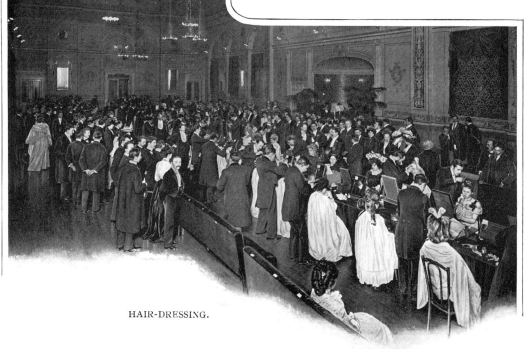

HAIR-DRESSING.

AWAITING ELECTION RESULTS.

night. They are invariably the possessors of nice, soft hair that is easily waved. The competitors and the models are arranged in a row. The competitors dress the hair in various styles. The best style produced most artistic-ally is awarded the prize. Nine professors make a jury for the higher grade competitions. For the Gold Medal contests the jury consists of eleven professors— one for each school. The grand exhibitions are announced as those of the Amalgamated Hair-dressers' Schools of London.

Typists and shorthand writers have annual contests for gold medals, and occasionally there are window - dressing contests among the West-End shop assist-ants, but these do not appeal to the general public.

There is, however, a public for the contests which take place here and there, generally in a minor music-hall or in a small concert-room, for clog dancing and singing by amateurs of the humbler sort. Prizes are frequently offered by an enterprising show-man for young ladies of the coster calling, who dance and sing with tremendous vigour before a critical audience. Many members of the audience know the performer by her Christian name and encourage her with the frank familiarity of old acquaintance. Our illustration on the opposite page represents a singing contest at the Sadler's Wells Theatre.

with stupendous effect. Then the prize winners are announced, and the bandsmen hasten back to London to catch the special trains which are to bear them and their instruments home. Many of the performers are miners or factory hands. They present a curious spectacle as, with their huge instru-ments under their arms, they crowd the big thoroughfare which leads to Euston, to St. Pancras, and King's Cross. This brass band contest is something to be heard and seen and never forgotten.

Trade contests are not numerous, but the hair-dressing fraternity make their competi-tions not only interesting to the general public but highly artistic. Shaving contests have a flavour of the variety show about them, and are not common, but hair-dressing contests are held in West-End halls, and are most fashionably attended.

The contest for the Gold Medal of Hair-dressing takes place at St. James's Hall. The contest for the higher grades of Figaroism are brought off at the Swallow Hotel, Regent Street. The Société du Progrès de la Coif-fure is the French School in London ; there is a German School, and there are English Schools. For the grand.contests living models are selected, who are paid five shillings per

At most of the institutions and local halls there are competitions for recitation and public speaking. A public speaking contest is sometimes an " impromptu speaking con-test." A certain number of subjects are written down on separate pieces of paper and placed in a hat. The competitor steps upon a platform and draws a paper. Whatever the subject may be that he has drawn he is expected to dilate upon it for ten minutes. It sometimes happens that the competitor is so unfamiliar with the subject Fate has allotted to him that he stands for a moment paralysed, gasps, and beats a hasty retreat. In one or two " discussion halls " which still remain in London subjects are introduced for debate open to anyone who may be present to take part in. Occasionally a young barrister or a Fleet Street journalist will air his eloquence, but the glory of the discussion hall has departed.

Bicycle and motor contests, and within certain limits rowing contests, are dealt with elsewhere, but a word must be given to the angling contests in which London fishermen delight, although the scene of their achievements is generally some distance from the metropolitan area. But if they catch their fish out of London they bring them carefully back to it. In many a homely tavern where anglers meet and have their special parlour you will find stuffed specimens of the prowess of a local professor of the gentle art, and you may hear some marvellous fishing stories. There is an anglers' club in the neighbourhood of the Adelphi, and the principal room is crowded with glass cases of fish caught by the members, some of them being the catch that caught the prize. It is dangerous for the non-angler who is

permitted to visit this club to indulge in criticism.

There are other minor phases of "London Contests"—quoits, bowls, basket carrying, bird singing, public-house dog showing; curious contests into the niceties of which only the born East-Ender could enter; contests in connection with porters' work at Covent Garden, Billingsgate, etc.; contests in which the humble donkey of the hawker plays an important part; contests specially arranged for the Fire Brigade at their sports; butchers' contests, and odd contests which occasionally take place in the bar of a public-house and sometimes end in a coroner's inquest on the winner.

But the contests which I have briefly dwelt upon are those which attract the greatest attention either among the masses or the classes, and they afford a fairly comprehensive view of a phase of Living London which is a welcome relief to the monotony of daily toil to many hundreds of thousands of its citizens.

SINGING (SADLER'S WELLS THEATRE).

130

WITH OLD WHEELS.

TOPS.

PICKABACK WRESTLING.

SOME LONDON STREET AMUSEMENTS.

By EDWIN PUGH.

STILTS.

IT is Saturday and all the streets in this mixed neighbourhood are a riot of children. "Are you out?" says one boy to another; and it seems a superfluous question. Translated, however, it means: "Are you on some vexatious errand for your mother? or are you at liberty to join in any fun that may crop up?" The boy replies that he is out, and joins the noisy, moving crowd.

Men must work and women must weep, says the song; it might be added that children must play. Even the ill-used, half-starved child of the London slums can find surcease from the horrors of its lot in a world of make-believe. Rag dolls and paper balls serve the purpose just as well as the more elaborate toys of richer children; and perhaps there is compensation for the lack of such luxuries in an inevitable quickening of the imagination. Of course there are things to be enjoyed in the streets of London that are, comparatively speaking, quite aristocratic of their kind and out of the reach of the very poorest. I refer to such subtle delights as riding in goat-shays, and flying kites and air-

balloons; even marbles, balls, tops, and skipping-ropes are not to be acquired without some small outlay. But effective substitutes for these things can often be made at home by means of a little ingenuity and some miscellaneous lumber. Carts and toboggans can be constructed out of soap-boxes and the wheels of disused perambulators. It is just as easy to be happy with a rusty iron tyre, a hoop off a butter-tub, a kite made out of a bit of cane and a page from a copy-book, a tin lid with a piece of string passed through a hole in the centre that revolves merrily on its edge as you run, a lump of soft clay and a catapult or a rhubarb-bind, as with a genuine shop-made article.

In a few years the sport will be out of these children. They will be playing "pitch and toss," and "banker" with a

MARBLES.

penny pack of cards ; they will, on high days, do their best to make the town hideous with painted horns, and "ticklers" and "tormentors"; they will have money in their pockets and "fags" between their lips ; but they will not be as happy as they are now.

It is mostly in the better streets that children play alone. Here is one whipping a top ; another is trundling a hoop ; a girl is skipping ; a boy on a pair of stilts seems anxious to achieve something complicated in the way of a broken nose ; a very superior young person is engaged in the prehistoric pastime of battledore and shuttlecock. A man has lately passed through this by-way with a barrow laden with paper windmills and flags; these he has offered in exchange for old jars and bottles and has emphasised his offer with flourishes on a bugle. Now the street is gay with his wares. Yet this clean, tidy boy, for instance, who has both a flag and a windmill, and who occupies his time between bouncing a very handsome ball and counting his "alley taws," has an air of aimless boredom. Another boy is skating on rollers; he, too, appears dissatisfied. Suddenly he takes off one skate, lends it to the first boy, and in an instant both are happy, for here is companionship to stimulate healthy rivalry. It is this spirit which animates the children of the London streets and enables them to play with an earnestness which seems to denote that, knowing their

childhood will be but a short one, they are bent on making the most of it.

Some of their games seem to be of a rather spiteful nature. Here is a party playing "Ugly Bear." One boy crawls on the pavement and the rest belabour him with

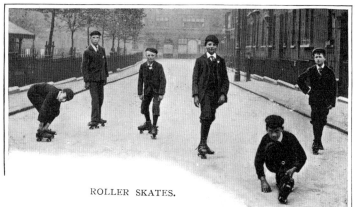

ROLLER SKATES.

caps attached to lengths of string. Here are others playing "Egg Cap" and "Mondays and Tuesdays." If you are a muff at this you will have to lay your open hand against a wall and allow a boy to shy a ball at it. "King of the Castle" and "No Man Standing" are just red savagery set to rules ; "Release" is plain fighting with the anger left out ; whilst "Leading the Blind Horse" is merely an elaborate practical joke, the point of which is to blindfold a trusting innocent and then to maltreat him in any handy way that his defencelessness suggests. Better games than these, though dangerous still, are in progress. Notable among them is tip-cat, but this is perilous only to onlookers.

These urchins who are engaged in throwing pieces of the roadway at other pieces of the roadway are playing "Gully" or "Duck"; they have just been playing "Castles," a game in which loose stones also play a big, shin-shattering part. "Horny Winkle's Horses," in which one set of boys stoops down and makes a bridge of backs against a wall, and other boys ride them to a thrice-repeated chorus of "Charley Knackers—one, two, three !" or, until they collapse, is another boisterous game. In this category come also "Rounders," a game resembling baseball ;

TIP-CAT.

"Chevy Chace," a form of prisoners' base in which one unit of a "side" is captured and held to ransom until a comrade rescues him; "I-spy-I," or hide and seek; "Tom Tiddler's Ground," "Red Rover," and "Puss-puss," which resemble one another in that one player is prominent above all the rest.

This is also the case in "Follow-my-Leader" and the various sorts of Leap-frog— inch-it, foot-it, "Fly-the-Gar-ter,"and Span-ish—with the difference that whilst in "Follow-my-Leader" the prominent figure is rather heroic, in leap-frog he is the butt. This butt or sport of for-

ROUNDERS.

EGG CAP.

tune is known as *He*, and appears in many games. In the various forms of "Touch"— "Touch Wood" and "Touch Iron," "French Touch," "Cross Touch," and "Widdy-widdy-warny" — it is invariably *He* who has to catch the others; it is *He* who comes in for all the indignities. The insane-looking urchin holding his knee is playing "French Touch"; he was touched on the knee by the last *He*, and must not remove his hand until he touches somebody else. This band of six or seven, all clasping hands and stretched across the road, are at "Widdy-widdy-warny." "Kick-pot" and "Strike Up

and Lay Down" are games in which one player opposes all the rest. The last-named is a rough form of trap, bat, and ball; but the trap is dispensed with and the ball merely bounced on the ground. The fielder of the ball endeavours to hit the bat (usually a rough piece of wood) which the striker places flat on the ground. "Straights," cries the fielder; and, if the striker has omitted to shout "No straights," he is at liberty to stand in a line with the bat.

Other robust games, but which belong—either properly or of necessity—to the winter, are "Chalk Corners," which is "Hare and Hounds" (only the hares blaze a trail by drawing arrows on the pavement instead of by dropping paper), and snowballing, and sliding. The fashions of street cricket and football overlap at one period of the year, and both are being played. An amusement for the boys that is an exasperation for the girls will crop up when two blithe spirits snatch a skipping-rope and run down the street, entangling all the indignant petticoats within their sphere of influence.

In the midst of the prevalent turmoil there are boys at games that might be called "quiet," if only the players would refrain from argument. "Buttons" can be played without any adjuncts at all, or in

HORSES.

conjunction with a ball, a peg-top, or a knicker —the last a heavy, leaden disc. There are some curious conventions connected with these games that are religiously observed. You may not, for example, use iron buttons or buttons below the regulation size; and if the peg of your top measures

LEAP-FROG (SPANISH).

less than an average thumbnail it is a "mounter" and may be thrown over the house by any boy who can get hold of it. Other "quiet" games of a competitive

SOLDIERS.

sort are "Buck, buck! how many fingers do I hold up?" and, in their season, "Cherry-bobs," and "Conquers," i.e., horse-chestnuts. A fascinating toy for solitaires is a disc of wet leather on the end of a piece of string which will adhere fast to the ground or, by adhesion, raise a cellar-plate. This is known as a "sucker."

Besides all these regulation games there are others which owe their origin to some passing London show or predominant public interest. War always fires the boys. A military exhibition may inspire them to a pickaback wrestling tournament But, as a rule, such games have a brief vogue,

the genius of organisation not being common in children. A notable exception to this *dictum*, however, was to be found during the Boer campaign in the wonderfully drilled regiments of juvenile soldiers that paraded the London streets. It was a memorable spectacle to see these bands of little ones, to whom some tiny *vivandières* were usually attached, marching along in perfect step through the mire or dust of the road, wearing their helmets and tunics, carrying their weapons, also an "ambulance," beating their drums and blowing their toy trumpets, with that dignified gravity of which only children know the secret.

But, generally speaking, the best games of make-believe are either rooted in tradition or founded on the everyday life of the participants.

HOPSCOTCH.

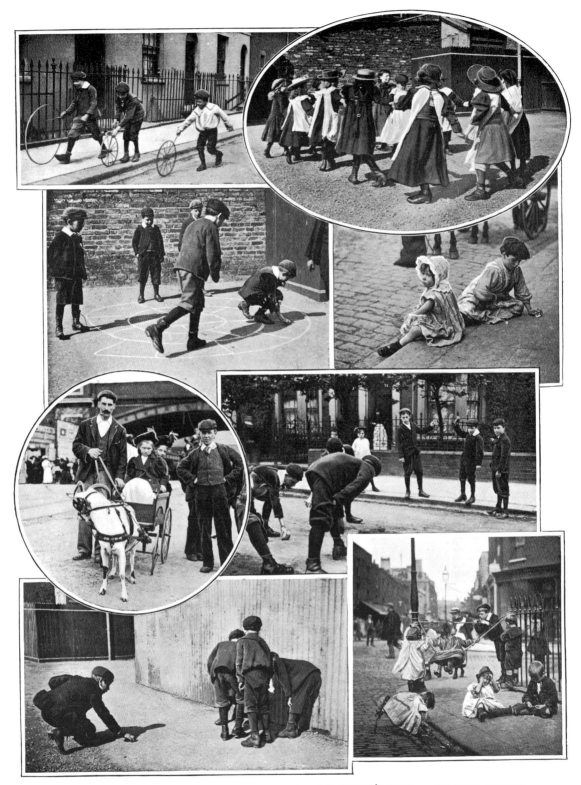

I. WHEELS AND HOOP.　II. KISS-IN-THE-RING.　III. SPIDER'S WEB.　IV. FIVE STONES.
V. GOAT-SHAY.　VI. GULLY.　VII. CHERRY-BOBS.　VIII. SWINGING.

Boys are not so fond of these games of make-believe as girls are; but you will find them playing at "Horses" with reins of rainbow wool which they weave on a machine constructed of a cotton reel and four pins; or, with lanterns, puffing and steaming along in imitation of a train. A thunder-shower will set them to floating paper-boats in the flooded gutters. Mud, at all times, will move the younger fry to make pies. Sometimes, if they are of a gentle disposition, they will join the girls in a mimic domestic drama of "Mothers and Fathers," or "Schools," or "Shops." They will reel about the pavement in dreadful pantomime as "father"; they will buy imaginary wares with imaginary coin; or submit to be cross-questioned or cuffed as the pupils of a small but imperious mistress. They will take part in "Kiss-in-the-Ring" and the other innumerable love-making games: "Ring o' Roses," "Poor Jenny is a-Weeping," "Bingo," "London Bridge is Broken Down," "Wallflowers," and many others. Their name is legion, and a recital of the rhymes that are chanted in a sing-song accompaniment to them would fill many pages. The ruling principle is invariably that a boy or girl shall choose one of the opposite sex, kiss, and then leave the other to pursue a similar policy of selection. These little ones seem to play at love for practice; they blush, and are tremulous and constrained; the boys cut awkward capers to show how terribly they are at ease; the girls are fiercely competitive for the favour of their particular sweethearts.

There are games in which the sexes mingle that are not love-making games: "Oranges and Lemons," "Here We Come Gathering Nuts and May," "Several Men Come to Work," and "Honey-pots." The first two of these games resolve themselves into a tug-of-war. "Several Men Come to Work" is a game in which trades are represented by dumb show. In "Honey-pots" you are trussed up, with your hands clasped under your legs, and swung to and fro by two other players. These things are shrouded in a mystery impenetrable to the mere masculine intelligence, even among juveniles.

No boy ever really arrives at the true inwardness of Hopscotch, for instance. It is as baffling as feminine human nature itself, whether it be of the variety that depends on a series of circles and numbers, or on a drawing known as "Spider's Web" which rather resembles a periwinkle-shell in outline and has initials written on it in set spaces. The tiny maids, hopping on one leg, kick at a piece of china or a flat stone; and if they fail in their incomprehensible endeavours they seem to go on just the same, and if they succeed they are as pleased as a cat in the fender, though it seems to make no difference either way. Then there is "Five Stones," better known as "Gobs," at which they will play for hours without tiring, though the game consists merely in sitting on a doorstep and bouncing a big marble and picking up stones and catching them dexterously on the back of the hand. They will nurse a doll, too, in an abstracted way, all by themselves; or swing on a rope attached to a lamp-post or the railings, monotonously, backward and forward with pathetically intent faces, showing no sign of pleasure. When they play together they are noisier; but you rarely see them smile. At the game of "Higher and Higher," which begins and ends in jumping over a rope, they display an amazing agility, whisking their bodies into the air by a revolving action and clearing almost their own height.

And all the while, in many cases, they have to play another part of little mother to younger brothers and sisters. They ape, with a cruel fidelity, the methods of stern parents, sometimes covering their charges with abuse, slapping, shaking, touzling them; but they are very solicitous for the little ones' safety all the same. In short, they are serving their apprenticeship to life. Whilst the boys are being Red Indians and pirates, and yearning to run amuck through the Ten Commandments with a cardboard sword, the girls are learning how to be mothers. For, though she plays, the poor little girl of the London streets is never quite a child.

A LECTURE AT THE ROYAL INSTITUTION.

SCIENTIFIC LONDON.

By JOHN MUNRO.

LONDON, of course, is the scientific centre of the British Empire. Over a hundred learned societies of renown have a home there, without speaking of smaller local bodies more or less of the Pickwickian order. They are scattered throughout the heart of the Metropolis, but, like certain trades, they show a tendency to cluster in certain parts owing to kindred societies in the neighbourhood and to suit the convenience of members. Comparatively few lie east of Temple Bar, and they seem to gravitate towards the West-End. New Broad Street, E.C., has an important Institution of Mining and Metallurgy; Finsbury Circus, besides the London Institution, has the London and Middlesex Archæological Society—dealing with antiquities of the city. When we come to Bloomsbury, we find not far from the British Museum the Royal Photographic Society, the Society of Biblical Archæology, and the Egyptian Exploration Fund—the last pair devoted to the study of Scriptural countries.

In quiet nooks off the roaring Strand are planted the famed Society for the Encouragement of Arts, Commerce, and Manufactures, better known as the "Society of Arts," the Institution of Naval Architects, which aims to perfect ships of every kind, the "Society for Psychical Research," engaged in the eerie task of investigating "ghosts," hypnotism, presentiments, and other uncanny phenomena of the mind, the Royal Statistical Society, and the Victoria Institute or Philosophical Society of Great Britain, which is concerned with all nature, from stars to atoms and from men to microbes.

Larger still is the scientific settlement of Westminster. Here the Royal Meteorological Society puzzles its brains over the caprices of the weather, the Royal Horticultural Society records experiments in growing flowers and fruit, and the Society of Chemical Industry is deeply engrossed with the preparation of dyes, gases, fertilisers, and so on. Here, above all, are the engineering societies, and first the noble Institution of Civil Engineers, whose roads, railways, and canals have changed the face and even the life not only of Britain but of the world. Their hall, adorned with busts of great engineers, is one of the handsomest in London; and it is a notable sight to see the bronzed, manly tamers of brute forces, the pioneers of civilisation, as they listen to a distinguished comrade on the irrigation of the Punjab or the damming of the Nile.

In the same room are held the meetings of the Institution of Electrical Engineers —a younger brother who bids fair to outgrow the elder in bulk and prestige. The motto of its alert, prompt, ingenious members, whose frames are seasoned to every clime and whose thoughts are as quick as that subtle "demon" they direct, might well be "Ubique." The electrical engineer is a compound of traveller, sailor, engineer, physicist, and merchant. A poet may sing for love alone, but an engineer does not run a telegraph or build a dynamo without considering whether it will pay. Watch an audience

while some inventor describes his new contrivance—for instance, a Marconi on his wireless telegraph. All are attentive to understand the novelty, but their opinions as to its merits are very diverse, and these come out in the discussion. One takes only a scientific interest in it, and foreseeing its possibilities is enthusiastic in its praise. Another is a cable engineer or manufacturer, who feels his professional interest threatened and is disposed to slight it. A third, lacking imagination or judgment, cannot discern its capabilities; a fourth is envious because he did not invent it himself, or is thinking how he can improve it, whilst his neighbour determines to keep his eye upon it as an addition to his present business or the opening of a new career.

Close by other branches of engineering are represented by the Institution of Mechanical Engineers, which is concerned with machinery of all sorts, and the Iron and Steel Institute, with other societies or clubs for engineers. It is perhaps not without significance that far away in Kensington is the Aëronautical

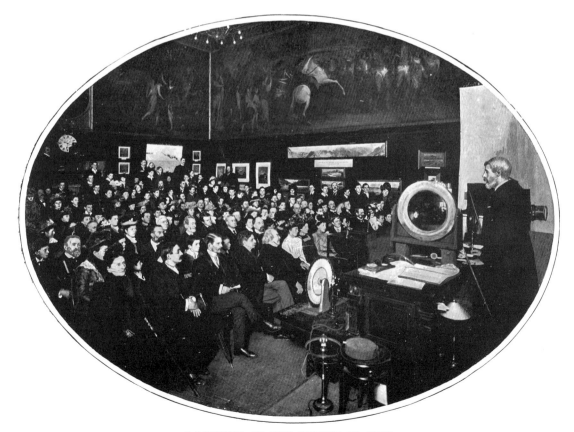

A LECTURE AT THE SOCIETY OF ARTS.

Society, which is occupied with the flying machines and air-ships of the future.

The principal scientific quarter of the Metropolis, however, is in and about Piccadilly, where, in Burlington House, a group of celebrated corporations, theoretical rather than practical, are dedicated to the great kingdoms of nature. There is the patriarchal Royal Society for science in general, which may be said to draw its members from all other scientific societies at home or abroad. A man, if neither prince nor premier, must have distinguished himself in original research to be elected a Fellow. That is a proud moment when the successful candidate signs the roll and shakes the hand of the President. The Royal Astronomical Society is a band of celestial explorers, many of them amateurs in the sense of working for love in observatories of their own provision. It is not for gain that such men watch the heavens night after night, and they are sometimes rewarded by the magnificent spectacle of a comet or eclipse, and the glory of discovering a new star or planet. The Royal Geographical Society holds its meetings in Burlington House, and is, of course, the most famous body of travellers, for no other nation has done so much as ours to open up the unknown regions of the earth. In the same building is the Geological Society of London, which reveals the geography of past eras, and includes experts who can draw you a picture of an extinct monster from its bones, even from its tooth. The Linnean Society, which is deep in the lore of plants, the Chemical Society and the Physical Society, which are throwing light on the properties of dead matter, the Society of Antiquaries, and the British Association, not to speak of more, congregate in the same place. Now and again some important "find" draws public attention to one of these sectional societies, but as a rule their quiet proceedings are only interesting to the specialist.

The British Association for the Advancement of Science, to give its full title, is, however, an exception. Indeed, one of its functions is to bring the results of the other societies before the world, and its brief autumnal session, which is held in some large town of the United Kingdom or the Colonies, is the great scientific holiday of the year. The jaded scientist, after long and patient labour in the solitude of his laboratory, pursuing a law or inventing an apparatus for the benefit of his fellow men, has now an opportunity of shaking the dust from his mind and receiving the applause or hospitality he deserves. Membership is open to the public, ladies as well as gentlemen, and the programme is usually very wide.

Near Burlington House is the Royal Institution — a classical establishment in Albemarle Street, with around it the London Mathematical Society, the Aristotelian Society of Psychology, the Royal Asiatic Society, and the Society for Promoting Hellenic Studies. Farther back, in Hanover Square, lie the Royal Microscopical Society, the Zoological Society, the Anthropological Institute, given to the observation of living races, particularly savages, and including not a few ladies among its members, the Royal Agricultural Society, the Royal Archæological Society, the Palestine Exploration Fund, and the youthful Röntgen Ray Society.

Perhaps the Royal Society and the Royal Institution are the nuclei of these western groups. The Royal Society is the most ancient of our scientific societies, and ranks in fame with the Paris Academy of Sciences. Its rooms are decorated with portraits and busts of past presidents, from Newton downwards, and its proceedings are attended with traditional state. The President, grave and dignified, sits on a high-backed chair, between the secretaries, with a mace in front. Surely never was the symbol of order less needful, for there no political passions rage, abstract thought is master, and the speeches are of quite impersonal cast. Yet even Fellows of the Royal Society are human and have their weaknesses. After months of careful and obscure labours, a member brings his experiments or his invention before his compeers, but his pride and pleasure at their congratulations are often grievously marred by adverse criticism. A rival has invented a similar apparatus before him and rises to claim the priority, or some eminent authority on the subject opens mighty guns to bombard his methods or demolish his conclusions. Thus, instead of joy or triumph, he reaps vexation or chagrin, and realises that his wearying toil and trouble have been in vain.

"LADIES' NIGHT" AT THE ROYAL SOCIETY.

Two *soirées* are annually held—one in May for gentlemen only, and the more brilliant "Ladies' Night" in June. The first is the more serious and scientific, but "Ladies' Night" is an event of the London season, "lions" of all sorts are present in large numbers, and the scientific bow is relaxed in deference to the fair sex. Sometimes a Royal personage or a foreign ambassador puts in his appearance. A Premier jostles an editor who attacks his policy; an Archbishop jokes with a Darwinian, perhaps to the advantage of both; antagonists in science are able to converse and understand each other better. The discoverer expounds his results in person, and receives the homage of the public; the inventor picks up hints that in the fulness of time may suggest a new machine; and the scribe gathers knowledge for a book or an article.

The rooms of the Society are filled with scientific instruments or curiosities, and popular lectures are given in the halls. Only the hackneyed and purely commercial element is taboo. It is not an industrial exhibition, and we shall not meet there any patent water taps or stoves. We shall see instruments of precision that will split a hair, measure a jiffy, or weigh an iota. Illuminated microscopes on the tables reveal their splendid secrets, photographs of the sun and planets

make us dream. There are diamond-bearing meteorites from the waste regions of space, grains of some new metal isolated by the chemist, flasks of liquid air and hydrogen, the latest Röntgen radiographs, wireless telegraphs, and many other novelties. In perambulating the galleries we may stumble on some hoary investigator renewing the pastime of his youth and blowing soap bubbles to calculate the dimensions of a molecule. How far his thoughts have travelled since he puffed them in childish glee! We need not be surprised to meet some rare orchid from the tropical forest blooming in the heated atmosphere. Its next neighbour may be a garland of withered roses, amaranth, and myrtle from the funeral feast of an Egyptian mummy. Here lie autographs and relics of departed worthies, there fragments of ruin, perhaps a cloudstone from the tomb of Tamerlane, and yonder some freak of nature—a stick of square bamboo or a four-legged bird from the Amazon.

If the Royal Society is the fountain-head of science in London, the Royal Institution is its main channel of distribution. It has laboratories of research which Davy, Faraday, and others have immortalised, but its popular

A LECTURE AT THE ROYAL GEOGRAPHICAL SOCIETY.

lectures form one of its chief characteristics. They are delivered in the winter sessions by specialists of repute, and range over the whole intellectual domain. Science, however, is the chief attraction, and the " Friday Evening Discourses," as well as the Christmas or Easter Lectures to Juveniles, are the salient features. Our illustration on page 272 shows a well-known professor initiating the young mind into the secret of " ripples," whether in water, air, or ether, and leading it up from the circles made by a stone falling in a pond to the signals flashed by an electric spark from Cornwall to Newfoundland. The children, mostly boys, sit wondering and expectant, ever ready to clap their hands with delight over some brilliant experiment. One or two, perhaps embryo philosophers, are more staid than the rest. They are accompanied by a sprinkling of their elders, including learned greybeards, who enjoy the lecture quite as much as the bairns do, although one or two may have discovered the phenomena themselves years agone.

The lectures at the Society of Arts are usually on applied science, and, as the commerce of this country is based on that, are of national importance. The subject of our picture on page 273 is a discourse on photography by an eminent specialist, who is conducting his audience from the first crude origins of the art up to its latest developments in colour photography, " X " rays, and the cinematograph.

If the Society of Arts disseminates practical science and fosters trade, the Royal Geographical Society brings home new products from every clime and opens up new markets. Ladies attend the meetings, especially when, as shown in our photographic reproduction on the opposite page, a famous traveller is relating his adventures in some wild country. Surely it is one of the contrasts of life to find yourself lecturing in evening dress to cultured ladies with your cheeks tanned by the fierce light of the jungle and your heart full of hair-breadth escapes from flood and fever, savage beasts and men. The plaudits of fair hearers and the vote of thanks from some distinguished man are probably deemed a flattering compensation for the trials.

Agriculture and seafaring are the founda-

MAKING AN OBSERVATION AT THE ROYAL
OBSERVATORY.

tions of our prosperity, and as both depend on the weather the Meteorological Office in Victoria Street, Westminster, now calls for a visit. Here the storm warnings are issued to ports and fishing stations, barometers and other instruments are kept and lent, pilot charts are prepared for vessels, and weather forecasts are sent to the newspapers or by wire to individuals. The forecasting is done in the morning, after eight o'clock, by two or three of the staff, in a bare front room lined with atlases of old charts. However magical its results may appear, the work itself looks tame, because it is largely mental, and beyond the Morse telegraph instrument clicking the messages, the deciphering of the blue tape, the scheduling of the results, and the marking of them on the big forecasting chart, there is little to see. The chart is merely a skeleton map of Europe dotted with the sites of the observing stations. On it the elements of the weather, the height of the barometer, the force and direction of the wind, the rainfall, temperature, and so on, are indicated. Then, from long experience, the forecaster judges by the state and tendency of the weather now what it will be during the next twenty-four hours. Finally, he submits the chart and his deductions to the approval of his chief—as shown in our photographic picture below—who sanctions their publication.

Astronomy is not less important than meteorology to seamen. The Royal Observatory at Greenwich was founded to help navigation, and its astronomers are so busy observing "clockstars" or the sun to correct the clocks of the country, and also the orbs which, by the Nautical Almanac and the chronometer, enable mariners to calculate their place at sea as well as the perturbations of the magnetic needle affecting compasses, that they have little time for discovery, and some have never seen the grander spectacles of the heavens.

Our picture on page 277 shows an observation of the sun at noon with the new altazimuth instrument—a useful "telescope of all work." The field of view is crossed by a grating of spider lines, and as the disc of the sun touches one line after the other, an observer presses a button on the eye-piece, makes an electric contact, and sends a current which marks the instant on a chronograph,

while an assistant on his left makes notes. The time is computed from such observations, and the standard clocks corrected by electrical currents. Time signals are also wired to the General Post Office for distribution at ten and one o'clock, other currents drop a time-ball at the Observatory and at Deal to regulate the chronometers of ships in the river and in the Downs. By-and-by, perhaps, they will also be sent by wireless telegraph to vessels at sea.

Chronometers are tested at the Observatory for the use of the Royal Navy and other purposes. There are hundreds of them chattering away like insects, while a standard clock beats the seconds loud and clear. At intervals an assistant calls out the error of each, and his companion jots it in his note-book. A certain romance is buried in the old "log-books" of these timepieces. One went with Livingstone across Africa, another perished with Franklin in the far North, a third lies in Davy Jones' locker with the crew of the *Birkenhead*.

The most important occasional work of the Observatory is the great star map which eighteen countries have combined to make. As the stars which look so fixed are ever changing, this record of the heavens now will hereafter be of practical value, since in one way or another it is the heavens that rule the earth and all it contains.

WEATHER FORECASTING AT THE
METEOROLOGICAL OFFICE.

IN THE AYAHS' HOME (HACKNEY).

MISSIONARY LONDON.

By ALEC ROBERTS.

THE missionary activities of London are a fascinating and an uplifting theme. Their range and their diversity are prodigious. Their aggregate of enterprise and achievement is one of the most impressive facts in human history. Volumes would be needed to set forth in anything like detail the scope of those numerous organisations which have their headquarters here; but we are concerned now rather with the metropolitan than with the imperial aspect of London's missionary activities. "Imperial," by the way, is a word of too restricted import in this connection. The noble zeal of our missionary agencies is not bounded by the limits of our Empire. It ranges from pole to pole. Thus need has arisen for the British and Foreign Bible Society to supply the great missionary agencies with complete Bibles in 100 languages; New Testaments in nearly 100 others; and portions of the Scriptures in 150. The Bible Society is not the only worker in the literary field. The Religious Tract Society has already made use of 250

languages. Then there is the Society for Promoting Christian Knowledge, which has many ramifications at home and abroad, and there are numerous denominational agencies ranging from the Catholic Truth Society of the Roman Communion to the Unitarian Society and the New Church or Swedenborgian Publishing Society.

Occasionally in London there are missionary gatherings of vivid interest and picturesque aspect. Such gatherings occur chiefly when the May Meetings of the various foreign missionary societies are being held. Then you may see men and women from the four quarters of the globe—some of them garbed like the native races amongst whom their lot is cast. They come from Indian bazaars and zenanas; from the cannibal isles of the South Seas; from the Far East, where comrades of theirs have earned the martyr's crown; from labours amongst the Eskimo of Greenland or the Hottentots of South Africa. They come even from the shunned abodes of lepers, where the living stalk like hideous phantoms—the abhorred and accursed cast-aways from their own kin. In the noble work of succouring these most wretched of human kind, the Moravians led all other Protestant organisations, as, indeed, they did in various missionary enterprises from Labrador to Cape Colony. As showing what regard is paid even to the outcast of different lands by beneficent agencies in London, it may be noted that the Spectacle Mission—originally concerned only with ministering to the needs of poor people at home—now sends tinted spectacles to protect the eyes of lepers from the hot sun. The Zenana Missions—Church and Nonconformist—afford a fine example of women's work for women. Lady missionaries, skilled in medicine or nursing, are a blessing to the jealously-guarded women of heathen and Mahommedan lands. Amongst the various training institutions for medical missionaries one of the most interesting is the Livingstone College, Leyton, which commemorates the famous African pioneer. Mention of Livingstone recalls his connection with the London Missionary Society, which

has sent out other famous men, such as John Williams, Moffat, Morrison (the first missionary to China), and Chalmers of New Guinea. Its museum in Blomfield Street is grimly interesting. Strange gods before whom the heathen in their blindness bowed down are here in fantastic deformity ; here, also, are curious implements of peace and war.

But our account is rather with London as a field of missionary activity, not merely as the headquarters thereof. Of Greater London's population of over six and a-half millions more than half are quite outside all the churches. In some districts only one person in eighty enters any place of worship. A third of the crime of the whole country is committed or discovered in London. Many thousands are habitually starving. Multitudes of children are the victims of neglect and poverty. From the seething cauldron of sin, misery, and unspeakable degradation which London represents, all the churches and all the sects are striving in generous rivalry one with another to rescue and to save.

Not all of them get credit for as much

CHINESE LANTERN SERVICE (WESLEYAN WEST-END MISSION).

IN THE LONDON MISSIONARY
SOCIETY'S MUSEUM.

as they are doing. Examination reveals, for example, that the Friends, or Quakers, have nine centres in some of the most densely populated and poverty-stricken parts of the Metropolis, and have many social activities— these ranging from free Sunday breakfasts to a labour department. Comparatively few Londoners may be aware of a useful mission known as the Christian Community, which, founded as long ago as 1685 by the Huguenots, still preaches the Gospel and relieves the distress of the poorest classes. The Unitarians are not lagging behind the "orthodox" organisations. They also seek to ameliorate the lot of the poor—to help the widow and the orphan. They have their "Poor's Purse," and their "Old Clo'" rummage sales. The Jews, who are never lacking in philanthropy towards their own people, have their charitable and missionary agencies. East and west, north and south; in the slums and in the streets; on the river and in the parks; in attic and cellar; in every nook and cranny London's missionary enterprise is manifest. The hungry are fed, the naked are clothed, the homeless are sheltered, the poor have the Gospel preached to them. None have sinned too grievously or fallen too low to be beyond the range of pity or the helping hand. London's missionary activities, moreover, follow the whole track of human life from the babe

in the crèche to the aged pilgrim in his home of rest. The lame, the maimed, the halt, and the blind are all objects of commiseration and aid. Christian philanthropy even provides homes for the dying poor, as, for example, the Wesleyan "Home of Peace," and the unsectarian "Hostel of God" at Clapham.

The foreigner within our gates is an object of as much solicitude as our own people. In Soho—where the Wesleyan West-End Mission had its birth—various agencies are at work amongst the foreign population. The City Mission is active here, as it is down by the docks, where it labours amongst the 20,000 Indian and African seamen who come to London annually as well as amongst Europeans. At Hackney the City Mission has its Ayahs' Home—a great boon to the Indian women who come and go between here and India as nurses or attendants on ladies and their children. In connection with the St. Andrew's Waterside Mission there is a mission to Lascars, carried on by native Indian ministers at Victoria Docks. At Tilbury, which hundreds of Japanese who come to our shores make their chief port, a mission has been founded and a home opened for their benefit. But, indeed, the scope of compassion is not limited to humankind. The fourth Sunday after Trinity is

APPLICANTS AT ST. GILES'S CHRISTIAN MISSION, BROOKE STREET, HOLBORN.

building devoted to business. It is a peaceful oasis in the strenuous life of the City. Here the flowers intended for distribution are wired and have texts or slips attached to them. The Society of Friends has its Flower Mission too; and the Church Army has its "God's Garden Guild," which encourages country folk and others who have gardens to provide for the replenishment of slum coffers — also flowers for distribution among the sick poor.

"Animal Sunday" in the churches, and there are various societies which, on ethical and religious grounds, inculcate the humane treatment of the lower animals.

No one can give consideration to the noble purposes and the splendid achievements of London's missionary zeal without his soul being stirred to its very depths, however little he may have recked of such enterprise previously. The resourcefulness of those engaged in the work is also impressive. They seem to overlook nothing, nor is any means of betterment disdained. Thus we have " Evangelical Brass Bands" in the streets, to say nothing of the Salvation Army's cheerful lilt, and we have the Chinese lantern services of the Wesleyan West-End Mission—services out of doors at nightfall with harmonium accompaniment. The Methodists, though staid folk, have had their Central London Brigade of frock-coated and silk-hatted " sandwichmen," carrying boards announcing meetings and services. One very charming idea which finds manifestation in connection with missionary work in London is the association of flowers with religion. The City Mission acknowledges the value of the Bible Flower Mission, inasmuch as the gift of a nosegay is a pleasant introduction to religious ministration. The Bible Flower Mission has its headquarters in Cannon Street, high up in a lofty

But the flower cult is only one of many. The Pleasant Sunday Afternoon, the Mothers' Meeting, and the Sunday Night Service in the theatre are recognised as means of grace. So are texts in tramcars and omnibuses. Thanks to its provision of a Poor Man's Lawyer, the West-End Mission claims to have recovered £10,000 for a poor client. If religious bodies had their way, they would leave you bare indeed. Church and Nonconformity are eager competitors for your old clothes. Excellent freebooters in the sacred cause of charity, they would not be absolutely content with your raiment if you would permit them to remove articles of furniture also. The Church Army has its "Old Clo' Mission," and, like numerous other organisations, it has its needlework guild. Truly, what is said of one religious body may almost be said of all. The Roman Catholics unobtrusively undertake works of benevolence amongst the poor. The tenderness and the devotion of the Sisterhoods are amongst the sweetest things imaginable. They shrink from no task, however arduous or unpleasant. Even menial offices at Nazareth House—one of the noblest charities in the world — are performed by the Sisters. The Roman Catholic community has its hospitals, its retreats, its refuges, its orphanages, and its homes of mercy.

As a result of what is known as the "Anglican Revival," the Church of England has its Brotherhoods and its Sisterhoods in London now engaged in ministrations amongst the poor, the afflicted, and the irreligious. The Evangelical section of the Church of England has its deaconesses who, without taking vows, labour amongst the poor. So, too, has Nonconformity. This is notably the case with Wesleyanism, which has its Sisters of the People. They are chiefly engaged as ministering angels, but they do not disdain romps with poor children, who have come to regard them as "fairy godmothers"; they enjoy "musical chairs" with workhouse dames, and they entertain guests at People's Drawing Rooms. The Baptists also have their Deaconesses' Home and Mission. The Church has its guilds and its missions,

There is no mission work so searching and none more potent for lasting good than the domestic. The London field is so enormous as almost to daunt enthusiasm. But in the bright lexicon of missionary zeal there is no such word as despair, though the multitude of workers is all too few for the work to be done. They represent every important missionary agency, from the London Diocesan Mission of the Church of England to the Salvation Army. Every denomination has its devoted labourers—men and women. The Salvation Army is particularly successful in its invasion of the slums, for its agents know just how to tackle the people in whose service they labour. "The slum officer," say the records of the Army, "is called upon by night and by day to act in the capacities of doctor, nurse, adviser, relieving officer, policeman, and minister of religion." The City Mission is active in this sphere as in every other. The St. Giles's Christian Mission, though largely concerned with

WITH JACK AFLOAT (ST. ANDREW'S WATERSIDE MISSION).

representative of the universities—with their hostels and settlements—the public schools and the professions. These last include the Guild of St. Luke, which comprises physicians. The Inns of Court Mission, supported by the English Bar, has the Lord Chancellor for president of its council, and works in the neighbourhood of Drury Lane.

the transformation of criminals into worthy members of society, has been house to house visiting for many years. The light skirmishers known as tract distributers and colporteurs are also assiduous. The St. Giles's Christian Mission just spoken of is described as "a hospital for moral diseases." Its aim is to bridge the gulf between the prison cell and the workshop. Right nobly it has worked, and well it has deserved the official tributes its long, patient, and successful service have evoked. It annually provides 20,000 free breakfasts for discharged prisoners, and assists an average of 6,000 of their number to obtain employment. Friendless juvenile first offenders are received into its homes, and the superintendent never loses sight of them from the moment he has made their acquaintance till they have undergone a course of regenerative and otherwise useful training. The Church Army has facilities for visiting prisoners in gaol, and it welcomes them on their discharge into its homes in order that they may work out

POLICE COURT MISSIONARY VISITING THE CELLS.

their social redemption. The Salvation Army has its Prison Gate Mission, and it has the proud distinction of having been served as missionaries by seven ex-criminals who themselves were in durance vile for an aggregate of 210 years. An unsectarian Prison Mission to Women is one of the philanthropic agencies founded by Mrs. Meredith. It is now under royal patronage. The design of the lady benefactress was to provide work for every female discharged prisoner, and to give her sufficient payment to support herself. Every morning in the London police courts, before magistrates take their seats on the Bench, the missionaries of the Police Court Mission are busy seeking the prisoners in cell or waiting room, listening to their stories and sympathising with their misfortunes or their self-induced degradation. The Mission, whose splendid success in the

salvage of human wrecks has excited widespread interest, is a branch of the Church of England Temperance Society. It has now a boys' country home for first offenders. Nearly all religious missions and philanthropic agencies have regard for youthful waifs—notably the Ragged School Union, Dr. Barnardo's Schools, and the Field Lane Refuges. And for the moral and physical discipline of respectable lads are there not the various Boys' Brigades? The saddest, but, perhaps, the noblest, work in which good and sensitive women can engage is rescue work amongst their own sex. Yet from the Dominican Sisters of the Roman Catholic Church to the "Quakeresses" of the Society of Friends, the womanhood of various religious bodies is engaged in it. There is also a "Midnight Mission," independently and exclusively devoted to the compassionate reclamation of the Magdalen.

One of the most remarkable phases of London's mission work is the attention devoted to specific classes. It ranges from inebriates to policemen ; from railway men to barmaids ; from telegraph messengers to commercial travellers. The City Mission is particularly assiduous in respect of specialised work. There is even a mission to theatrical *employés*. The Theatrical Ladies' Guild is not a mission, but, from the nature of its work, it might almost be called a "Clothes and Comfort Guild." Tommy Atkins and the Handy Man of the Navy are not forgotten. Both have their Scripture Readers' Associations and their Guild of the Holy Standard. The Army Scripture Readers who work in London's barracks are men who have served in the Army themselves ; consequently they know all the soldiers' trials and temptations.

The Soldiers' Christian Association and the Wesleyan Army and Navy Committee are likewise doing good work. Mercantile Jack is not neglected. Various organisations are eager for his welfare. The St. Andrew's Waterside Mission looks after him afloat, as well as ashore in many lands, but is particularly mindful of him in the port of London from Gravesend to beyond London Bridge. It has its steam launch so that clergy and distributers may board incoming ships, and it has its boats on the river. The once notorious "Old Mahogany Bar" near the London Docks is now a branch of the Wesleyan East London Mission. The Seamen's Christian Friend Society not only attends to the spiritual and social condition of sailors, but gives temporary assistance. Seventy-two mission vessels, and boats "propelled by steam, sails, or oars," are in use by the Twelve Roadstead Missions. The Thames Mission, like the St. Andrew's, is a Church organisation. So is the Order of St. Paul—a community for men, "priests, and laymen dedicated to the service of God and our merchant seamen in holy

religion." It has a branch at Greenwich. The British and Foreign Sailors' Society, with its institute at Shadwell, aims at "the religious, intellectual, and social elevation" of seamen. The Missions to Seamen—under royal patronage—not only works amongst sailors and fishermen in British waters, but is represented in every part of the world. The club for Roman Catholic seamen near the London and St. Katherine's Dock, founded by the Catholic Truth Society, is the first of the kind in Great Britain.

Said we not truly that the range and the diversity of London's missionary activities are prodigious?—that the devotion and resourcefulness of those engaged in the work are impressive? Tongue cannot adequately tell, or pen indite, the heart-moving story of London's missionary zeal. The mere contemplation of it inspires the observer with profound admiration, not unmingled with self-reproach. It makes those things which worldlings strive for seem but the fleeting baubles of vain desire, and it invests the humblest worker in the vineyard with a nobility that kings might envy.

AN ARMY SCRIPTURE READER AT WORK.

THE COMMERCIAL SALE ROOMS
(MINCING LANE).

SCENES FROM EXCHANGE AND OFFICE LONDON.

By CHARLES C. TURNER.

BOUND for London, speeding under steam and sail from the far Antipodes and the sweltering tropics, from north and east and west, in infinite variety, comes the produce of every land and sea. But, swallowed up in the great city's prosaic greyness, the wonder and romance of this vast commerce are seldom appreciated.

Yet they are worth a thought. Consider the varied labour and various labourers in every clime : black, brown, yellow, red, and white men and women, toiling under the sun every minute of his twenty-four hours' course ; undergoing peril and privation that we may eat and drink and clothe ourselves comfortably, revel in luxuries, and delight in things that are beautiful. Let us see for ourselves the process by which London's great commercial maw swallows and digests the world's tribute.

We are in the London and India Docks warehouse in Crutched Friars. On all sides of the big courtyard are offices, storehouses, and lifts. Also there are direction boards pointing to various salerooms. One leads to the "Shell Room,"

another to the "Fur Sale." The one we will be guided by points to the "Crude Drug Department." If we are members of the trade, we are at once admitted to a room containing samples of drugs which will be sold by auction on the following day. This sample-room contains much that is mysterious and instructive. There is the dried juice of aloes in gourds, and even in monkeys' skins ; and there is sarsaparilla from Jamaica. We see cinchona, camphor, and strophanthus, a deadly poison from Africa. There are drugs in horns, and in barrels ; bottles of musk, sold by the ounce ; a parcel of musk skins ; bales of ipecacuanha; gums, myrrh, eucalyptus, sandal-wood, and turmeric.

At other warehouses of the Company are periodical sales of ivory. There are even sales of birds' skins. The drug sale takes place in the Commercial Sale Rooms—the great Exchange for foreign and colonial produce. On any day the Commercial Sale Rooms present a busy scene. Hundreds of brokers and merchants in the fine marble hall, standing in groups before the handsome fire-place, overflowing into the vestibule and street, are talking, bargaining, and recording transactions in pocketbooks.

The precincts are full of the offices of dealers in the goods to which the Exchange is devoted; and also, like all Exchanges, of the offices of auxiliary trades, such as packers, barrel-makers, and shippers. Home and foreign news agencies also have offices in the neighbourhood, and cabled prices and other information are eagerly watched by the dealers. The Commercial Sale Rooms form an Exchange of more than average interest, for here meet the dealers in tea, sugar, coffee, cocoa, wines, spirits, raisins, dates, rice, spices, and similar goods.

In Mincing Lane are frequent feather sales. Sometimes in one month upwards of 60,000 lbs. of ostrich feathers alone will be sold; and since it takes about 150 feathers to weigh a pound, and the price is somewhere near £2 10s. per ounce, it is evident that the trade is enormous, both for quantity and value. The osprey and the egret are still more expensive, the latter selling at over £4 per ounce.

Mark Lane, famous as the headquarters of the corn trade, runs parallel to, and within a few yards of, Mincing Lane. The Corn Exchange, which wields such a fateful control over the " staff of life," and where the ruddy grain seems to lose its character as the chief constituent in our daily bread, and takes to itself such wholly irrelevant titles as " Spot," " Shipment," and " Future Delivery," is referred to and illustrated elsewhere in " Living London."

Coal is bought and sold, in " parcels," in Lower Thames Street, in the handsome Coal Exchange. On Mondays the Exchange assumes its busiest aspect, when the crowded hall and the eager, keen bargaining present a striking scene viewed from

any of the three galleries that circle the building. Here the dread plot for raising the price of fuel at the approach of cold weather is hatched.

The Wool Exchange is in Coleman Street. The periodical sales, which run for several days at a stretch, take place in a semi-circular, theatre-like building with seats rising in many tiers from the centre. The wool merchant, by the way, is specially dressed in view of the wool-flakes with which he gets covered. One sees the same busy scene here as at the Coal or Corn Exchange, though there is, of course, something characteristic about the brokers and merchants of each trade.

If this is fancy in the cases mentioned, it is hardly fancy when we come to diamonds. In Hatton Garden we see the dealer in precious stones. Behind one of the most prosaic exteriors in this famous street, in studied seclusion, is the Diamond Merchants' Club. A glance inside reveals Dutchmen and Jews in large numbers, so much so that the physiognomy of these races is said to characterise the diamond merchant. The dealers in gems are apparently quite careless with their goods. They trust each other implicitly, passing the stones to and fro with familiarity

A FRUIT SALE ROOM (MONUMENT BUILDINGS): TESTING SAMPLES OF FRUIT.

A SHELL WAREHOUSE (QUEENHITHE).

and smaller quantities of mangoes, persimmons, and other fruits halt at this Exchange on their way from ship to consumer.

Two important Exchanges lie south of the river. Hops, foreign and English, are sold at the Hop Exchange in Southwark; and butter, bacon, and other provisions at the Home and Foreign Produce Exchange in Hibernia Chambers, close to London Bridge.

This brief list of the principal Exchanges may convey some impression of the enormous extent and variety of one department of London's commercial activities. It is safe to assume that the average citizen who is not connected with Exchange life has no conception of its importance, its great interest, or of the huge army of somewhat modest and exclusive men devoted to it. For instance, who, after schooldays, ever casts a thought to the Hudson's Bay Company? Yet London is still the centre of the world's fur trade. In Lime Street is the warehouse of the famous Company, whose explorers, huntsmen, and trappers occupy such a great and noble part in the literature of the boys of Britain. As a matter of fact, nothing in fiction exceeds in daring and romance the daily doings of the servants of the Company. The wild red man even in the twentieth century still furnishes a quota of precious furs, not omitting to add an additional spice of danger to the white man's life; and the Company's service is still organised on military lines. London for two centuries and a half has had its annual fur sale in the middle of March. Buyers from the farthest regions

and trustfulness born of long practice. No guard seems to be kept on their treasures. This carelessness, of course, is only apparent, as the outsider would soon find were he to assume membership of a trade in which every man knows his neighbours.

The Dutch element, mingled with the Spanish and the American, is conspicuous in the tobacco trade. Tobacco is sold at the London and India Docks warehouse, and also at the salerooms in Fenchurch Street.

Perhaps one of the most interesting Exchanges is that for shells at Bull Wharf, Queenhithe, where no one would expect to find such picturesque commerce. The auctions here are attended by buyers from America, Germany, France, Spain, indeed from almost every country. They buy shells for manufacturing cameos, buttons, and all sorts of everyday articles. The finest come from Australian waters, and the price ranges from 10s. to £8, and more, per cwt.

At the big Fruit Sale Room in Monument Buildings one gets a vivid impression of a great city's appetite. Enormous quantities of all kinds of foreign fruit are sold here every Monday, Wednesday, and Friday. Oranges and bananas in their millions,

of the world, even from China and Japan, are represented. Furs of bears, foxes, seals, martens, sables, beavers, leopards, lions, and many others, form the trade. Over 50,000 caribou skins alone pass each year through the Company's books. The value of furs is astonishing, a single skin of silver fox having fetched as much as £500. The fur auction is decidedly the most interesting that London has. By comparison the great Metal Exchange in Whittington Avenue seems tame.

All this merchandise involves shipping, and we must pay a visit to the Shipping Exchange in Billiter Street, where merchants with goods to carry meet ship-owners with freightage to quote. The prices named in the daily newspapers under "London Freights" are chiefly quotations from this Exchange. Sales of ships, barges, and yachts are held here from time to time. In connection with the Shipping Exchange is the Baltic, which is the market for Russian and Scandinavian produce, such as grain and oil. Many members of the Corn Exchange also subscribe to the Baltic, and in connection with the latter it is necessary to mention the dealings in seeds and oils which take place daily at the Royal Exchange, when its doors are for a brief interval closed. It should also be mentioned that, in addition, there is held here twice a week the Foreign Bill Change. But this stately building is also a great rendezvous for City men.

The Royal Exchange, too, is the centre of a collection of offices of various marine insurance companies and big merchants. The chief is Lloyd's. The Merchants' Room at Lloyd's is provided with a library, where the famous "Index" is seen. This is a huge affair, kept strictly up to date. With its aid the condition and whereabouts of every British ship can be ascertained. Then there is

133

the "Captains' Register," which contains the history of every commander in the mercantile marine. The Captains' Room is the place where captains meet owners, and where ships are occasionally sold. At its entrance is the inquiry office, where relatives and friends of those at sea may get the fullest information of the vessel on which their thoughts may be anxiously bent. Sometimes when a disaster has occurred truly pathetic scenes are to be witnessed here.

The Underwriters' Room is always full of excitement and bustle. There is a continual rushing to and fro of clerks and members with their notebooks, and the frequent recitation of names pronounced in a fine, sonorous tone falls on the ear. At the barrier, which only members may pass without challenge, sits a beadle in a most gorgeous uniform, the combination of scarlet cloth, black velvet, and gold lace being very impressive. In full view, his pulpit

A BUSY HOUR AT LLOYD'S (UNDERWRITERS' ROOM).

surmounted by a sounding-board, stands the "crier," who proclaims the names of members for whom inquiries have come. These calls proceed incessantly throughout the day. The same functionary has to announce the fate of ships as to which there may be speculation. Lloyd's is an intelligence system which has no equal. Its agents are spread all over the world, many on lonely out-lying rocks whence they can announce by cable the passing of ships. Its status will be appreciated when we consider that each member has to deposit £5,000 as security. The secretary is trustee for three and a half millions of money so paid in. You can insure almost any risk at Lloyd's, any unusual contingency leading to a risk not covered by the ordinary forms of insurance. For instance, on the approach of Budget day, merchants protect themselves against possible increases of duty on certain goods.

The danger from fire run by great treasures hoarded up has resulted in the growth of an elaborate system of fire insurance. There are some forty fire insurance companies in London. They stand to lose big sums of money in certain contingencies, and they find it good policy, besides subscribing to the London Fire Brigade, to support the Salvage Corps, whose traps, so often seen in London streets hastening to answer "a call," are fitted with waterproof cloths, axes, buckets, hand-pumps, shovels, crowbars, and even lime-light apparatus. When the fire-extinguishing brigade have won their victory, the men of the Salvage Corps remain on duty to secure and guard all that the fire has not destroyed. Many exploits and adventures are on record in the books stored in the basement of the headquarters in Watling Street.

The burglar is the next great enemy of property, and against burglary risks there are, besides the big safe deposits, some five or six insurance companies. The uncertain element in the life of boilers necessitates a special insurance, and two or three companies in London undertake this risk. In addition, there are a great number of accident insurance companies, some of which specialise on particular risks, such as railway accidents, mishaps to horses and carriages, motor cars, cycles, and so on. Then, since the liability of employers for accidents to their servants was recognised by the State, there has sprung up an elaborate system of employers' liability insurance. There are companies which arrange for weekly payments to those prevented by sickness or accident from following their occupation. Specific diseases, such as small-pox, may also be insured against. One company insures against blindness, and there are plate glass insurance companies. Live stock and latch keys can be insured ; and risk of damage to crops from hail can be provided for. Life assurance is so general that it is only necessary to remark that it forms one of the most important sections in London life. Many of the offices are more like palaces, supporting staffs of several hundreds, and paying claims amounting to millions of pounds per annum.

To realise the extent of insurance business it is necessary to go over one of the great offices and see the serried ranks of clerks at their desks ; or, in a special room, a score of experts doing nothing else all day but making out new policies ; or to another department, where claims are considered and met, for these come in and are paid by the hundred per day. More impressive still is the paying-in of premiums to the company's banking account, especially after quarter-days, when big collections come in from agents scattered throughout the length and breadth of the land. Finally we must mention what is known as re-insurance. It may be said that an insurance company will engage, on suitable terms, to take any risk. But supposing it finds on its hands an unusual concentration of liabilities, then, to use a sporting phrase, it can "hedge" by re-insuring in other companies.

People with whom we all do business are the parcel carriers, second only in importance to the General Post Office. Messrs. Pickford's, Sutton's, Carter, Paterson & Co.'s, and the London Parcel Delivery Company's vans are seen in every street and for miles out in the country. They employ armies of drivers, warehousemen, and boys. Their warehouses cover acres of precious London

IN THE COAL EXCHANGE.

land. And this is only for the carrying of goods within the Metropolitan area. Representing London's great over-sea trade are the offices of the shipping companies. The great passenger lines possess magnificent offices. A visit to one of them enables you to realise what the running of a big line of

a man of millions. He is a knight and an alderman, but he comes down to his office every day, "takes the wheel," and steers the great ship of his business through the boisterous ocean of modern competition. Naturally it is only the larger issues which are referred to him. His private secretary,

AN INSURANCE OFFICE
(OCEAN ACCIDENT AND
GUARANTEE CORPORATION).

A SHIPPING OFFICE (PENINSULAR AND ORIENTAL STEAM
NAVIGATION CO.).

immediately on the great man's arrival, lays before him a list of the day's engagements, and acquaints him with questions and problems that await his solution. One by one these are dealt with. Big schemes are approved or disapproved. Callers are continually announced. Cheques have to be signed, lawyers consulted, the

steamships means—the scores of clerks, the crowds of customers and inquirers, some paying for passages, others inspecting cabin plans or the lists of sailings and arrivals, the splendid maps, or the beautiful and costly miniature ships.

But a word about the master-minds that govern the great businesses scanned in this article, the merchant princes of London. Come into the office of one, a typical one,

bigger financial problems dealt with, and, in the middle of it all, there is a Court of Aldermen to attend, or a company meeting to preside over. Towards five o'clock the day's engagements are nearly covered, and the merchant prince goes out through a hushed throng of clerks, past emulous office-boys and saluting commissionaire, to his neat brougham, or automobile, and so to his mansion in the west.

ARRIVAL OF A MILK TRAIN (PADDINGTON).

LONDON'S FOOD SUPPLY.

By A. ST. JOHN ADCOCK.

MILK.

ONE half of London lives by feeding the other half. That, at all events, is the conclusion we arrive at in the course of our survey of this subject of London's Food Supply. It is an inexhaustible subject, beginning anywhere and having no end; so, as it matters very little where we open it, let us go to Paddington by way of a start and see how the milk arrives at one of the great railway termini.

Here, as elsewhere, milk trains are arriving at intervals of the day and night, but *the* milk train at Paddington comes panting fussily in a little before eleven every morning. A stationary procession of carts, stretching out beyond the gateway of the milk platform, up half the length of London Street, is waiting for it. A long line of carts driven in and backed all along the rear of the platform is waiting for it, too; and on the platform itself a numerous congregation of blue-aproned milkmen is also waiting. No sooner is it here than its doors are opened, and brisk porters who have swarmed into the train are handing heavy cans out with the quickness and dexterity of long practice; while the blue-aproned milkmen, crowding forward, seize the cans as fast as they are set down and trundle them, rumbling dully, this way and that, and muster them in groups according to their ownership. Carts are filling up and rattling out momentarily, and as each drives off another is backed into the vacant place.

A similar scene was enacted here, on a smaller scale, earlier this morning, and will be enacted again and again later in the day; for the milk trade is never at rest.

There is more peace for the baker—that is if he bakes nothing but bread. So far as the actual baking is concerned, he gets through with it while his customers sleep; but you can no longer perambulate London on rainy nights and know every time you are passing a baker's by the suffocating blasts breathed up at you from tropical basements and the warm, dry patches in the wet pavement, for modern sanitation requires the baker to build his bakehouse beside or behind his shop instead of underneath it. But the mammoth bakeries of certain of the great catering firms are more suited to our present purpose, so we will take a look over one of these in the west of London, where work is going on all day in some of the departments, and in others all night.

MAKING BREAD
(MESSRS. LYONS).

Numbers of white-garmented bakers are busying themselves everywhere—rolling paste for pies, constructing sausage rolls, buns, cream tarts, jam tarts, and such things as it makes the mouth water even to name. Here is a room where there is nothing making but French pastry, and the bakers are natty artists from Paris; here is another devoted to Vienna loaves, twists, and rolls, that are fashioned with astonishing rapidity by light-hearted, light-handed Viennese, who whistle and sing over their labours as cheerily as birds in an aviary. There is less poetry about ordinary bread-making, but the largest hall in the place is reserved for it. When the men in other departments have put away the various instruments of their art, and are beginning to go home, the electric lights are turned on in that hall and a mighty staff is getting to work there— superintending the automatic mixing of dough in big tubs; kneading it, bare-armed, in big troughs; moulding it into loaves, and deftly passing the latter into the cavernous ovens whose row of iron doors darken all one side of the white walls. On the top floor is the storeroom, piled high with sacks of flour, and having at its inner end a ponderous apparatus in which flours are blended automatically, and a shoot for

POTATO MARKET (YORK ROAD).

passing them to the floors below. The ground floor furnishes covered accommodation for delivery vans that will go on their rounds in the morning with what is baking to-night ; and the establishment is so self-contained that it includes even its own printing works.

We have been " Round London's Big Markets " elsewhere in this work, and the difference between most of those we saw on that occasion and those we did not see is practically only a difference of size. Very early in the mornings all manner

In Monument Buildings, near Eastcheap, is a foreign fruit market—the only one of its kind in London. On either side of the lane are the offices of merchants and importers, and if you go into their showrooms, upstairs or down, towards eleven o'clock you find them alive with prospective buyers sampling consignments of apples, pears, onions, tomatoes, lemons, pineapples, grapes, and bananas, that are bursting invitingly out of opened cases, hampers, barrels, and boxes ranged up and down the rooms. Sale announcements pinned to the doorposts tell you that these consignments are from Spain, Portugal, Italy, Russia, the Americas, and the Indies ; also you learn from some

UNLOADING EGGS (MILLWALL DOCKS).

of burdened vehicles flock into the Borough Market, as they flock in greater numbers to Covent Garden ; there are country carts, driven by sun-burnt, sleepy countrymen, toiling in with masses of cabbages, carrots, and turnips from the market gardens of Kent and Surrey ; you may see railway and carriers' vans bringing sacks and hampers and cases of fruit and vegetables from docks and railway stations ; and an hour or two later the carts of retailers will come jogging in, and the market will be a roar of buying and selling.

At Spitalfields or Stratford or Columbia Market you may see pretty much the same thing over again ; but Portman Market is a happy hunting-ground for retail stallholders, and, like Farringdon and Leadenhall Markets, deals in fish, meat, poultry, and game as well as in vegetables and fruit.

of them that tinned fruits have arrived in abundance from the British colonies and foreign parts. The sale commencing at eleven, you procure a long printed catalogue and proceed to the auction-room, which is approached by an unpretentious doorway half way down the lane.

This auction-room is a lofty, square, plain hall that in its general aspect is a compromise between a court of justice and an amphitheatre. Its sweeping semicircle of tiered seats is densely crowded with all sorts and conditions of men, and each man holds what might be either a legal " cause list " or a circus programme, but is really his sale catalogue ; and a helmeted policeman poses under the clock to keep order. The illusion is so strong that if a wigged and gowned judge entered down below and mounted the bench behind the long, crescent-shaped barrier fronting the amphitheatre it would not seem surprising; on the other hand, if a young lady in undeniably summer costume rode in on a bare-backed steed, followed by a clown holding hoops for her to jump through, that would not seem surprising either. But neither of these things happens. Instead, an unromantic frock-coated auctioneer seats himself at the table behind the barrier, with, to right and left of him, two or three clerks, who write diligently in ample ledgers while he is offering the lots he has for sale and calling upon his audience to bid for them.

At Shadwell there is a riverside fish market which is a sort of younger brother to Billingsgate; and in York Road, King's Cross, there is a long row of warehouses, with a railway-siding behind it and a covered way before it, which is so exclusive in the matter of vegetables that it is a market for potatoes only — a sort of potato reservoir, in fact, from which the other vegetable markets are largely fed.

Also in the York Road is a railway depôt for cattle. Far up the straggling yard you come to a platform bristling with cattle-pens, and here, as at similar platforms on every line that enters London, cattle are landed almost daily. You shall see them detraining here from the North in misty winter mornings when snow and slush are underfoot; in golden, hazy mornings of summer, and in summer mornings that are not golden, but grey and chilly with dismal rains that make the littered yard squalid and desolate. Whatever the weather, two or three mornings a week, at least, drovers and their dogs shepherd their bleating or lowing droves hence across the road to the Caledonian Market *en route* for Smithfield.

Foreign and colonial cattle are landed at Deptford, and dead and frozen meat at Victoria Docks, where you may see it swinging up out of icy holds and being lowered by means of cranes into barges anchored alongside the ship that has brought it, or dispatched down lengthy shoots to railway refrigerator vans that are waiting for it ashore. Most of this frozen meat is New Zealand or Australian mutton, but it includes an increasing quantity of American beef. From

America, too, as well as from Holland, Denmark, and Canada, comes no little of the Londoners' cheese and bacon and ham; and from America, again, as well as from India, Russia, Turkey, Egypt, Argentina, and our own colonies, wheat, flour, meal, and the like are shipped up the Thames to us.

Day after day cargoes such as these are unloaded at the docks, and borne off by barge or rail to wharves and granaries and warehouses that border the river as it flows through London. To see a ship discharging large live turtles on the quay has, perhaps, a smack of novelty about it; but to see cargoes of fruit and vegetables, or of tinned meats or fish, landed is as matter-of-fact and unsensational as seeing macaroni coming ashore from Italy, rice from China, Japan, India; butter from Denmark, Canada, Russia; eggs—but it would be easier to say where our eggs from over-seas do not come from than where they do. They come principally from Russia, Denmark, France, Holland, and Canada, and the bulk of them reach London by rail from Harwich; but regularly on Monday mornings, before the suburbs are out of bed, you may see a Danish or Russian vessel invade Millwall Docks, to be boarded by a gang of dockers, who extract cases and tubs of eggs and butter from the depths of it, and lower them from pulleys or roll them down shoots to the landing-stage.

A good deal of this foreign foodstuff is transferred to the warehouses of foreign provision importers, who set up their brass plates in every division of London, and are nowhere, perhaps, more plentiful than in Tooley Street. Cross London Bridge and stroll down Tooley Street almost any hour of the day, and there are carts and railway vans bringing in or taking away hams, bacon, eggs, butter, and cheeses of foreign origin; glance aside into Hay's Lane, at the two towering lines of warehouses whose restless cranes are whirling goods up from or down to the tangle of vehicles below that are unloading or loading; go round behind the warehouses here that back on the river, and there are barges unloading at their wharves or emptied and stranded on the mud till the tide rises.

Such of the frozen meat as is not required

DETRAINING CATTLE (L.N.W.R. DEPÔT, YORK ROAD).

for immediate distribution is deposited in one or other of the vast cold storages that are inseparably associated with the food supply of modern London. Going to one of these storages on a hot, sunshiny afternoon, the dimness and coolness that envelop us the moment we enter are grateful and comforting. Passing a sliding door, that is promptly shut behind us to exclude the warmer airs without, we are in a long vaulted passage that strikes us as distinctly chilly, and massive doors open from it into various cold chambers.

There are forty-seven of these chambers, opening on a series of those chilly passages. Go into one, and your surroundings become Arctic immediately. The moisture in the air has condensed round all the refrigerator pipes across the ceiling into a crisp coating of snow that glistens bleakly in the white glare of the electric light; walls and ceiling are as white as if the place were a cave hewn in a snow-bank, and the frozen, white-shirted sheep lying in rows or standing stiff on their fore legs might have been literally frozen to death here, if the

MILK.

absence of their heads did not suggest a different fate.

It is difficult to remain shivering down here and believe that outside the sun is blazing and men perspire, and that in Cannon Street railway station, immediately overhead, people in straw hats and airy suitings are booking themselves to cool places for summer holidays. In the forty-six other cold chambers there is more and more frozen mutton from Australasia, frozen beef, butter, fish, fowls, hares, rabbits, fruit; and in each chamber the temperature is delicately regulated to suit the exact requirements of its contents. When we have thawed ourselves near the furnaces in the engine-room and ascertained how much heat goes to the making of all the cold we have been through, and when we have had a glimpse of the river at the back, up which refrigerator barges bring provisions to be stored here until the markets are ready for them, it is time to inquire the way out.

LOADING WAGGONS (HAY'S LANE).

MEAT.

It is a good thing to look into the Corn Exchange down Mark Lane, and see the merchants and factors there arranging "deals" in connection with those foreign cereal supplies we saw coming in at the docks and with similar supplies cultivated at home and carried systematically into London by road, and rail, and river. It is a good thing, too, to wander through London warehouses where teas are blended; and it is another good thing to peer into quiet, decorous offices and agencies where small samples of various teas are set out in very small bowls, and expert tasters are brewing sample spoonfuls in small teapots and sipping the results critically from infinitesimal cups. It is a better thing still, though, to loiter and watch the unshipping of those teas, or of coffees, or cocoas, in chests and cases branded with glamorous names of remote places in India, China, Japan, and the Antilles—names that halo the coolie-haunted East and West India Docks with glimmerings of romance.

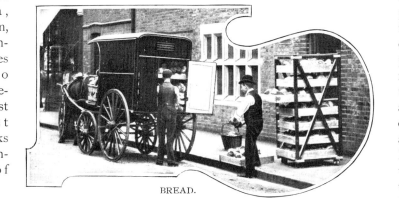

BREAD.

But we must not go back to the docks again, especially as we have visited them in another article in "Living London." For the same reason we must only glance at breweries and distilleries, and factories in general, and pass by on the other side; though, to be sure, such luxuries as jam and marmalade are not to be lightly dismissed, seeing that nowadays they count as common items in the daily bill of fare.

We sit to our breakfasts in London and eat, with no sense of the wonder of it, rashers of bacon that are rich with memories of some Canadian farm, or crack without emotion an egg that a hen laid for us in a Russian village. Lunching at pleasant restaurants, we trifle with compressed vegetables, with sauerkraut, or delicatessen despatched to us from the heart of Germany, and are as familiar with them as with homelier sausages and collared brawn compounded in our own city by men of our acquaintance. Dining at our big hotels, we give no grateful thought to the alien artists who, last night in Paris, prepared our sweetbreads, cutlets, fillets, packed them, and sent them across channel to arrive in London by rail for us this morning.

But, if it is only to gather a fuller idea of the magnitude of this task of feeding London, it is worth while giving a thought to these things, and to the myriads of men and women employed in London itself on that same business. Consider the thousands of dockers busy daily unloading food from ships, and of porters unloading it from trains; of barge-men, lightermen, carters, and carriers transporting that food; and of clerks, packers, and miscellaneous toilers, male and female, engaged in and about London warehouses, wharves, factories, stores, and distributing agencies to which it is transported. Add to these the numbers of merchants, agents, and middlemen, with their multitudes of employés, through whose hands such food supplies filter to the retailers, with their equally multitudinous shop assistants and armies of men and boys who drive carts, push barrows, and carry baskets and cans to deliver bread, meat, milk, and all manner of eatables and drinkables at the doors of customers. And this is to say nothing of costermongers of both sexes who sell provisions on stalls in the streets or hawk them on carts or barrows; nothing, either, of proprietors, chefs, waiters, waitresses, and scullery hands of every variety of eating - house; and nothing of cooks and kitchen - maids in private families——

But ere this you will be glad to abandon the bewildering calculation, and accept our preliminary axiom on trust.

THE LONDONER OUT AND AT HOME.

By GEORGE R. SIMS.

THERE are things so familiar in the life of a Londoner that he is astonished when they excite non-Londoners' attention. Taken as a whole, the dweller in the capital is a creature of habit and groove. The business man goes about his business the leisured man goes about his pleasure, in much the same way year in year out. And this monotonous regularity takes so much romance out of his existence that he sees very little in it that could possibly be of interest to anyone but himself. But the observant stranger finds in the daily life of the London householder much to note, much to criticise, and a good deal to marvel at.

Let us for the moment be intelligent strangers, and study the Londoner in his home.

In his home he is quite sure to be constantly harassed. He rarely gets up in the morning without finding something to grumble at, something to be irritated by. His grumbling may have begun before he rose, for the noises of the day frequently disturb the Londoner's sleep while he reckons that it is still night. The early milk-cart laden with rattling cans will often herald the dawn before even the crowing cock of a neighbour has discovered it, and the milk-cart's matutinal round is succeeded by the vocal efforts of the chimney-sweep and the newsboy, the interval between the two being frequently filled in by the bells of a neighbouring church ringing the faithful to early prayers. The steam whistle is another "unnecessary noise" of the early hours which gives the Londoner broken rest, and brings him to the breakfast table in none too sweet a temper if his bachelorhood is past and he has family responsibilities.

Even the Londoner who is a pattern of promptness with his tradespeople is given to taking the longest credit allowed by the law in the matter of rates and taxes, for Londoners look upon the preliminary printed demand notes with equanimity, and the tax collectors and the rate collectors know that they will be put off by the wealthiest householder until the "final" has been delivered. Then they will probably receive payment owing to the nervousness of the Londoner's wife, who, even in middle-class life, has a haunting terror of the summary proceedings of a Government kept out of its money. And the staunchest patriot, the most enlightened citizen, is given to adverse criticism of the powers that be when the rate papers and the tax papers stare him in the face. His house is his castle, but it is a castle besieged by brigands.

When the census paper is delivered to be filled up by the "head of the family," there being nothing to pay, good humour invariably prevails. Paterfamilias assumes the position of a magistrate at his study table, but there is a smiling twinkle in his eye as he calls his domestics before him and warns them of the awful consequences of giving in a fictitious age. It is, however, inside the space devoted to "relation to the head of the family" that the greatest humour is developed. Men who have never been known to make a joke at any other period of their lives are sorely tempted to be facetious in answering this portion of the domestic inquisition.

The London householder has other troubles which are less legitimate. He is constantly persecuted by people who call about their own business, and refuse to go about it until they have seen the master or the mistress. There are canvassers, collectors for charities, directory agents, gentlemen with samples of tea and wine merchants' touts to be kept at bay, and shrewd and skilful rogues who are constantly lying in wait to enter either at the front door or the back and help themselves to a little portable property. A list of the knocks and rings to which the Londoner in his castle is subjected would fill a page of this work. The postman in some districts knocks or rings every hour of the day between 8 a.m. and 9 p.m. The tradesmen ring in the morning when they call for orders, ring succeeding ring, for they rarely arrive together, and during the day they ring again when they call to deliver; the telegraph boy rings outside, and the telephone bell rings inside; and the man with the draper's cart knocks or rings loudly with the parcel for which the money is to be paid on delivery. The newspaper boy rings morning and evening, and frequently in the afternoon if you take in weekly periodicals. Visitors ring, and the members of the family ring when they come from school, from shopping, or from a walk. Only the head of the family refrains, because, as a rule, he provides himself with a latchkey, and if he is of independent habits prefers letting himself

taking out a licence. He has, if he is a man of means, to take out so many. He has to have a licence for each of his dogs, a licence to have armorial bearings on his notepaper and his carriage, a licence to have his footman's hair powdered, a licence for his two-wheeled and his four-wheeled carriages, a licence for every male servant he employs in livery, and a licence to carry firearms.

The Londoner making up the list of his establishment licences and drawing a cheque for them in the gloomy days of early January is frequently a pathetic picture.

There is only one licence that, as a rule, he applies for with a smiling face. That is a marriage licence. Most readers of "Living London" are familiar with the various processes, but I am assured by one who knows

FILLING IN THE CENSUS PAPER.

in to ringing and waiting on his doorstep for admission to his own house.

There is another matter over which the Londoner is occasionally perturbed, and that is

that the most trying form of this experience is applying at the office of the local registrar. Many men have been known to walk up and down in front of the building for half an hour before summoning up the courage to enter. There is a painful feeling that every eye is upon you, and that every passer-by, from the cabman on the crawl to the nurse-maid with a perambulator, is aware of your particular business with the official inside.

The great carriers are constant visitors to the London householder. Messrs. Carter, Paterson and Co. and the London Parcels Delivery Company furnish him with printed cards which he sticks up in his window to let the passing carmen know that they are to call to take a parcel away. Messrs. Pickford and the vans of the various railway companies deliver goods sometimes too bulky for the area steps, and so it comes about that packing-cases are brought in through the hall. The brewer's man delivers his beer, and the coal merchant delivers his coal. "Having in coal" is a daily feature of Living London. In poor districts it is delivered in small quantities. The coal-carts pass slowly, and the goodwife comes out and buys. But in the West-End and the suburbs where substantial householders dwell several waggon loads arrive at once and form a line. Then men, grimy, strangely habited, proceed to lift the round plate let into the pavement, and shoot the coal sack by sack into the cellar which lies below. A considerable amount of coal lies on the pavement around the aperture until the delivery is completed, and then one of the men takes a broom and makes an apology for a clean up.

The washing is delivered by

BOOK CANVASSING.

covered carts bearing the name of the laundry upon them. The name is frequently poetical — "Sunshine Laundry," "Rosebud Laundry," "Meadowsweet Laundry," and the like suggest sylvan drying grounds and pastoral surroundings. The suggestion is frequently unjustified by the facts. The visit of the washing man is sometimes a source of considerable anxiety to the householder who keeps a dog indoors. All dogs have a rooted and inherited objection to the man who comes with the washing.

The clock winder is not always beloved of the dog of the family, and care has to be taken that the animal shall be locked in a clockless room before the winder proceeds on his tour of synchronisation. "The man who winds the clocks," if he has a large local connection, must have a very wide knowledge of the *vie intime* of a neighbourhood. To his credit be it said, he is not given to gossip, but some day one may write his memoirs.

There is one feature of domestic life that years ago was interesting—that was the sale of waste paper. All the newspapers were kept, and taken at a price by the butcher. But of late years papers have multiplied to such an extent that they are a drug in the market. The *Times* is about the only "old

DELIVERING A SUMMONS.

paper" that the butchers of to-day will take away and pay for.

There is a matter which occasionally engages the householder's attention when his wife is of a frugal mind. That is the selling of old clothes. Some housewives give their old clothes away, send them to hospitals or charities, or it may be to poor relatives. But others make a financial transaction of the annual clearance of the wardrobe.

There are established in many parts of London enterprising business women who have a large connection with society ladies, and who purchase from their maids dresses and garments scarcely worn. These women have a large connection also with ladies of a slightly lower social standing or smaller means, who are glad to pay a fair price for fashionable attire which would cost them double or treble first hand at one of the great millinery houses or Court dressmakers.

But the big business in second-hand clothes is done by women who call themselves "wardrobe dealers," who send out cards and call by appointment, and bid for anything and everything the householder or his wife may be willing to part with.

The idea of the dealer with regard to "fair prices" will frequently be in striking contrast to that of the seller. But the bargain is eventually struck, for second-hand clothes shops abound all over the Metropolis, and they are usually stocked to the full limit of their space. If the faded finery of a second-hand clothes shop could speak, it could tell many a tale of the great human comedy, and, alas! of the great human tragedy also.

The male householder is subject to a form of persecution which is the penalty of living among law-abiding citizens. He is liable to be summoned on a jury. To escape this particular duty of citizenship the majority of householders resort to many subterfuges. Nearly all are prepared with an excuse, which

in only a few instances is accepted. To serve on a jury when the case spreads itself over several days is an experience which lingers long in the memory. The unfortunate juryman taken away day after day from the Court, locked up in an hotel, and only taken out for exercise under the watchful eye of a Court official, has had stories and even plays written around his miseries.

Occasionally a summons makes the householder a party to legal proceedings. He is summoned at a Police Court for allowing his dog to be out without a muzzle when the Muzzling Act is in force, or without a collar when it is not. He is summoned if his chimney catches fire; he can be summoned if his daughter plays the piano too loudly; he can be summoned if his wife hangs out clothes in the garden; he can be summoned if his coachman collides with somebody else's brougham; he can be summoned if his servant neglects to have the snow swept from his doorway. I hesitate to complete the catalogue; it is really difficult without devoting a lifetime to the study of the subject to know what a householder may *not* be summoned for.

His tradespeople may summon him to the

RATE COLLECTING.

A SECOND-HAND CLOTHES STORE.

County Court over a disputed account or his neglect to pay an undisputed bill. The County Court procedure is, as a rule, short and summary, and the atmosphere is rather poverty-stricken.

A day in a County Court would dishearten a Mark Tapley. The whole surroundings are depressing : there is an air of seediness about the little crowd of defendants, and the plaintiffs appear none too confident as to increasing their stock of ready money with the law's assistance. There is always plenty of hard swearing in a County Court, and the County Court judge takes a cynical view of humanity. But he is practical, and in most cases when poverty is pleaded makes an order for payment by instalments which the plaintiff considers preposterous. The defendant who fails to keep up the instalments may, if the plaintiff is a man of energy and determination, find himself in prison for contempt of court. There are men well dressed, well groomed, and living in apparent luxury, who are constantly hovering between the County Court and Holloway. Contempt of court has become a habit with them.

The Sheriff's Court, which is situated in Red Lion Square, is generally associated with breach of promise cases and the reading of love letters which cause considerable amusement. But the householder who has never brought a smile to the lips of Jove by a lover's perjuries may still have to make his appearance before the Under-Sheriff. Here arbitration cases of a certain character are decided, and here compensation claims are settled in connection with premises required by railways and public improvement schemes.

Among the occasional annoyances of the London householder are accidents to the kitchen range and the kitchen boiler, necessitating considerable disturbance in the culinary department. But nowadays, thanks to the spread of " flat " life, there are many facilities for obtaining " a sent-in meal " which were unknown to the past generation. The " kitchen on wheels " is an institution which is largely patronised. The company responsible for the innovation will deliver at your residence a dinner of many courses " all hot," as the clown used to sing in the pantomime ; or they will put upon your table direct from your front door a hot chop, or a hot fried sole, or a tureen of steaming soup. In poorer neighbourhoods this perambulating kitchen will accommodate the inhabitants with hot fried fish and hot chips or hot sausages delivered at the doors.

There are companies to-day which will do a considerable amount of household work for you by contract. The window-cleaning company sends men to your house to clean your windows systematically, and the nervous housemaid perched on a window-sill at a giddy height is no longer a scandal to the Metropolis. Another firm of contractors will keep your window-boxes supplied with flowers or greenery all the year round; and there is now a firm which will even save you the trouble of sending your maid to the pillar-box. A box is placed at your own front door, from which the postmen on their rounds will collect at stated intervals by arrangement with the postal authorities.

Gradually the minor household burdens are being lifted from the shoulders of paterfamilias. He can now even contemplate the family holiday with equanimity, provided his balance at the bank is satisfactory. The old horror of the family impedimenta—the huge trunks, the portmanteaux, the bandboxes, the bicycles, the spades and buckets, banjoes, mandolins, and sewing machines—has departed. The railway companies collect the day beforehand, and deliver at the country house or the seaside apartments before the family arrive. The householder's wife can obtain all the newest books, his daughter all the newest music, by paying a small subscription; and there is a company which for a shilling a year will supply Fido, the poodle, with a metal number to wear on his collar, and will pay the reward for him if he is lost.

We have seen the discomforts and annoyances the Londoner has to endure in his home; we have glanced at the efforts which a progressive age is constantly making to relieve him of them. May the relief continue until there is nothing left for him to grumble at but the rates and taxes. These will always be sufficient to keep him from a too sleek contentment.

A KITCHEN ON WHEELS.

INDIAN AND COLONIAL LONDON,

By HENRY THOMPSON.

AUSTRALIAN COMMON-
WEALTH FLAG.

INTO this ever loudly throbbing Heart of the World from the uttermost frontiers of the Empire the representatives of the "Britains beyond the seas" are ceaselessly flowing. The stay of some is but short — merely a glimpse round the "Big Smoke," then home again to bush, plain, veldt, or jungle. Many of these visitors, however, fall under London's unexplainable fascination, and remain for more lengthy periods, finding in a plethora of Colonial clubs, societies, and other institutions that they are indeed handsomely catered for socially, officially, and commercially.

The great India Office, in Whitehall, swaying the fortunes of hundreds of millions of British subjects, and solely concerning itself with grave questions of State, occasionally unbends, and, to honour visiting Indian princes and other notabilities from the mysterious East, holds one of those formal receptions which for brilliance and glittering splendour are unequalled in Europe. On these occasions the King and Queen, or other members of the Royal family, may be the presiding dignitaries, and the lofty, magnificent central hall is superbly lighted and decorated, the ceiling representing a clear blue tropical sky irradiated with myriads of stars. The gorgeous dressing of the princes, maharajahs, rajahs, and others, their turbans ranging from rose through all shades to the palest blue, their robes from gayest orange to sedatest grey, and all richly decked with a veritable rainbow of precious, and in some cases priceless, gems, is to one unused to Oriental splendour a dazzling

spectacle. When the ancient East comes to meet the modernised West it has the exalted traditions of centuries to live up to, and even on ordinary occasions the passing of gaily attired Indian personages in our thoroughfares lights up for a moment the prevailing dull greyness.

Some of these potentates, having crossed the seas, settle here, take English wives, and enter into public and political life in the hope of benefiting their fellow countrymen. The arrival in London of a high native dignitary provides a striking sight for the usual loungers at Victoria or Charing Cross Station. He will be accompanied, perhaps, by over 100 servants, and 50 or 60 tons of luggage. There are portions of the latter that no railway porter is permitted to touch, for they may contain gems and valuables worth scores of thousands of pounds, or, still more important in Hindu eyes, even a sacred god. This last will be in a casket by itself, with handles for the priests who act as bearers. A miscellaneous collection of pots and pans of beaten brass, cooking tripods, etc., complete a truly imposing display.

Of the lesser Hindus, Parsees, and Mohammedans who come to London, the first and third are mostly students, and the second favour commercial enterprise in various shapes. Their extraordinary analytical faculty and hair-splitting subtlety make the majority of the students adopt the law as a profession, a few become doctors, and fewer still visit South Kensington Museum to study technical trades, weaving, cloth making, etc. For the comfort, education, and assistance of these strangers there are several agencies. The National Indian Association strives to extend a knowledge of India and arouse an interest in its people. Meanwhile it safeguards and guides the student, takes charge of wards and their allowances, gives them advice and information, introduces them

A RECEPTION OF INDIAN PRINCES AT THE INDIA OFFICE.

to suitable residences, entertains them with lectures, soirées, and excursions, and publishes a monthly magazine. The Northbrook Club likewise makes pleasure instructive and knowledge attractive; while the Royal Asiatic Society exists for the promotion of science, art, and literature in relation to Asia, and offers a gold medal for competition, among the seven great public schools, in Oriental learning. The Parsees are specially provided for by the Zoroastrian Fund, which has acquired a reserved burial ground at Woking and built a chapel thereon. It also helps Zoroastrians financially, and makes translations of instructive works for Parsees.

Speaking the same tongue, bearing a white skin, and dressed in English garb, the Australian, Canadian, South African, New Zealander, and others born of British parents abroad become to the ordinary passer-by but units among London's teeming millions. Nevertheless, they have their own particular rendezvous and celebrations. In Victoria Street or in the City their High Commissioners or Agents-General are the official representatives of Commonwealth, Dominion, or Colony. The duties of these officials are multifarious. They deal with contracts or loans

to be placed on the English market, control depôts or stands exhibiting and advertising the products of their States, give trustworthy information — not advice — to mining and other intending investors, collect diverse details and statistics required by their home Governments, and register the names of visiting Colonists for invitations to various social and other gatherings. The Crown Agents, having offices in Downing Street and the City, represent Colonial Governments who are without Agents - General. They are appointed by the Secretary of State for the Colonies, who also, through the Colonial Office, deals with all matters of weighty importance, outside India, concerning the Empire abroad. Most of the big Colonies have their own London newspapers, such as the *Canadian Gazette*, the *British Australasian*, the *British Columbian*, etc., and their leading home newspapers have central

IN THE LONDON OFFICE OF A COLONIAL NEWSPAPER : THE READING ROOM.

APPLICANTS AT THE WOMEN'S EMIGRATION ASSOCIATION OFFICES (IMPERIAL INSTITUTE).

offices here, where on the arrival of the mail eager Colonists may be seen scanning the latest news of their kith and kin at home, as shown, for example, in the photographic illustration of the

THE WRITING ROOM OF THE
COLONIAL INSTITUTE.

reading room of the Melbourne *Argus* office on the opposite page.

The great and most important meeting place of the Colonial visitor to, and resident in, London is the Royal Colonial Institute in Northumberland Avenue. It came into existence in 1868, and now numbers many thousands of members. An invaluable and most extensive library is provided, with reading, writing, and smoking rooms, and a museum for the collection and exhibition of Colonial and Indian productions. The newspaper room is a systematised wilderness of Colonial journalism, and is unequalled anywhere. The Institute at its meetings has papers read and discussed on all subjects likely to interest or instruct its members, for example: "British Guiana and its Boundary," "Swaziland," "A Canadian Polar Expedition," or "The Expansion of Trade with China." Altogether the R.C.I. is a well furnished, well appointed, and invaluable institution. For the manufacturer, importer, or exporter there are Colonial chambers of commerce, commercial bureaux, and wine and agricultural depôts. The social side is looked after by the Colonial Club, the Australasian Club (principally for City men), the African Society (founded in memory of

Mary Kingsley, and serving also as an information bureau for Africa generally), and the West Indian Club. The last named, though of restricted membership, is not lacking in energy, and, in addition to holding a fortnightly dinner, is instrumental in bringing to England cricket and shooting teams to meet us on our own ground. The Dominion Day dinner, the Burma dinner, the gatherings of the East India Railway and the Indian Political Service, and other such festivals all serve to gather together periodically Colonists who have laboured, lived, or been born far across the seas. To bring the Colonies closer in touch and sympathy with the Motherland there are various leagues and federations, all doing good solid work in an unostentatious manner for the Empire.

To the practical business Colonial desirous of cultivating a product or initiating an industry in one of the Colonies the imposing Imperial Institute at South Kensington and its minor, but more convenient, branch in the City afford a wealth of valuable information. At these he may learn about the grasses suitable for weaving or working into useful articles, the appropriate soil and climate for cereal and other nurture, the uses and adaptability of various timbers, and a host of other things likely to facilitate the opening up and development of a virgin colony; the whole being based upon the knowledge of experts. It is in the magnificent building of the Institute that the British Women's Emigration Association is installed, and here may be seen daily applicants for free or assisted voyages to the newer lands where Christmas-time is mid-

London receiving home a day or two before starting. After medical inspection, they are escorted on board, and the matron divides them into small parties, each supervised by one girl, who helps the matron to

DRILL-HALL OF THE KING'S
COLONIALS : A ROYAL VISIT.

Photo : Elliot & Fry, Baker Street, W.

summer. Men preponderate in the majority of the Colonies, so the British Women's Emigration Association is a busy concern. The main office, with the honorary secretary surrounded by a dozen lady clerks, is quite a spectacle when intending emigrants are inquiring as to the best country to go to and how they shall get there. Every detail of information is supplied to them. Those from the provinces are recommended to comfortable, but moderate, lodgings, accompanied by a matron to the sailing port, and also in the vessel to their destination. The West Australian Government gives from time to time free passages to fifty girls selected by the B.W.E.A. They are gathered into the

see that the regulations are carried out. Everything is done to make the voyage enjoyable, and, to a restricted extent, an improvement to the girls educationally. On arrival at Fremantle the emigrants are installed in a Government depôt until situations are found for them. With the reservation that no girl shall be allowed to take a position as a barmaid, these are readily secured, and the girls begin life anew under the Southern Cross. In Cape Colony, where no Kaffir is allowed to sleep in the houses of whites, there is a little earlier rising for the female domestics, and in the evening all work after six o'clock falls to their hands, as the blacks must leave at that hour. In addition to a dozen other emigration societies and funds — many of a religious nature — scattered throughout London, there is the main centre, controlled by the Home Government, under the title of the "Emigrants' Information Office" at Westminster. This issues most accurate and fully detailed information about every British Colony, with illustrated hand-books plentifully besprinkled with maps.

Of immense Imperial significance is the raising of a London regiment of Yeomanry entirely composed of Colonials. The Prince of Wales is the honorary colonel, and the "King's Colonials," as the force is called, bear as a crest the popular three feathers and the motto "Ich dien." It numbers about six hundred of all ranks, divided into four squadrons. The first is the British-Asian squadron, and comprises Colonials from India, Ceylon, Burma, Hong-Kong, Singapore, and the Eastern Dependencies; the second (British-American) squadron includes the Dominion of Canada, West Indies, and Dependencies in the Western Hemisphere; the third (British-Australasian) represents Federated Australia, New Zealand, Fiji, and the South Sea Islands; and the fourth (British African) Cape Colony, Natal, Rhodesia, Transvaal, Orange River Colony, and other African Dependencies. In addition there are a battery of machine guns, a corps of signallers, and an ambulance corps, making the King's Colonials a complete and independent unit. Both full and undress uniforms are of khaki cloth with scarlet facings. Each squadron wears a distinctive metal badge showing the

INDIAN PRINCES IN LONDON.

portion of the Empire they represent. Thus, there is a kangaroo for the Australasians and an ostrich for the Africans.

A hard-and-fast rule of the regiment insists that every officer and man either be a Colonial born or of Colonial parentage, the only exception being, at the discretion of the

commanding officer, those who have rendered special service to any British Colony or Dependency or to the King's Colonials. Drills are held nightly, and for fifteen days annually the men go into camp at Sidcup. A commodious drill hall at King's Road, Chelsea, provides sufficient surplus accommodation to allow of a suite of rooms for social purposes.

The "Children of the Empire League" is the name of another active force which has for its centre London, for its scope wherever the British flag waves, and for its aims the impressing upon the youth of the Empire the duty of loyalty and patriotism. The League encourages parents to have their offspring taught the history and geography of the Empire, also its needs and how they may best fit themselves to meet those needs. Children are provided with correspondence comrades, boys are assisted to join cadet corps, etc., to practise shooting, to learn not only to ride but to saddle and groom their horses, and to acquaint themselves with some useful handicraft.

It will be seen from the foregoing that even a cursory glance at the Indian and Colonial side of London discloses a wide and varied field, and depicts really the condensed spectacle of the whole of the Britons beyond the seas dwelling in touch and sympathy with their own Colonial interests in the big Metropolis. Of the many cricketers, riflemen, oarsmen, lacrosse players, and athletes generally who visit us from time to time, in search of the Mother Country's laurels to deck Colonial records, little need be said here but to bid them a hearty welcome, for their presence among us is indeed a promising sign for the continued success and stability of the British Empire.

IN A BOARDING-HOUSE: DINNER.

FROM LONDON TENEMENT TO LONDON MANSION.

By P. F. WILLIAM RYAN.

THE millions of this great, weary, over-grown capital are sheltered by about seven hundred thousand houses; and of these some are veritable palaces of art, temples of luxury and beauty, while many, many more are meaner than the hovels of the poorest countryside.

Let us plunge at once into that wilderness of life called East London, and, entering one of its poorest streets, make acquaintance with a tenement house. A troop of noisy children are playing hopscotch opposite to the street-door, from which the weather has worn the paint, leaving on its panels as sole embellishment sundry names, dates and rhymes—rude memorials to the general usefulness of local pocket-knives, nails, and hairpins. To disturb the unhappy-looking knocker is a gratuitous waste of energy, for it is nobody's business to heed its summons. Moreover, the door is ajar. A slight push and you are in the passage, noting the dirty broken

walls, to which cling a few patches of greasy wall-paper. The stairs are straight ahead. There is no sunshine to speak of outside. It therefore matters but little that the window on the first floor lobby is thickly coated with dust and cobwebs, save where a child has impressed—as children will—his open hand with well extended fingers on the centre of one of its panes. Children are wrangling over marbles on the landing. Curiosity concerning the stranger quells for a moment their strife. Women with unkempt hair and unwashed faces pop their heads out of half-opened doors and eye the intruder with a rather aggressive air. Visitors are not welcome here, for they too often represent the Law, or the School Board, or philanthropic societies—all disagreeably meddlesome institutions!

A glance at one room suffices for all. A crazy dresser stands in one corner. It contains a jug without a handle, a tin can blackened from long service in the capacity of a pot, and some blue cups and saucers showing so many suspicious-looking cracks that their functions must be taken as purely decorative. A few canisters that once held cocoa, mustard, and so on flank like sentinels the crockery ware. Cooking utensils there are none; evidently the tin can has to do regular duty as a teapot. A plain deal table is covered with a newspaper as an

AN EAST-END ONE-
ROOMED TENEMENT.

apology for a table-cloth. One chair has the upper bar of its back missing. There is another, but it has no back at all. By its side is a small tin bath full of soapsuds. The fireplace is empty, but as it is summer that is unimportant.

The tenement house is not to be found only in the east. The west, too, has its slum districts where dilapidated house-fronts, broken casements, slatternly women, and neglected children are eloquent of the horrors within. Occasionally, the occupant of a one-

roomed tenement sublets a corner of his holding. The slum lodging-house keeper sometimes contrives that her beds may earn a double rental, by arranging to have them occupied by day as well as by night; so that one sleeper has hardly risen from his couch, when another slips into the still warm blankets.

It is in the homes of those very far removed from the well-to-do, yet distinctly beyond the grip of poverty, that one is most chilled in London. There are miles upon miles of obscure streets, some clean, some untidy, all melancholy, where every house is outwardly like its neighbour from chimney-pot to basement. The "workman's dwelling" is, of course, unknown in the City proper and the regions bordering

MODEL DWELLINGS (FARRINGDON ROAD).

thereon. It is equally a stranger to the fashionable quarters of the west. But in practically every other district these monotonous four- and six-roomed houses may be seen running at right angles to well-known thoroughfares. But we must wander far from tram and omnibus route to realise how vast is the area dedicated to these cheerless-looking abodes. In the smaller of these streets the houses are only a couple of storeys high. The interiors are as a rule pleasantly disappointing, for though all is plain and homely, even perhaps a little rough, yet there is generally simple comfort. The housewife in these small dwellings is almost invariably a thrifty, tireless soul. Were she less so, instead of having her own humble roof-tree she and her husband would be lodgers in some tenement, little less squalid than that into which we have already peeped. In some streets at a distance from the centre of the town houses of this class often have tiny front gardens, in which miniature plots of grass struggle to be green.

Now and again when exploring London one lights upon a huge barrack-like structure some five or six storeys high, with tiers of iron balconies running along the face of the building. It belongs to the class known as Model Dwellings for workmen. The balconies are seldom without groups of gossiping

women. Here and there one may notice baby faces peering through the iron bars at the far-away life of the street below. Mr. Peabody, the American philanthropist, first introduced places of this kind to the Metropolis, and buildings called after him are now found in many districts, such as Spitalfields, Islington, and Southwark. The County Council and Corporation buildings of the same class are designed on similar lines, those at Millbank being especially representative of the work of the former body.

Step into a train and let us away to a suburb, with its villas detached and semi-detached, its roads with their avenues of saplings and bay-windowed houses. Every suburb is, in fact, a town in itself, with villas standing in their own grounds proclaiming the presence of an aristocracy, while democracy is represented by terraces of four-roomed and six-roomed houses, a great number of which receive lodgers. Somebody has said the London suburbs are sad. They are only peaceful. The door of one of those eight-roomed houses where live the people who are neither poor nor rich stands open. We shall pause a moment here. A baby's carriage waits in the short, narrow avenue, its canopy covered with some spotless material edged with lace. The snowy pillow will soon be the sweeter for a little flaxen head. The young mother is in the hall adjusting baby's cloak and bonnet, in the intervals of kissing the bright young face. The walls are hung with a few popular prints. There are flowers on the hall table. A couple of tennis rackets are fixed crosswise near the hat-rack. You can see the staircase over the young mistress's shoulder; it is covered with linoleum, and the brass rods are glistening. Baby is settled in his carriage. Final

TEA IN A SUBURBAN GARDEN.

directions are given to a young maid who is to take him for his airing and do some shopping at the same time. The mother snatches her very last kiss, which is also a very long one, and waving her hand to the laughing mite watches with beaming eyes the royal progress of his majesty. There is much to be done while the young rascal is away. A sitting-room in which a piano, a sideboard, a sofa, a mirror, a davenport, and centre table are the chief

A BACHELOR'S QUARTERS IN THE TEMPLE.

pieces of furniture has to be dusted and rearranged. There is no luncheon to be prepared. The master lunches in the City. At 6.30 he will be home for a cosy little dinner. Homeliness, represented by varying degrees of comfort and refinement, is the keynote of suburban life. See that broad road fringed on either side with deep bands of green lawn ; on each lawn a villa, with flower-beds, shrubs, and trim hedges for its framework. Very bright and inviting are these homes. Each has a name of its own, painted either on its gate or on the post in which the gate swings. Behold a pretty picture. A summer-house, overgrown with a rambler rose and a canary creeper, is the background. A corner of a croquet green is in the foreground. Around a table a party of charming children and their father are paying their devoirs to the lady of the house as she presides over afternoon tea. A little shrubbery at the far end of the croquet-green divides it from a kitchen garden in which lettuces, peas, and other vegetables flourish. Peach and pear trees are trained against the boundary wall.

Flats are becoming more and more a feature of metropolitan life. They may be had for eight shillings a week in certain suburbs. In a fashionable neighbourhood the rent is counted by hundreds a year. It is possible to get an eight-roomed flat in a central locality for £150 or £200 per annum, while smaller places in dingier streets can be had for half the money. Let us peep into palatial flats close to a well-known square. The entrance hall is spacious and handsome. Palms large and small, and other plants, thrive behind the plate-glass panels let into the carved wooden framework of the hall door. No need to touch the electric bell. Scarcely have you stepped on to the huge rubber mat just inside the threshold, when a uniformed porter assumes that your want is "to see the vacant flat." The lift whisks you to the third floor. The vacant flat includes two reception-rooms, one a drawing-room, the other a dining-room, both furnished brightly. Something is wanting. It is the photographs, the bric-à-brac, the hundred and one trifles that mark the homes of refined people. Elsewhere there are flats of three or four rooms. Such rooms ! If an ordinary-sized table were used the tenants would need to retire to the hall. One of the drawbacks of flat life is the lack of privacy. In a fashionable flat it is hardly possible to battle with genteel poverty without your neighbours suspecting your circumstances. If finances are still more straitened, and, as often happens in humble life, the bailiff takes possession on behalf of a creditor, secrecy is hopeless.

LAWN TENNIS AND CROQUET (ONSLOW GARDENS, S.W.).

A WEST-END DRAWING-ROOM.

Certain districts are practically given over to boarding-houses and lodgings. Every pocket, every taste, every nationality is catered for. Some boarding-houses provide the guests with every comfort which could be expected at an hotel, combined with a greater degree of domesticity than could be hoped for in a public hostelry. The dining-room in such places gives the guests an opportunity of becoming acquainted with each other. After dinner the ladies meet in the drawing-room, where music, cards and gossip are indulged in, while some of the men adjourn to the smoking-room, which may also be a billiard-room. There are boarding-houses in really desirable districts which receive guests for as little as a guinea a week, this sum including the cost of at least two meals a day. Of course, the amount of the *pension* depends very much on the quality of the bedroom the guest happens to occupy. It is scarcely necessary to say that for a guinea a week the sleeping-room would be very little larger than the tiny bedstead contained within its four thin walls. In many of the more remote suburbs the boarding-houses range from fifteen shillings a week upwards. For this sum respectable lodgings and wholesome if frugal fare can be obtained ; while for a few hundreds a year the "paying guest" may find himself—more often herself—one of a household with relatives known to Debrett or Burke.

The lodging-house must not be confounded with the boarding-house. The boarding-house is quite an institution in certain well-known localities of the West and West-Central districts, but the lodging-house is indigenous to no particular suburb or borough. It is to be found everywhere, even in the sacred precincts of Mayfair itself. The lodging-house keeper merely lets out her rooms on certain terms ; and for board her tenants are at liberty to go where they will. In this particular there is, however, no set rule. In houses where good servants, and an adequate number of them, are kept, the landlady is generally ready to meet her lodgers' wishes in the matter of meals. In the cheaper localities, where possibly the landlady does all the household work with the assistance of a charwoman, cooking is regarded as a nuisance, and the lodger who merely occupies his room at night, leaving before breakfast, approximates very closely to the ideal. To the citizen of the world, an inspection of a large lodging-house in a moderately expensive neighbourhood is full of human interest. In the dining-room apartments are, perhaps, a young clerk and his wife. In the drawing-room suite is a man who can afford to pay two or three guineas a week in rent. As likely as not he is only in London on temporary business. If he wished he could live in an hotel. This suits him better. The floor above is made up of bed-sitting rooms. In one dwells a middle-aged civil servant who was a young man when he entered for the first time that plainly furnished apartment, rented at sixteen shillings a week. Now he is more than middle-aged. The landlady had seen his hair grow thinner year by year, and its colour change, the while the wrinkles silently mobilised round her own eyes. He has no secrets from her. Not that he ever exchanged words with her beyond what was rendered necessary by their relative positions ; but landladies often enjoy peculiar powers of intuition ! Next to him is a commercial traveller, a lively blade who divides the greater part of his time between commerce and music-halls, having but little left for his bed-sitting room, though it is a cheerful apartment enough, with a piano and a neat little suite of furniture upholstered in some crimson stuff.

On the same floor is a very small room let for a few shillings a week. Here is one of the tragic contrasts of London. Its tenant is part of the wreckage of the great city. He hungers and thirsts every day of his life, while the men who breathe the same air as he spend as much money each evening on dinner as would relieve his misery for a week. Once, doubtless, he could spend money as freely as they. Ascend higher—now you are deep in the drama of everyday life. In one room live a couple of young actresses out of regular employment. Next-door to them sleeps at night an old young man, whose days are passed grubbing amongst books at the British Museum. In the next there lives a boy clerk. The same roof which shelters the dining-room and drawing-room shelters them, but miles divide them. They are literally near the stars, but socially they are in the depths.

Bachelors' apartments are as various as bachelors. The Inns of Court are favourite residences for others besides barristers and law-students. Chambers for single men can, however, be had in all quarters of the capital. Here is a wretched room containing only a bed and a table. The man in the bed has written things at which thousands of Londoners have laughed. He might live in comparative luxury but for one thing—there is a bottle on the table! Ramble towards Regent's Park. Here are two pretty rooms on the topmost floor of a large mansion. The sitting-room walls are hung with expensive prints and theatrical photographs. The tenant is a solicitor's articled clerk, happy enough in single blessedness.

The citadel of fashion lies in the district known as Mayfair and Belgravia. When the sun is kind the gardens here are musical with the voices of ladies and children at play on the croquet lawns and tennis courts. Park Lane is the holy of holies so far as Society is concerned. Here the interiors of the houses are as perfect as wealth and art can make them—from the nurseries where satin-skinned children laugh and prattle and weep unconscious of their good fortune, to the kitchens where cooks devote their lives to designing dinners which shall be eaten with relish and blissfully digested. We step into a drawing-room whose contents represent thousands of pounds. There are Sheraton cabinets with fortunes in bric-à-brac visible through their glass panels. Exquisite miniatures are painted on the satinwood frameworks. There are parquet floors and inlaid tables, bronze statuettes the perfection of grace, and china of every tint that blooms in the garden or reigns in the sky. The centre of the ceiling is an oval of blue as soft and uncertain as a gossamer cloud. That is the background, and from it emerge forms of matchless cupids and the wonderful maidens of a great artist's fancy. In the dining-room a different note is struck. The table and chairs are of mahogany. The mantelpiece is a magnificent Chippendale creation, with a fantastically carved canopy. Turn into the library. Here the bookcases and chairs are of carved oak.

In the very heart of Mayfair there are tiny houses, "bijou residences" the agents sometimes call them, and jewels indeed they are— to be paid for accordingly. All rich men, however, are not devotees of fashion, and the charmed circle has no attraction for them. Lording it over all this amazing forest of stone and brick are the historic houses bearing names known from Tokio to Washington — mansions like Devonshire House, Stafford House, Holland House, and Apsley House — the homes and rendezvous for generations of those who have helped to make and mould the Empire.

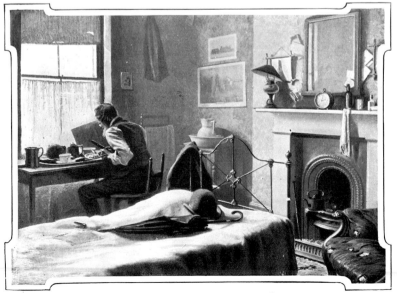

A BED-SITTING-ROOM (ST. GEORGE'S, E.).

AN ENCAMPMENT (BATTERSEA).

VAN DWELLING LONDON.

By T. W. WILKINSON.

READY FOR SWEETS.

PETULEN-GRO at the Agricultural Hall! The thing seems wildly incongruous; yet there he is, or somebody very much like him, during that rural carnival under cover, the World's Fair. Not that all, or even most, show people are gipsies or of gipsy descent. Let that be made perfectly clear. Still, a number of the van dwellers who congregate at Islington realise one of the finest characters immortalised by George Borrow.

The World's Fair is the great event in the showmen's year. As Christmas draws nigh van dwellers come to town from east and west, north and south, and pitch their tents at Islington. In the yard of the Agricultural Hall their movable dwellings, a few of them exceptionally commodious and well furnished—low, ornate "living waggons," having about double the cubic space of an ordinary caravan—are massed together, and life runs its course much as in other encampments. Though the owners of some betake themselves to fixed houses for the season, there are the usual scenes in the little colony, for all the world as if it were situated in the backwoods of England. Children play about the "living waggons"; out of business hours olive-skinned, black-haired men lounge against their caravans; and at meal times the air is laden with savoury odours from sizzling frying-pans or seething pots perched on top of braziers that stand near the steps of some of the homes on wheels. Even in London in mid-winter the open air has no terrors for most of the show folk.

Close by is another feature of the fair ground, though this is private—the clowns' dressing room. And here, as the hour for opening approaches, you can watch the

VAN DWELLERS IN LONDON.

professional jesters perform the delicate operation of "making up." The paint is laid on with an uncommonly heavy hand; but then it has not to bear scrutiny through illusion-dispelling opera glasses. It is, in fact, intended to be seen.

In the office there is a school for the showmen's children, surely the only one in the wide world that is held in a company's board room. During the morning, and the morning only, about a score of swarthy youngsters bend over their lessons under the superintendence of one of the London School Board's mistresses. There is also a Sunday school, in connection with which a treat is given by Mr. Joseph Wright, of Glasgow, to all the children — and they number about sixty — in the fair. Naturally, the bairns look upon this as a most important function, more important by far than even the annual meeting of the Van Dwellers' Association, though that body, with the showmen, *did* have the honour of presenting a miniature carriage, a set of silver-plated harness, and a well-matched pair of Shetland ponies to the children of the Prince and Princess of Wales. The Agricultural Hall, however, is the van dwellers' Parliament.

To all seeming the showmen are fixtures at Islington; but in reality their stay is short. Soon comes packing up time. Then for some days the hall has a peculiarly after-the-fair aspect. A ring is all that remains of the circus. Through the smoky air can be dimly seen the pole of a roundabout, sticking up without much visible support, like the mast of a partly submerged wreck. Cases, canvas, engines swathed in tarpaulins, bundles of sticks, odds and ends innumerable, lie scattered about everywhere. It is after the fair, indeed! Some of the companies of itinerants have meanwhile departed, and a day or two later all have scattered—many not to meet again till Christmas comes round once more — and the hall is a barren waste.

That is one side of Van Dwelling London. If you want to see another, you must travel further afield, to the ever-extending outskirts of the Metropolis. Some morning you come on a regular encampment on a piece of waste ground well inside the county boundary. Last night it was bare; now a colony is spread over it. Sheeted vans are scattered about the plot, and among them rise bell-shaped tents—the children's bedrooms. To each of the "living waggons" a horse is tethered, while underneath it crouches the indispensable dog, one of the bread-winners of the family. No need for him to see a gamekeeper; he can smell him a mile off. About the steps dishevelled children, their toilet

THE FAMILY WASH.

not yet made, play light-heartedly, indifferent to the curious gaze of the passers by ; and here and there groups are gathered at breakfast—a vastly more substantial meal to these invaders than it is to most Londoners.

By and by the vans will crawl through suburban streets, and the brown-eyed syrens —greatest living exponents of the art of blarney—and the tall, lithe men will " drop " a brush here, a basket there, a flower-stand somewhere else.   So they will pass away,

In certain districts on the other side of the Thames, also, van dwellers' encampments last all through the winter.   Though a good many of such colonies are situated in Wandsworth—where some of the hibernating nomads lay up their movable dwellings, go under a fixed roof, and become conventional, rent-paying householders—Battersea contains more than any other metropolitan borough.

Let us visit a typical specimen—Donovan's Yard.   It is a plot of ground near the South-

PREPARING MEALS (AGRICULTURAL HALL).

and London may see them no more for years.

On the borders of Epping Forest, about the northern limits of Finchley and Hampstead, and round Wembley, there are numbers of more permanent and more squalid encampments.   Pitiable indeed is the condition of some of the nomads in these settlements. When the air bites and stings, when there is a wind that you can lean against, whole families have no other home than the peculiar squat tent of the gipsy or a wigwam formed of an old cart and a few yards of canvas.

Western line, commanding an unpicturesque prospect of palings, walls, and arches, in one of which the Ragged School Union carries on a highly useful work, started by Mr. John Dyer, having for its aim the social and spiritual welfare of the van dwelling class. Two long lines of " living waggons," broken here and there by a firewood dealer's hut, run the length of the yard.   Instantly the eye travels along them you miss something.   Ah ! the horses !   They have long since gone. The steps are down in the places they occupy while the movable houses are on the road. When the van dwellers come to town about

October those who own steeds usually sell them, to save the cost of keeping them in idleness during the cold months, and purchase others just before taking to the road again.

On and between the lines there is a curious air of domesticity. Women, most of them stamped with their tribal characteristics, sit on the steps of the waggons, some at needlework, some merely gossiping. Other housewives are engaged on the family wash. Bent over tubs and buckets in close proximity to a fire, on which clothes are boiling briskly, they are rubbing and rinsing with a will, now and again

ON THE EVE OF DEPARTURE (AGRICULTURAL HALL).

CLOWNS MAKING-UP (AGRICULTURAL HALL).

dozen youngsters come forward in a body and clamour for sweets, their healthy faces aglow with expectancy and their pinafores outstretched, lest their hands cannot hold enough ! A moment later and they are happy.

Next, an interior. Go up the steps of a waggon, first noting that the ground rent for such caravans in Battersea is from 2s. to 3s. per week. The inside is a pocket edition of home as known to many thousands of house dwellers—the vast public of the one-room tenement. On the left is a tiny fireplace, over which hangs a collection of brass and copper ornaments and utensils that glisten like burnished gold. The other side of the van is mostly taken up with a table placed underneath the neatly-draped window. And, lastly, through some curtains at the far end of the van is a vista of a snowy-white bed which extends across the whole width of the waggon.

Big as the bed is compared with the size of the little house on wheels, it does not seem

going off for more water to a tap at one end of the ground. In a solitary instance a " mother's girl " is engaged in this important household duty, while close by another child is scrubbing the chubby face of a sister not much younger than herself. The offspring of the poor seem to learn the domestic arts in the cradle.

And now there is a diversion. Some half-

sufficiently large to accommodate all the family. Nor, in fact, is it. The children sleep underneath when their home is in London, and in a tent when it is in the country. Sometimes a man owns two vans, and in that case his children, of course, occupy the extra bed. One feature of the van into which we have intruded must be emphasised—its spick-and-span condition. It would meet with the approbation of a "house-proud" Lancashire woman, who may be taken as an extreme representative of the slaves to cleanliness.

Over the other encampments in Battersea we need not tarry. They are practically identical with the one in Donovan's Yard, though in some there are "movable" homes which have been made fixtures. Shafts, wheels, and axles are gone. Only the bodies of the waggons remain, and these are numbered among London's myriad and strangely varied dwellings.

All the encampments exist for about six months of every year, from October till the flat racing season begins. And it is not cold alone that drives van dwellers into town for the winter, but cold and "nothing doing" combined. Many are in the cocoanut-shy business, and may be seen on Hampstead Heath on Bank Holidays and at the various race meetings, chivalrously making a concession to one of woman's little weaknesses: "Ladies half way!" A still larger section work in the fields at fruit picking, hopping, and harvesting generally. Dead, absolutely dead, of course, are these industries during the winter; so they come to London, and for the most part trust to hawking to carry them on till spring.

And nobody welcomes it more heartily than they. Town is not their proper environment. They would rather hear the lark sing than the mouse cheep. But their spirits rise as the days grow longer, and when at last the Epsom meeting is at hand they rejoice at the glorious prospect that opens before them. Their period of hibernation is over. Sing hey! for the open road!

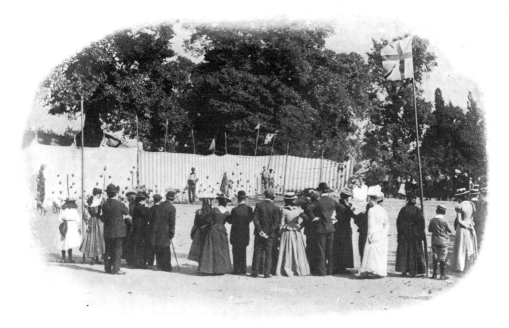

ON HAMPSTEAD HEATH : A COCOANUT "PITCH."

BOROUGH COUNCIL LONDON.

By C. DUNCAN LUCAS.

EXAMINING A LIST OF
VOTERS.

PROBABLY not one person in a hundred realises the importance of the work that is carried on by the Borough Councils of the Metropolis. Yet London is divided into twenty-eight boroughs, each one of which has its body of councillors who control to a considerable extent the lives of those whom they represent in the government of their district.

If the reader will accompany me to-day on a round of visits he will witness a series of spectacles of the deepest possible interest — spectacles which the average Londoner, engrossed in his own immediate affairs, seldom observes for himself. An easy walk brings us to a plain red-brick building which we have arranged to explore. It is the Borough Town Hall— a hive of civic activity. The pale, serious gentleman whom we meet in the corridor is the Town Clerk — a local governor in his way. He is responsible for the due execution of the Council's orders, and he draws a salary of a thousand a year. When he stepped into his office he had to give security for £5,000. The person he is talking to is the Comptroller, who is head of the Finance department. So vast are the sums that filter through his hands he has to find security for no less a sum than £10,000. Peeping into the various rooms, we see the Deputy Clerk in consultation with the Surveyor, the Sanitary Inspector instructing his staff, the rubicund beadle, an army of clerks writing furiously, and lastly, some very sober and harassed looking officials who are opening letters. They are the rate collectors—the best-hated and the best-abused mortals in the borough. Study the expression of the one in grey. As he withdraws from an envelope a greasy piece of paper and commences to read his brow darkens—he fancies he can predict what is in store for him ; but presently his face lights up and an inward chuckle escapes him. The

PUBLIC VACCINATOR AT WORK IN A PRINTING ESTABLISHMENT.

fact is that an aggressive householder, who has threatened to break his head if he repeats his call for the rates, has unexpectedly forwarded the money he owes. We shall encounter the rate collector again. He is ubiquitous.

A meeting of the Council is about to be held, and we must be in attendance. The chamber is pretty full to-day. On a daïs sits the Mayor close by are the Town Clerk and the Deputy Clerk, each armed with bulky docu ments; on the table below lies the sacred mace, the symbol o authority. At desks arranged in a square, on which are pens and writing paper, sit the councillors some grave some gay. Presently a grey-bearded little man, very self-important, is on his legs. He is discussing wash houses. A colleague in front of him and another behind are apparently bored, while the other members are mostly yawning. The Mayor alone is on the alert. Of a sudden, driven to desperation, he interrupts the flow of language and calls the attention of the Council to the speaker's continued irrelevance and tedious repetition. The latter is strongly advised by an impatient councillor to sit down, but refuses, and continues his discourse. Before long, however, he is pulled up effectually. He is reminded that, according to the bye-laws of

MAYOR AND COUNCILLORS ON THEIR WAY TO CHURCH
(HAMMERSMITH).

the Council, no member can speak for longer than ten minutes except by leave of the Mayor or the Chairman of the Council; and, as the Mayor is in no mood to afford the necessary permission, the prosy one, with a savage glance at his neighbours, resumes his seat. He is followed by a business-looking man, who speaks to the point and says all that he has to say in three minutes. In an hour the meeting breaks up, and the members slowly disperse, the Mayor retiring to his parlour, where his worship is visible to anyone who is able to show just cause for interviewing him.

Over the way is a church, by the door of which are a couple of men. They are anxiously scanning the recently-published lists of voters and jurymen, both of them hoping to discover that by some fortunate accident their names have been omitted from the latter. Another day, if we revisit this locality, we shall see the Borough Council proceeding to church in a body—the Mayor, aldermen, and councillors in their robes, the Town Clerk in his wig and gown, the mace-bearer supporting his mace, and the beadles with their staves of office.

Close by is the free library, the temporary resting place of rich and poor. Ladies of all ages are borrowing books, sporting youths are devouring the sporting news, prosperous

A MEETING OF A BOROUGH COUNCIL (HAMMERSMITH).

tradesmen with an hour to spare are immersed in the illustrated papers — almost every human type is to be studied in this very free library. But the out-of-works predominate. At one table there is a collection of them — old and young, ragged and footsore, their eyes sunken, a look of utter hopelessness imprinted on each one. Happily for these outcasts, although newspapers are spread out before them, sleep has overtaken them. For one brief hour they are strangers to the tragedy of life.

On our tour round the borough we meet the Surveyor. He superintends the cleansing, watering, paving, and lighting of the highways, the collection and removal of street and house refuse, the erection and demolition of buildings, the breaking-up of streets, the licensing of hoardings, and a hundred and one other things. The official wearing one of the Council's caps is his foreman. The Surveyor has just ordered him to keep watch over the street-orderly boys who are inclined to be frolicsome. The man who hurriedly passes the Surveyor with a smile of recognition is the Sanitary Inspector. He has his hands full to-day. His mission at the moment is the removal of a small-pox patient on the instructions of the Medical Officer of Health. But we will let him do that by himself; nor will we seek the company of his subordinates when they come to stop up every crevice of the rooms that have been occupied by the patient preparatory to fumigating them.

But we will be present at the interesting scene portrayed in the illustration on page 324. The public vaccinator has called to vaccinate a number of printers. Attending on him are two nurses, one in uniform and the other in private dress. One by one the compositors step forward, the operation is performed, and each man returns to his work. The public vaccinator is not an official of the Borough Council, but the latter issue notices encouraging the public of their district to be vaccinated, and probably do more than any other body to popularise this

method of preventing the spread of small-pox.

As all risk is probably now at an end, we will seek the acquaintance of the disinfecting staff at their headquarters. They have fumigated the apartments of the small-pox patient, and have taken possession of his clothes and his bedding. The big boiler-shaped contrivance which we examine is the disinfector, and the clothes and bedding are inside. They have been sprayed with a disinfecting fluid, as indeed have also the walls, the floor, and the ceiling of the premises, and are being purified by means

DISINFECTING CLOTHES.

of hot air. It is not a very safe operation, we remark, but the attendant tells us that he "never catches anything himself." He further explains that for bad cases the Council supplies him with a macintosh and holland overalls.

At this juncture we are introduced personally to a Borough Councillor, who offers to facilitate our progress. He shows us an inspector purchasing some doubtful eggs. The inspector will examine the eggs shortly, and, if they are very ancient, the vendor will hear something unpleasant from the Public Health department. Our notice is also drawn to sewermen, dustmen, pickers — men who sort the refuse at the wharves—bricklayers, garden-keepers, and gullymen. A Borough Council employs a whole regiment of work-people, and, by-the-by, every one—not even excepting the street-orderly boys—who has been in the service of the Council for twelve months gets a week's holiday in the summer without deduction of pay.

As we turn a corner leading into a slum, we meet our friend the rate collector whom we saw in the Town Hall. He is endeavouring to induce a dishevelled old hag to pay the rates, and the latter is flourishing a frying-pan in his face.

"My man ain't 'ad no work these four months," cries the lady violently, "and don't

PAYING EMPLOYÉS (WESTMINSTER)

you come worritin' 'ere no more, or I'll give you what's what."

The rate collector shrugs his shoulders, dodges the frying-pan, and tries next door. A man in his shirt sleeves, with drink stamped on every feature, thrusts his unkempt head out of the window, and withdraws it immediately. The collector knocks twice and thrice. At last the door is opened by a young woman. The result is *nil* as before. The excuse this time is illness. The occupier's husband has deserted her, her seven children are down with the measles, and there is no money to buy them food, let alone to pay rates. But the collector

is an observant being. He knows that the individual he has to deal with is upstairs, and that he spends most of his time lolling against a gin palace. He is also perfectly aware that the seven children who are alleged to be suffering with the measles are playing in the gutter. Summons after summons has been issued, but without effect, and the final act will be a distress warrant.

By an odd chance a distress warrant is being executed lower down the street. A crowd of unclean loafers is congregated outside a dingy hovel. They are jeering and swearing at the broker's men engaged in carting away the goods and chattels of an obstreperous ratepayer, who is smoking a clay pipe on the doorstep. They will confiscate as much property as they imagine will realise the sum that is owing. In this case every stick save the bed and the man's tools (which he never uses)—the brokers are prevented by law from appropriating a man's bed and the tools with which he is supposed to earn his living — will have to be forfeited.

The scene is not a pleasant one, yet the Council must have the wherewithal to perform their allotted task, and if ratepayers will not disgorge willingly payment must be enforced. In one of the southern boroughs from five to six thousand summonses for the non-payment of rates are issued quarterly, and one magistrate sits for an entire week to deal only with such cases.

Later in the day, when we return to the neighbourhood of the Council's offices, we watch the employés receiving their weekly wage. They are drawn up in rows, and there is an air of eager expectancy on every face. Hard by are officials in semi-naval uniform looking on.

Thus is the work of the Borough Councils of London accomplished. On the whole it is excellently done, and, if here and there fault can be found, one must remember that the councillors render their services gratuitously, and that each borough is in itself a large town.

NOMADS (HACKNEY MARSHES).

LONDON BEYOND THE PALE.

By GEORGE R. SIMS.

BASKING IN THE SUN.

THE force of circumstances may put our bodies outside the pale of society, the force of ideas may induce our minds to wander beyond the pale of knowledge. There is a closer connection between the two subjects I am about to treat in this article than may be at first apparent. The two subjects are Occult London and Tramp London. And yet the occultist mentally and the tramp physically have one quality in common. Both are seeking to order and shape their lives outside the pale which fences in and limits the sphere of action of ordinary citizens.

The occult and the mystic have ever had a fascination for mankind, and here, in the London of the twentieth century, are thousands of men and women of all classes and all degrees of intellect who daily resort to prophets and prophetesses, to seers and wizards, with as firm a faith in their power as the savages have in the priests of the Ju-Ju groves.

The commonest forms of modern magic are fortune-telling by cards, palmistry, thought reading, clairvoyance and crystal gazing. Spiritualism is commonly carried on by hundreds of professional mediums as a means of livelihood, and messages from the dead are rapped out nightly for the edification of the true believers. Methods of cure outside the programme of modern medicine are practised for a fee by Christian Scientists, and there are several weekly organs which advertise the names and addresses of the practisers of magic, black and white.

The scheme of this work compels it to abstain from criticism, and merely to present things as they are, therefore it must be understood that no opinion is herein offered as to the honesty or sincerity of these methods or professions.

The commonest form of fortune-telling

for a fee is that practised by certain "wise women" who live in a small back room, where for a trifling fee they "tell the cards" for servant girls of the humbler sort, factory girls, and the wives of working men. Sometimes the fee is a shilling, sometimes it is half-a-crown. The young woman who has her fortune told can, if she is able to part with more money, pry still deeper into the secrets of destiny. She can gaze into the crystal and see her future husband. If she is married already, and unhappy, she can see her second. If she is worried and has doubts about the constancy of her sweetheart, she can obtain of some of these backroom "witches" a powder which, put into the young man's beer, will induce him to make her an immediate offer of marriage.

For the aristocratic wife and maiden there are wizards and witches also, but the surroundings are very different. Instead of a back room in the slums, these fortunetellers have gorgeous apartments in the most fashionable West-End thoroughfares, and charge the fee of a physician for a consultation. Palmistry is the favourite occultism of the West, and the palmists, though occasionally harassed by the police

flourish and grow fat. Many of them advertise in leading society organs; some openly announce their calling and invite visits on boards carried about the West-End by sandwichmen. Palmistry and thought reading are also largely indulged in by amateurs who confine their efforts to their own circle of acquaintances.

Spiritualism engages the attention of a large body of Londoners, and among them are many thoughtful and intellectual people. There are spiritualists who require a large amount of manifestation, and there are spiritualists who are content to treat the mystery of communion with the dead from a higher standpoint than table rapping and other physical demonstrations of the presence of a departed fellow creature. The spiritualists have their own publications and weekly journals, their clubs and societies, and even their own hotel. Occasionally a medium who has produced manifestations of a novel and striking character becomes famous outside spiritualistic circles, and the press and the public help to swell his or her fame. But of late years Spiritualism has been more of a private creed and less of a public performance than it was in the days of the great American professionals who visited our shores.

Nor has London for a long time past had a first-class ghost. Haunted houses are occasionally rumoured, and sometimes crowds gather round them for a few nights, but a ghost to set the whole town talking has not yet given itself to the twentieth century. There are, however, many private citizens who see ghosts, and, in order that no effort may be spared to secure a ghost that can have no shadow of doubt cast upon its *bona fides*, there has been formed a most admirable society, known

FORTUNE-TELLING BY CARDS.

as the Society of Psychical Research. The members of this body are scientific men, and they undertake the investigation of haunted houses, phantom appearances, mysterious noises and spiritualistic manifestations.

The clairvoyant of "commerce," if we may use the term, is common enough. She is a young lady who, blindfolded, will give the ladies and gentlemen who have paid the price of admission the number of a watch, the date on a coin, the description of any article held up in the hand of the proprietor of the show, who invariably puts the questions. But there are also clairvoyants who take a loftier view of the gift they profess to possess. They are consulted by wives whose husbands are missing, by mothers whose children are lost. In the well-known case of a gentleman who had disappeared for many days, a clairvoyant told the wife where the body would be found. The result justified the prophecy. Clairvoyants are largely consulted by the ladies who have faith in the crystal, and occasionally large sums of money change hands over the revelations.

Mesmerism and its more modern form of hypnotism are practised privately for the benefit and instruction of the few, and publicly for the amusement of the many. The experiments of a "professor" on subjects induced to step up from the audience are always popular side-shows; sometimes small halls are taken by the professor, and the experiments make up an entire evening's entertainment. Hypnotism is also performed in connection with medical treatment, and is learnedly discussed in certain journals. But by the great general public it is still looked upon as either a mysterious power of the uncanny order, or as the hocus-pocus of the professional mesmerist arranged as an amusing exhibition.

The divining rod is always hovering on the border line. The papers will one day chronicle a successful experiment for the discovery of water by its means, and the

READING A PALM.

next day make merry over the failure of a diviner or divineress.

There are other forms of occultism practised in London into which it is not necessary to enter. Some of them are closely allied with religious belief, others border on insanity and are "beyond the pale" in the fullest acceptance of the term.

Tramp London seeks its existence as Occult London seeks its knowledge, beyond the pale; that is to say, it lives in a land not inhabited by the ordinary citizen. The tramps of London are, many of them, not only born tramps, but come of tramp families. In the workhouses, to which in bad weather most habitual tramps resort, the history of some tramp families can be traced back in the books for over 200 years.

The London tramp is, of course, frequently the provincial or country tramp taking London in the course of his tramping. He comes to the Metropolis in large numbers at certain seasons of the year, and always in the largest numbers for great public festivals and pageants. He does not come to see the sights, but to share in the *largesse* which is often a feature of these occasions.

Outside most of the London workhouses towards evening you may see a number of homeless wanderers waiting for admission to the casual ward. They are many in winter, but few in summer.

There are comparatively few genuine tramps who make London their permanent tramping ground, but there are always an immense number "passing through" more or less leisurely. Those who stay for a while cease to be tramps and become mendicants. They hang about well-frequented corners at night time and appeal in a confidential manner to a likely looking passer-by or loiterer for assistance.

But these poor wretches are not all mendicants. The spectacle of a man and woman with a child, woebegone and half famished, but still with the remnants of respectability about them, tramping through the streets that are paved with gold is common enough. For an honest artisan and his wife are often reduced by force of circumstances to travel in search of employment, and when the journey is a long one, and they are penniless, the travelling has

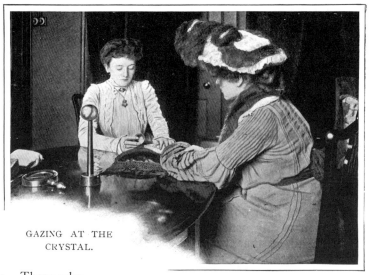

GAZING AT THE CRYSTAL.

to be done on foot. These are the best kind of tramps. The worst are the " 'appy dossers"—the men and women who loaf about London during the day and at night sleep in the open spaces, on the Embankment, under railway arches, on steps — or sometimes on the stairs of tenement houses in the slums.

On Hackney Marshes are occasionally to be seen nomads of two kinds. One kind is a small colony of homeless boys, who burrow holes in the great dust heaps for shelter, and live on what they can pick up. The other kind is of the genuine gipsy order. These nomads may be seen with their van, their tent, their horses, and their hens in our illustration on page 329.

Trafalgar Square is a favourite "pitch" of the tramps of both sexes. There are seats and cosy corners for the *al fresco* siesta, and a fountain is close at hand. In the photographic reproductions on page 329 and this page you may see the male tramps basking in the sun in this world-famous square, and two female tramps dreaming the happy hours away on an adjacent seat.

There are certain strange colonies of homeless outcasts in London who are to all intents and purposes gipsies, with the important exception that they are not peripatetic. There is such a colony in Regent's Park, where for many years they were known as

SLUMBERING.

the Park Gipsies. They have nothing in common with the Romany folk, as they follow no occupation and have no property. They are ill-clad, frowsy, dissipated looking men and women who camp daily under the hedges. They are turned out of the Park at closing time, and where they go is a mystery, but I have seen them waiting at the gates

camp in search of provender. As night gathers the camp breaks up.

You will occasionally see fresh faces among the Park Gipsies, but most of them are old stagers. Some of them have come to the same spot day after day in spring, summer, autumn, and winter for many years.

Of this class of "tramp"—if tramps they can be called, seeing that they spend their lives sitting and lying down—the great mystery is where they get the clothes that cover them. Be they careful as they may, the constant outdoor wear must eventually make the rags undarnable. Probably they have old garments given to them. The clothing marts of the better class tramp, the

TRYING TO SELL A " FIND."

for re-admission as early as 4 a.m.

About nine o'clock they make their toilet and smarten themselves up for the day. The ladies re-arrange their own hair, and perform kindly little acts for each other with pins. Occasionally they do a little cold water washing, laying the apron or handkerchief out on the grass to dry. It is at this hour that the men of the party stroll off in search of breakfast. Sometimes they return with dry bread ; sometimes they come back with bread and cheese and meat bones and a can of beer. After breakfast the men light their pipes and read any torn bit of newspaper that the wind may have wafted towards them. The ladies gather together and talk, perhaps scandal, perhaps " chiffon "—who shall say ? Noon is the hour of the siesta. The whole party generally reclines about this time in attitudes more or less graceful, and sleep is the programme for the greater part of the day. About five envoys again leave the

SUNDAY MORNING IN RAG FAIR.

man who when he gets a few shillings desires to renovate his wardrobe, are in the south and east of London, but the great resort is the celebrated Rag Fair which lies near Wentworth Street, Whitechapel.

The time to see this market in full swing is Sunday morning. Here you can obtain anything and everything in the clothing line, from an odd second or third hand boot to a fourth or fifth hand fur-trimmed overcoat.

Many working men and hawkers enter Rag Fair in their old clothes and walk away in second-hand splendour. The dealers are mostly of the Hebrew persuasion and work in couples. One man does the "patter"— that is the talk, the eulogising of the coats and waistcoats he has to sell—and the second man is the human block upon whom the coats are fitted, just to let the bystanders see what elegant articles they are. Our photographic illustration on page 333 will give the reader an excellent idea of the scene that to anyone unaccustomed to this form of reclothing the masses is decidedly startling.

With another class of men and women who live "beyond the pale," those who get a varying subsistence by mendicancy pure and simple, it is not easy to deal, because of the difficulties of classification. There are mendicants who combine trickery with appeals for charity, and who are dealt with elsewhere in "Some London Dodges." There are others who, though practically beggars, just evade the Mendicity Act by carrying some small article which they pretend to offer for sale. The mendicants who live wholly and solely by asking for alms without disguising themselves with a box of matches, a bootlace,

a bunch of stale flowers, or an affliction are, as a rule, among the most dangerous of London's pests. They terrify nervous women and young girls by following them in lonely suburban roads. They stand about in a crowded thoroughfare frequently only to assist and mask the operations of the pickpocket.

The house-to-house mendicant is less common in London than in the country, but there are men and women who, under pretence of begging for broken victuals, take stock of basements and kitchens for the future guidance of the area sneak. The begging letter impostor is a nuisance of the worst description, because he trades on the best feelings of humanity. His letter is written for him, as a rule, in the common lodging-houses, where the "screever" or writer keeps a list of charitable people, and sends the mendicant out with a written story to suit their particular "sympathy."

But the adepts in this art are hardly "beyond the pale," for many of them live in comfortable little houses, enjoying the rights and privileges of citizenship, and are able, when they bring actions against a periodical which has denounced them, to brief a leading K.C. to defend their "honour."

SORTING RAGS (REGENT'S PARK).

BANKRUPTCY COURT : EXAMINING A DEBTOR.

PUBLIC OFFICE LONDON.

By HENRY LEACH.

IN the course of some of the articles in this work it is shown how entirely is London the centre of practically every phase of national and imperial life that one could name, and how even the people in the provinces as well as those in the colonies, and farther away at the outposts of the Empire, are accustomed to lean upon the great departments in the capital for the proper arrangement of many of their affairs. But beyond these Government centres, which divide, as it were, the business of the country into certain definite and important sections, there are in the Metropolis many other public offices ; and though folk generally may have little knowledge of them and of their heads and staffs, yet they are all-important to the nation as a whole. They each control a section of the life of the kingdom. Suddenly abolish a single one of them without at the same time making some provision for its work to be carried on elsewhere, and it would very soon be apparent to a considerable proportion of the population that one of the screws of Great Britain was decidedly loose.

Consideration should, perhaps, first be given to the Heralds' College, or College of Arms—to make mention of both its titles—which has its abode in a building which stands back from Queen Victoria Street in the City. It looks unpretentious enough, but in a far-gone age it was the town house of the Earls of Derby. If there is not much to look at outside, the College within is so impressive to anyone who has respect for age, and tradition, and blood and lineage—the things upon which our old families most do pride themselves—that the very atmosphere seems to have altogether changed in stepping from the busy, murky thoroughfare in which it is situated, till now it is redolent of anything save the prosaic twentieth century—redolent of the days of the Norman kings, of the Tudors, of the Stuarts.

The chief duties of the body which controls the College and attends to its working may be defined as the making out and preservation of the pedigrees and armorial bearings of noble families, and the conducting of such royal ceremonials as come within its province. Therefore, on the one hand, here, if you suspect that you have any "blood" in your veins—blood, that is, with a tinge of blue—you may set the heralds to work—for a consideration—and have your line of ancestry traced back as far as it will go, and for another consideration, if you are not already joyful in the possession of arms, you may have a set of them prepared in all the most beautiful colours and of historic and dignified appearance, with motto and everything complete ready for immediate use. All this is just what the College of Heralds is for, and there are times when it is very busy indeed. When the rich American comes over in the summer time he often feels that he would like to know just how he stands in regard to certain personages of the fifteenth and sixteenth centuries, perhaps, who bore the same name as himself. It might not be difficult to find a connection. Also when some great national ceremonial of historic import is about to be celebrated, and questions of right and precedence become plentiful, the archives of the College are stirred to the bottom in the settlement of them.

Then again, on the other hand, if there is any big proclamation to be made with trumpets and a great show of authority, invested with that touch of the mediæval which never fails to command the respect even of the most sordid cynic—a proclamation, it may be, in the name of the King himself—it is these heralds with their coats and their tassels of scarlet and gilt, they and no others, who will be permitted the honour of making it. When a new King succeeds to the throne they are down at St. James's Palace while others are abed, proclaiming him from a balcony which is old enough to match their uniforms. In the ceremonies of a Coronation, also, the heralds are at work, and these are the times when we become familiar with the names and duties of the Earl Marshal, who is over all, and with the three Kings of Arms, Garter—the chief—Clarenceux, and Norroy. We hear also of the six heralds, Chester, Lancaster, York, Somerset, Richmond, and Windsor, with Surrey Extraordinary and Maltravers Extraordinary, and of the four pursuivants, Rouge Croix, Bluemantle, Rouge

Dragon, and Portcullis. It is all very old, all so intensely respectable, and nothing short of a revolution can ever dim its dignity.

There is another public office about which not so much is known, but it is one of the most important departments in the whole world to those who are constantly sailing upon the seas, and especially to those who get their living by doing so. It is Trinity House, and a very interesting place it is. Not one man in a hundred of those you meet in the street would be able to tell you even vaguely what Trinity House is, or what it is supposed to do. The nearest he could come to answering your question would be that Trinity House "has something to do with the sea." Probably only a small proportion are aware that there is really a "House," not among the mermaids, but away on Tower Hill, hard by the Mint. What Trinity House, the department, really does in these days is, in the first place, to attend to all pilotage matters, grant licences to pilots—and take them away again — control the lighthouses, buoys, beacons, and so forth, so as to make navigation for British seamen a thing less fraught with danger than it would other- wise be. Occasionally, too, its senior representatives attend at the Admiralty Court to act as assessors, and they also advise the Board of Trade in matters nautical which landsmen could not be expected to understand properly. Over and above all this, it gives pensions to worthy sea captains who have need of them, and what with this and the other duties which have been named the Corpora- tion manages to get through the sum of £300,000 per annum.

At Trinity House there are Board days and Court days when the Brethren, as the members of the ruling body are designated, assemble in the noble apartment which is devoted to their meetings. The doors to this and many other chambers in the whole build- ing, tall and thick and of the most beautiful Spanish mahogany, are the pride of the Brethren, who say they can hardly be equalled in London. On the walls of the board room are magnificent paintings of the King, of the Prince of Wales, Palmerston, Wellington, and many others

PUBLIC RECORD OFFICE : VISITORS SEARCHING THROUGH VOLUMES.

PATENT OFFICE : PREPARING PUBLICATIONS FOR PRESS.

of the officers of the department, past and present, for the most part displaying in these portraits in naval uniform the scarlet cuffs which are the badge of the House. On Court days, when the Brethren sit round their semicircular table in uniform, this touch of scarlet is always very pronounced. On these occasions it sometimes happens that the royal Master, the Prince of Wales himself, takes the chair of presidency. His Royal Highness has his own private apartment adjoining, handsomely fitted up and with the inevitable model of a lighthouse on a stand in one corner. Such models, and others of buoys and the like, abound throughout the place. The entrance hall is filled with them, and they ornament the library. Trinity House smacks of the sea, as it should do, and with a fine regard for the remembrance of old times, the Brethren call the landing on the first floor,

decorated with busts and pictures of the worthies of Trinity House, not a landing, as we should, but the quarter-deck. It is a wonderful place in its way; long may it survive.

Then, to continue our look round the public offices, there is that huge and strong looking building in Chancery Lane which is known as the Public Record Office, where are deposited the archives of the nation. The Public Record Office looks what it is, for it was designed for safety from the demon fire, and, though all the East Central district of London should be swept by a mighty conflagration, yet would this office in all likelihood survive. There is little or nothing of ornament about it; indeed, it is reviled by many for its plainness. But it is an achievement in brute strength in a modern building. It is made of iron and stone everywhere. The roofs and the doors are of iron, and the windows have stone mullions and iron lights. There are as few fireplaces as possible and only electric lights. That is because there are here preserved by the million and by the ton all the most valuable papers which concern the progress of the nation from the earliest times —the records of the rise of England. The people may come here and consult them, as they do, discovering for their own satisfaction some nice point of official usage in the past or clearing up some doubt upon a matter of history. It is not exactly a show place; it is a place for the studies and references of people of solemn look, and you may see them entering and departing any day of the week, adding something new to their personal store of historical knowledge.

The Patent Office in Southampton Buildings is the monument of the genius of invention. Let there be a

HERALDS' COLLEGE : THE MANUSCRIPT ROOM.

man anywhere in the kingdom with a new idea for something to be made, which in his invariably enthusiastic opinion will help towards accomplishing in the future what has never been accomplished in the past, and the chances are at least even that before the finish he and his invention will find their way to this Patent Office, which has been the maker of many a fortune and at the same time the grave of many a long cherished hope. Here are stored the specifications of thousands and thousands of patents for all the most curious and wonderful inventions. If a twentieth part of them had proved really practicable, London would not now be recognisable to those people who had been absent from it for two or three years. One inventor is confident that he has discovered a new kind of traction which will make the minimum rate of locomotion under any circumstances 120 miles an hour, by road, by sea, by rail—yes, even by air. And another man has been spending months of his valuable time in discovering a method of dyeing pea-sticks yellow, and, having so discovered it, has duly registered his patent in this department. The comedy and tragedy of the Patent Office are remarkable in their variety, and the officials who regularly examine all the strange specifications and models that come in and prepare the departmental publications that all others concerned may know of what is happening have seen more of the strange results of human ingenuity than anybody else in the world.

Not far from here is another public office which—such are the disappointments which are inseparable from enterprise—often enters with the Patent Office into the history of a single life as a natural corollary. It is the Bankruptcy Office and Court, situated in a corner of Lincoln's Inn Fields at the end of Carey Street. Plain and prosaic enough in all conscience for the work it has to do is this office, which is dreaded by every man who finds that the gains and expenses of this world do not

PATENT OFFICE : EXAMINING A MODEL.

in his case make a satisfactory match. The Bankruptcy Court is the temple of ruin, and there come to it alike the greengrocer from the East-End, who after years of honest toil has failed for fifty pounds, and the noble lord with castles and estates who, just like his humble fellow bankrupt, is not able to meet his obligations. On the same morning they may attend here before the Registrar, and in answer to the painfully pointed questions of the Official Receiver, recount the story of their discomfiture. The material difference is that the lord goes back to his castle and his easy living, and the greengrocer tries to borrow a sovereign upon which to exist for a week.

Another public office which comes up for mention is one which exists for the service of all the others, and that is the Stationery Office, at Storey's Gate, in Westminster. Its duty is to supply every Government department in existence with all its needs in the way of paper and stationery of every description. It supplies the Premier and his Cabinet with the note sheets of the finest quality upon which they write to the chiefs of foreign Governments, and it supplies the Board of Trade with strong paper in which parcels may be packed. To the military schools at Gibraltar, Hong Kong, and elsewhere it regularly sends big boxes of stationery and general school utensils. It keeps vast stores of them, as well as account books, and Government publications of every description. The Stationery Office is more than usually methodical and careful, and it is an instance of this that each batch of paper which comes in is sent first to the examining room where it is subjected to every chemical and other test that is known lest the manufacturers who supply it should to the very smallest degree give less in quality than they are paid to do.

And there are many other public offices, each with its own special work to do. There is one devoted to the management of the National Debt, and another to attending to the preparation of nautical almanacs, which are of far more importance than might appear to the landsman at first thought. Whilst we have a public office for the disposal of Queen Anne's Bounty, we have another for the collection and adjustment of all revenues from woods, forests, and lands. Others serve their special purposes, and thus is the great machinery of the Government kept smoothly running, each little wheel being as necessary to perfect harmony in the whole mechanism as is the great driving shaft of the Cabinet itself. Our departmental system may not be perfect, but such as it is it has taken hundreds of years to evolve, and it is easier for a critic to suggest improvements than it is for Governments to bring them about.

STATIONERY OFFICE : PACKING STATIONERY FOR ABROAD.

RECREATION GROUND (FORMERLY A GRAVEYARD), ST. PETER'S, WALWORTH.

LONDON'S PLEASURE GARDENS.

By I. BROOKE-ALDER.

THOUGH elsewhere in this work we have dealt with the parks, with "Gardening London," "Cricket London," and "Football London," there still remains much to be said about the open spaces of the Metropolis.

The first example that presents itself is at Earl's Court. There, where on unconsidered trifles of waste space arose sundry buildings for the accommodation of more or less foreign or native exhibits, annually varied, gardens play a very important part. Not only do they serve with the aid of bridges to unite the disjointed exhibition sections, but they provide the visitor with most welcome diversion from the inevitable monotony of galleries and halls. Kept in excellent order, botanically speaking, and provided with plenty of seats, a selection of entertainments, and several bands, the grounds of the Earl's Court Exhibition are, in the summer months, a striking illustration of the possibilities of unpromising material when cleverly adjusted. The portion known as the Western Gardens is, from its favouring space, the chief point of attraction. There, whilst a military band discourses sweet music, dozens of Londoners and London's passing guests assemble to promenade or rest in shady corners, where cooling drinks

are considerately provided. The evening hours bring special features in the way of illuminations, fairy lights giving additional charm to the scene. Viewed from the comfortable lounge chairs scattered on the lawn of the Welcome Club enclosure, this attractive pleasure garden is seen at its best.

Time was when certain hostelries made bids for public favour by means of their grounds. Traces of the custom are still visible at the "Welsh Harp," Hendon, and like resorts, the existence of an extensive view often forming a great attraction.

In the matter of wide outlook the Park and Gardens surrounding the Alexandra Palace hold their own; and the survival of the Avenue where Dr. Johnson liked to walk when visiting his friends whose estate subsequently formed the nucleus of this enclosure, lends special interest to "The Grove." Hampstead Heath, the natural wild beauties of its scenery wisely left untouched, has also a fine position. The Crystal Palace grounds, too, with their unrivalled accommodation for various contests, such as football and cricket matches, and for displays of fireworks, are invaluable both to local residents and to chance visitors; while Kew

Gardens offer special botanical advantages to those interested in horticulture.

For the benefits enjoyed by Londoners in the matter of pleasure gardens, their gratitude is chiefly due to the London County Council and the Metropolitan Public Gardens Association. The latter organisation is supported exclusively by private persons sufficiently active on behalf of the general public to provide the means for the very valuable work that it carries on — acquiring by purchase or otherwise, and arranging for the use of our fellow citizens, spaces which would inevitably be secured as building sites; converting disused churchyards and burial grounds into gardens; and so on indefinitely. To the unremitting efforts of this Association we owe the preservation and beautifying of many picturesque old spots threatened with being ruthlessly monopolised by the modern habit of getting the best possible return in hard cash out of every available inch of land in this crowded city.

To fully appreciate the advantages offered by our London gardens and open spaces they should be visited at various times, and on every day of the week. Take, for instance, any ordinary morning, and see the children of the neighbourhood being wheeled in their mail carts or running beside their nurses, who take an occasional rest on the seats, in Highgate Woods; on Primrose Hill; at Richmond and Kew; on the commons of Streatham, Wandsworth, and Clapham.

See them again on a school half-holiday, and watch the boys and girls race about, enjoying their liberty; or be there later when business folk get an evening airing after office hours.

Go on a Bank holiday to Golder's Hill, and see the vast numbers of tired mid-Londoners lounge through the day, imagining themselves in the depths of the country because out of the noise and dust of their ordinary surroundings. There they stroll, and regather courage, under the fine trees that were once the pride of Sir Spencer Wells, the famous doctor. A scheme for purchasing for the public from his heirs this his Hampstead estate was initiated by the Metropolitan Public Gardens Association and leading Hampstead residents, and we are lastingly indebted to the voluntary committee formed to promote this purpose, by whose zeal and energy the £42,000 required was raised in a comparatively short time. Go also to Waterlow Park, another private garden given to the public (by Sir Sydney Waterlow), and see just such another crowd; and hear a sentimental daughter tell an admiring, though wondering parent, details of the career of Nell Gwynne which have never yet graced the published records of the time of Charles II., when the Drury Lane orange girl was to be met in the corridors of Lauderdale House, still standing over there on the terrace near the Italian Garden. The girl's brothers meanwhile are getting themselves disliked by the custodian of the lakes, who suspects imminent teasing of the water-fowl since the restraining presence of their father is temporarily withdrawn, he being too much fascinated by the contemplation of the well-stocked orchard and kitchen garden to follow quickly in their train. Local hospitals benefit by the household produce in which he is taking such keen interest. A repetition of similar scenes takes place at Clissold Park, Stoke Newington, with visits to the deer house and guinea-pig run by way of variety.

LISTENING TO THE BAND (ISLE OF DOGS).

Music adds much to

AN OASIS (RED CROSS GARDENS, SOUTHWARK).

the power of attraction of these and similar resorts, the band performances being thronged in summer. The Embankment Gardens at Charing Cross are a case in point. There, besides the mental refreshment provided in the summer by the musicians, excellent food is to be obtained at very low rates from the buffet, worked automatically.

There are many other examples of equally delightful pleasure gardens, which, like Golder's Hill, Waterlow and Clissold Parks, once private grounds, are now, through the generosity of the owners or the enterprise of the afore-mentioned two bodies that arrange such matters, thrown open to the public — as, for instance, Brockwell Park at Herne Hill; the Old Manor House, Lee; Ravenscourt Park, Hammersmith; Dollis Hill, Willesden; and Walpole Park, Ealing.

Hackney Downs, Primrose Hill, Parliament Fields, and Clapham Common are airy resorts made even more beneficial by the liberal provision of seats. Here may sometimes be surprised picnic parties, whole families taking a meal in the open, a proceeding

which adds greatly to the satisfaction of the younger members; though the alarmingly hearty appetites that they develop after some hours of play are apt to tax the elastic capacity of their peripatetic larder—mother's string bag.

The young men and maidens of various neighbourhoods avail themselves very readily of the tennis lawns in their vicinity. Highbury Fields, Peckham Rye, Victoria Park, Streatham, and Camberwell provide good specimens of this privilege. The Camberwell tennis courts are situated in Myatt's Fields, a park which once formed the cabbage growing enclosure and strawberry fields of a market gardener named Myatt. Other games find their advocates in humbler environment, hockey and bowls being much played in some of London's pleasure gardens. The gymnastic appliances in many of them are a never-failing source of enjoyment to young folk of either sex.

One garden, which is of very special value to its thickly populated neighbourhood, is situated in Usk Street, Bethnal Green. It is maintained by the London County Council,

A DISUSED GRAVEYARD
(DRURY LANE).

Thames, opposite Greenwich Hospital (which the local worthies vauntingly call "Wren's Master-piece") and the grounds of the Observatory. To sit on the terrace and watch the big ocean-going ships pass quite close, or to stroll round the well-kept flower beds, whilst listening to the band, comes as near perfect enjoyment for the inhabitants of the Isle of Dogs as anybody ever attains in this work-a-day world. A similar ground lower down the river is Victoria Garden, North Woolwich.

and having been secured and laid down by the Metropolitan Public Gardens Association, is named after Lord Meath, the indefatigable Chairman of that body. Here, in this transformed burial ground of eleven acres, pale-faced children, factory "hands," and workers of all ages spend every available moment; and the playing of the Wednesday night band in the summer constitutes their one weekly diversion. They are nothing if not critical, these East-Enders, as is proved by the remarks they make on the programme and its execution. Patriotic airs, and anything with an emphatically marked measure — such as marches and polkas—meet with unequivocal approval, testified with a sympathetic tapping of feet or bumping of sticks and umbrellas.

Sunday evening spent in the County Council's garden on the Isle of Dogs, Poplar, is an experience not easily to be forgotten: it shows working London taking rest in its best possible mood. This little enclosure is another veritable treasure to its frequenters, and unique in situation —on the edge of the

A favourable part in which to spend the daily hour of rest which comes at luncheon time to many grades of working Londoners is round about the Tower—in the flower-edged walks that have been made on the sloping sides of the encircling battlements, or on the broad, gravelled terrace that runs beside the river. Here, with the stately grey old pile on the one side, rich with memories of ancient feats of daring and records of dark deeds, and the new bridge, that triumph of modern engineering, on the other, there

ALMSHOUSES OF THE IRONMONGERS' COMPANY : IN THE GARDEN.

is food for reflection. But the ordinary frequenters of the Tower Gardens do not think much about the stirring associations of the place. They are chiefly young men and girls, clerks employed in the surrounding business premises, with a sprinkling of elderly shabby-genteel men, touchingly suggestive of the insurmountable difficulty now experienced by any but the brisk and enterprising in securing remunerative employment.

In the matter of increasing and beautifying for the recreation of its citizens the conversion of graveyards into pleasure gardens, a scheme which is as great a credit to the broad-minded opinions of latter day philanthropists as anything in the way of public good yet undertaken. For instance, there is the churchyard of St. Botolph, Aldersgate Street, which from the fact of its vicinity to the General Post Office, and its being extensively patronised by postmen when off duty, or between whiles, has become locally known as the "Postmen's Park." Among others there is the recreation

Photo : C. T. Brock & Co., Sutton.

FIREWORKS AT THE CRYSTAL PALACE.

hitherto neglected little plots of ground, London has bestirred itself very satisfactorily. In Red Cross Gardens, Southwark, is a good specimen of this valuable work, for there, in spite of the high buildings that surround this oasis on every side, can the inhabitants of that crowded part of the city rest in the open air in comparative quiet. Equally advantageous are St. George's-in-the-East Churchyard, the Benjamin Street garden, the riverside strip at Battersea, and Leicester Square—all small spaces, but turned to the best possible use by means of seats and flowers.

Under the same order of usefulness comes ground at St. Peter's, Walworth, made out of the former graveyard ; and there is the burial yard of St. Anne's, Soho, in the centre of the French and Italian colonies, which is quite as much used by foreigners as by our own folk. Cripplegate Church grounds, just off Fore Street, in the City, are equally noteworthy ; and in a disused Drury Lane graveyard the children have been specially considered, swings having been included in the scheme of transformation.

Amongst many little pleasure grounds in London for the exclusive use of children there is one in Southwark, at the back of houses on the west side of Borough High

SATURDAY EVENING AT EARL'S COURT.

Street, reached by an arched passage specially characteristic of this part of London. "Little Dorrit's Playground" is the appropriate name by which they call it, since it is close to the spot where once stood the Marshalsea Prison, grim playground of Dickens' poor little heroine.

Perhaps the most picturesque of London's pleasure gardens are the grounds belonging to some of our ancient almshouses, where selected communities of elderly folk spend the evening of their days. Take, for instance, the extensive garden enclosure in Kingsland Road, replanted and renovated by the Metropolitan Public Gardens Association at the cost of the Ironmongers' Company, and skirted on three sides by the almshouses belonging to the Company. Beautiful old trees, wide lawns, and borders full of flowers — not prim little patches of "bedding out" plants, but good old-fashioned marigolds, tiger lilies, Canterbury bells, peonies, and such like, and blossoming bravely under the fostering care of the Association, in spite of the somewhat uncongenial atmosphere of the capital. Much interest is taken by the inmates in their garden, common to all, and pleasant hours do they spend, these old men and women, pensioners of the wealthy Ironmongers' Company, sitting in groups under the trees, and strolling along the paths. Theirs is a peaceful way of going gently down the slope and out of life—with a neat little set of rooms, a nurse within hail, and a chaplain holding weekly service in the little sanctuary within the grounds.

Noteworthy, too, is the dwelling place of the pensioners of the Trinity House—old seafarers, Merchant Service captains—in Mile End Road: sixty-nine little homes grouped round a large T-shaped garden, with a chapel in the centre and a library in one corner. Delightful stories can these old salts tell of the days of their youth, of eventful voyages, perils by sea, and strange adventures in other lands — embroidering truth, perchance, in course of telling; but who cares for just the ordinary bare record of unvarnished fact when it is a matter of ancient mariners' thrilling yarns !

The year 1695 saw the founding of this valuable Hospital by the Corporation of Trinity House, but then it was on another site, and provided for but twenty "decayed masters and commanders of ships." The almshouses are sufficiently roomy to permit each old captain to bring his wife or some other female relative to share his quarters, and keep things ship-shape for him. In the library and reading-room the men find neutral ground on which to meet their comrades as well as to discuss the affairs of the nation. There is a uniform belonging to

ON THE GRASS.

the Trinity House almshouse men—navy-blue cloth with brass buttons—which is donned every Sunday for chapel. A charming custom survives from the very foundation of the Corporation of Trinity House, with which the pensioners have always been associated —the assembling of all the members, from the Royal Grand Master downwards, for service at St. Olave's Church, Tooley Street, on Trinity Monday. This annual expedition makes an agreeable break in the ordinary routine, and provides many a fresh topic wherewith to wile away a sunny hour on the seats in the almshouse garden.

To be able fully to grasp the very important part which open spaces play in the geography of the Metropolis, it is necessary to see a chart of the County of London, and notice how numerous are the little green patches which stand for London's Pleasure Gardens.

BALLOONING LONDON.

By the REV. JOHN M. BACON.

LOUNGERS in the London parks, sighting a little globe sailing above the far horizon to the south-west, stand and watch it while it climbs the sky. There is some strange fascination about the tiny translucent ball, for in every open space people turn their gaze and mark its graceful form as momentarily approaching nearer it sails up majestically towards the town.

Presently the passers in the streets catch the unwonted object against the sky, and heads are craned upwards, and 'bus drivers with raised whip indicate its flight to outside passengers. Then, soaring far aloft, it floats overhead, and so on without pause, passing once again into a mere tiny speck before it vanishes out of sight in the distance over the northern suburbs.

This is one of the balloons which rightfully belong to the great city, hailing from the Crystal Palace, where Londoners have flocked in thousands to enjoy the attractions provided for a summer holiday. Let us join the crowd which is eagerly watching where vast folds of silk spread on the turf are growing into a shapely globe, and presently taking our seat—or rather seats, for the writer, bound on a scientific voyage, is to be joined by his daughter as chief assistant—let us view all Living London in one grand survey from the standpoint of a mile aloft.

There is eager excitement among the crowd, not unmixed with nervousness, as the balloon begins to catch the wind which in heavy gusts sweeps up from the lower ground, and the old hands, struggling with the straining gear as they attach the car, strive to make all taut and "snug." The feeling is akin to that evinced in the last busy half-hour before a Cunarder leaves the docks; but now the nervous tension is greater in proportion, as the risk to ship and passengers is greater. Sandy Hook once passed, the well-found liner is assured of safe and easy landing. It is otherwise with the balloon, whose ultimate haven is always uncertain and unknown. Then restraining ropes are cast off, and

"WELL AWAY."

bag after bag is dropped with a thud on the turf as the balloon, with the passengers already in their places, is "weighed" and balanced, and the next moment, with one last bag overboard, the fragile craft is free and in the air.

When the aëronauts next have leisure to look round, the Palace roofs, glittering in the sun, are a slant mile in the rear. To right and left, away to a far sky line, stretch the smiling suburbs, but the object which claims the whole attention is a long,

INFLATION (CRYSTAL PALACE GROUNDS).

low belt of murky haze that bars the view to northward. Behind that curtain lies earth's greatest city, all unseen. Yet not for long. Rapidly the fretted face of earth glides by below, and soon in dim outline mighty Living London opens out. The river, flinging back the sunlight, shows its silver loops dotted over with moving objects — the first signs of active life. Then the larger buildings on both shores plant themselves prominently on the fast unfolding map. Spires stand white and clear, and vacant spaces develop into squares and parks. Next the interlacing threads of grey among the dun broaden and lengthen out into familiar highways, and all the town lies etched in plan below.

But before this there has been other evidence than that of sight of the life with which the vast scene is instinct. The ear catches the pulse of the mighty city. The air, lately so devoid of sound, palpitates with a harsh discordant murmur, growing every moment till it becomes an intense and quivering roar—the ceaseless din of traffic from the unending streets. In truth, to the eye the thoroughfares appear to have no limit. Oxford Street, seen throughout its entire length and prolonged indefinitely in either direction, lies below, coursing like some main artery from Turnham Green to Stepney. Black spots are dotted irregularly along its length, strangely minute, and seemingly also strangely few, considering that they represent the entire moving life of the great thronged highway ; but the fact

is that to the passengers the streets always necessarily appear more crowded than they really are. Viewed from above the pavements are but sparsely speckled with humanity, and vehicles in the roadway are for the most part far between. Here and there the larger dots are grouped in patches. These patches are the congested traffic at street corners. But, misled by the perspective which but a slight elevation affords, the man sitting on the top of a 'bus is apt to form a wrong impression of the throng about him.

From our present point of view the familiar blocks of buildings appear but as fringes of bricks and mortar, with courts and clearances within. Nevertheless, to the voyager a mile overhead London has lost none of its greatness. On the contrary, the same law of perspective which opens out the ground below, showing in plan each several building and the units of the human hive, has closed in the scattered suburbs, and now within the limits of vision— narrowed, no doubt, by haze—all and everywhere is London.

But the precious moments of a rare opportunity have flown all too fast. It is but seldom that a balloonist in clear air finds himself sailing fairly over the city, nor is he ever allowed more than a passing glance. In the moment of identifying familiar objects they have passed from view, and before we have leisure to note the change the town is already transformed. The quaint intricacies of the older streets have given place to the monotonous regularity of more modern districts. Huge unlovely roofs lie below, marking the familiar railway termini, with outgoing trains speeding northward. The tops of clustered gas-holders yawn at us 1,000 feet below, sadly lacking in the picturesque, but interesting to the sky-voyager who recognises in them the source whence he gains his powers of flight. To the north-east gleam sheets of water, sharply outlined — the huge basins of the water companies. On our other hand more than one large plot covered with weathered stones tells where the dead are sleeping, and beyond all stretch the pastures and deep woods of verdant Hertfordshire. Our rapid transit over London is ended. We shall presently resume our aërial survey from other aspects and from other heights — by night too, as well as day ; but to gain a clearer insight into Ballooning London let us first visit a famous school where ballooning is learned, and where balloons and all that appertains thereto are made.

One large oblong building in the north of London, with a well-lighted roof, contains the workroom, with all necessary plant, of the largest balloon factory in England. Here, at a busy season, many balloons in all stages may be seen in progress of manufacture, and at first sight it seems surprising on entering that so much and varied work can proceed without confusion within so limited an area.

"ALOFT" : THE WRITER AND HIS DAUGHTER.

But a glance at the workmen themselves suffices to dispel the mystery. With many of them the weather-beaten face, the easy attitude, the deftly working fingers, at once betray the old sailor. Indeed, it may be stated that among the male hands the majority are either old sailors or have had a sailor's training. The rigging and fitting of the balloon belong essentially to the craft of a mariner, who needs but little elbow-room to work in.

Spread out over nearly half the available floor space lies a balloon lately come home from active service, which is being overhauled and examined in every detail, or if necessary inflated with a rotatory fan for better inspection. Hard by another balloon is receiving its coats of varnish. On a long side table the gores of a new balloon are being cut out with the sweep of a razor, while upstairs women are sewing the huge lengths together. Hanging from a line across the far corner a net of gigantic mesh, worked by hand, is assuming large proportions ; while elsewhere carpenters are at work upon the wooden valves, and cars, with their appropriate hoops, are being fitted and rigged. Nor is this all, for under the same roof hot-air balloons and their parachutes are to be seen, also a navigable air-ship in actual course of construction.

Trophies of various kinds adorn the walls —such as the mercurial barometer, in its special case, used by the famous Charles Green in olden days before aneroids were known, and the apparatus provided for a recent climb of six miles high. Suspended, too, from a nail may be seen a Davy safety lamp for use in night voyages. It is of a certain occasion on which this instrument was required that we would now speak.

It occurred to the writer that the story of Ballooning London in the small hours of the morning had never yet been told, and, though the difficulties of accomplishing the needful voyage were great—everything depending on

wrong impression if he supposed the streets to be empty. No sooner had we risen above the house-tops than a dozen voices hailed us. To those who were abroad the balloon, large and black against the sky, was an object sure to attract attention. At a greater distance, however, we might well be missed, and, as small objects below were indistinguishable from above, a special device was employed to learn how far this quiet quarter of London was yet awake. Using a large speaking trumpet, and pointing it in all directions, we challenged the neighbourhood

A MISTY VIEW OVER THE CITY.

the winds aloft, which are not easy to determine at night-time—yet in the end complete success was met with.

Stamford Bridge Athletic Grounds, Chelsea, were chosen as a starting point, and three on an August morning as the time of departure. At that hour commercial London requires practically no one to be abroad. Social London, too, affords few late gatherings in the latter half of this month, and early trains would not be running for two good hours. It would naturally be supposed that London was sleeping; and it is true that a pedestrian might at that hour traverse many thoroughfares and meet not a single passenger. But he would form a totally

around; and we were quickly answered. Right and left shouts rang out, and were taken up and repeated again and again from points far and near. Nor, owing to the night silence, were the voices indistinct or incoherent. It was a strange experience to be carrying on speech in London with someone two or three streets away; but it was a fact. A far-off friendly greeting in lusty bass belonged, beyond all doubt, to some guardian of the peace. In higher key came many questionings as to the direction we were taking. Youthful voices were among them. One individual continued conversation for a long period, and presently explained the fact by saying that he was pursuing us on a bicycle.

GAS-HOLDERS AS SEEN FROM 1,000 FEET UP.

have been expected, for many craft were moving with the tide, and those which were moored would have their watch. For all that, it was surprising to hear the watermen hail in chorus, and proceed by way of salute to blow their hooters far up stream and down.

Presently we rose higher, out of the range of voices, and then to the view the immensity of London opened out. In day hours the light coming from the sky and illumining the dust motes floating in the lower air raises to the eye of the sky-voyager a haze that always more or less veils the distance. But under the black night sky the case is different, and far as the eye can reach the lights of earth are seen. With us the circumstances of the situation were unique, and probably the limits of modern London had never been so well defined as then. Eastward the town seemed literally without limit. Human dwellings, clustered on both sides of the great waterway, stretched in lines of dwindling light till they met the sky. To the right it was otherwise: London

It was a new and astonishing revelation of night-time in Westminster and Chelsea: here even in the dead hours London was really alive and watchful. It was easy to understand now how crowds will so quickly gather at any hour of the night on an alarm, as that of fire. More remarkable yet, however, was the wakeful life on the river, which for a while ran near us, and which we presently crossed. This, of course, should

ONE MILE ABOVE TRAFALGAR SQUARE.

faded out in an irregular fringe somewhere in the middle distance, and far beyond other clustered lights shimmered in the sky, marking distant Kentish towns—Rochester maybe, or Maidstone. The far left, on the other hand, over Essex marshes, was comparatively blank.

But all beneath us lay an enchanted city, extending for miles and miles, a very maze of lights ; with roadways in dark lines, fringed with pavements shining white like frosted silver. And yet it was truly and unmistak-

a patch of the Milky Way had fallen on the earth.

But the balloonist's survey of London would be incomplete without a nearer view, and, though in these days a perfect web of electric wires is seen to be spread over all parts of the town, making it doubly hazardous to approach the roofs, yet it sometimes happens that a balloon, dipping near the house-tops, may be allowed to skim low for a little while in certain quarters, affording such a close scrutiny of the town as no

A CORNER OF A BALLOON FACTORY

ably London. There were the well-known open spaces, each a broad flood of light, framed by black blocks of buildings ; Westminster, Trafalgar Square, the West-End circuses, the broad, bright thoroughfares of Club-land, the lesser lights of riverside London ; and winding through it all a gap of utter blackness, streaked with bars of reflected light, and bridged in places with double rows of lamps, where silent Thames was flowing. So on and on for miles we floated over the fairy scene, till the lights below frayed out in lines and patches, and lost themselves in open country. Our last view of London ere dawn broke was a broad distant track, studded with faint points of light, as though

creatures, save, perhaps, the pigeons, may enjoy. This is a rare and extraordinary experience for the aëronaut which comes as a surprise. His actual high speed of travel, perhaps twenty miles an hour, is then peculiarly impressed upon him. At no other time has he traversed the same streets or parks, except in the imprisonment of a train, so swiftly, and the rapidly changing scene gives him a new idea of London.

Never as then is he made to feel what close neighbours here are poverty and plenty. One moment he is crossing over a prosperous, or maybe fashionable, street. The next he is hovering over a squalid court, hemmed in by mews or dingy workshops or blank walls—

the promenade of starveling cats. Here is a throng of well-dressed idlers; hard by an alley full of ragged children. The experience is as instructive as it is novel, and the question naturally arises whether this fascinating view of London, hitherto so rarely enjoyed, cannot be brought within the reach of all who wish to explore the varied ways and life of our great city.

The practical answer to this question has been given by the air-ship, the embryo of which we have already looked at. The graceful and easy flight of the aërial motor, as performed to-day over suburban pleasure grounds, and its ready obedience in favouring winds to the will of the helmsman, are convincing proof that this newest mode of transit is fully capable of providing pleasure trips across the breadth of London so soon as meteorologists can give a surer account of the way of the winds.

To the casual observer the air-ship may, indeed, appear a simple aërostat, and as our photographic illustration below almost suggests, little more than a balloon of altered shape; but in truth its design involves a problem in aërial dynamics of extreme difficulty. When called upon to oppose the wind in any degree the strength of its frame and fabric is put to the severest test, while, inasmuch as it floats wholly in air with its length extended horizontally, the maintenance of its balance becomes a matter of the greatest nicety. The cross currents that would twist it from its course, the ascending and descending air-streams that would upset its equilibrium, demand of the pilot the utmost skill and nerve; and it is only because the air-ship is no mere inert balloon but endowed with powers of motion—for the while a thing of life—that its management becomes possible.

And this fact applies particularly over London. The turmoil of the busy town may seem to terminate with the level of the houses; but in truth it is not so. The gusts of wind sweeping through the streets, when stopped by opposing buildings, find their only egress upwards towards the sky. The air lying over heated roofs and pavements rises constantly in a vast tide through day hours to be replaced by cold down draughts at night. And this is Nature's own mode of providing for the ventilation of our vast Metropolis—affording, among very much that is deeply impressive and instructive, perhaps the happiest aspect of all in the aërial survey of London.

Photo: Spencer Bros., Highbury, N.

" FULL SPEED AHEAD ! "

THREE A.M. AT A GOODS STATION (KING'S CROSS).

LONDON AT DEAD OF NIGHT.

By GEORGE R. SIMS.

THE Mother of Cities slumbers not nor sleeps. Her children are restless, and never once allow her to sink into repose. But there are two hours of the twenty-four when the great heart of London beats more slowly, when her breathing is more rhythmic, when the hush of the night is upon her, even if dreamless sleep be denied. "In the dead of the night" is the poet's phrase. It is in the middle period between the hours of 1 a.m. and 4 a.m. that the London night is deadest.

At one o'clock there is still plenty of life of a kind in the great thoroughfares. It is but half an hour since the restaurants and the public-houses closed their doors "by legislature's harsh decree," and those who have been satisfying hunger and thirst up to the last moment allowed by the law have to make their way home. This process, in a city of the vast extent of the capital, takes a certain amount of time.

But soon after 1 a.m. the sleepers-out have settled down into their *al fresco* slumbers, and so the Embankment presents a picture of mingled magnificence and despair that is perhaps without parallel in the world.

The great hotels, the palatial residential chambers, are still lighted up. Dreamy waltz music may be heard floating out upon the quiet night from the colossal Cecil or the sumptuous Savoy, where there are always a large number of resident guests, and frequently big supper parties for which a special licence has been granted. You may linger on the Embankment sometimes till the dead of the night has yielded to the first faint flush of dawn, and be soothed by the strains of music.

Strangely out of harmony with the sweet sounds are the scenes that will meet your eye as you take your way along the broad tree-shaded pavement by the river side. The lamplight shining through the branches of the trees makes a dainty tracery upon the flag-stones. The sentinel stars in the sky look down upon the black waters of the mighty river, never so beautiful, never so mysterious, as when it reflects only the lights of the bridges and the dull red lamps of the craft that lie at rest upon its bosom.

On a fine autumn night the Embankment is a scene for the painter's brush, for the poet's pen. "All save the spirit of man is divine." The spirit of man upon the Embankment is, alas! more suggestive of Dante's "Inferno" than of Milton's "Paradise." Here the lost souls wander gloomily. Here the homeless vagabond and the prowler in search of prey herd together. Men, old and young, grey-haired women, and girls just come to womanhood crowd together in sheltered corners, or sleep huddled up on the garden seats, which were certainly not intended when they were placed there to be free dormitories for London's tramps and outcasts.

Here and there a policeman in silent shoes lurks in the shadow, waiting to emerge at the sound of danger and arrest the culprit before he has time for flight; for there are desperate men among the Embankment "dossers"— men who would not hesitate to fling their stunned and despoiled victim into the Thames if the opportunity were given them.

A dozen of these men will appear suddenly from steps leading to the river, alarmed, perhaps, by the voice of a policeman ordering some burly ruffian to "move on." I have seen such a group spring suddenly into view from apparently nowhere, and had they been photographed as they stood, and described as a gang of desperate criminals in the Old Bailey dock, no one would have hesitated to accept the picture as genuine. Fortunately for the police the Embankment roughs of both sexes are cowards. I have seen them run and scatter in every direction, like startled deer, at the sound of a policeman's whistle.

But not all these children of the night are criminals or roughs. Some are the sons and daughters of despair. The seats on the Embankment are the last refuge at night of many a man and woman who has fallen out of the ranks of labour—sometimes out of the ranks of the brain workers—from sheer misfortune. "No chance" is writ large upon the furrowed faces of many of them.

To cross the bridges in the dead of night is to see the Embankment misery repeated on a smaller scale. Some of the bridges are brilliantly lighted, and, as no one likes a strong light in his eyes during the hours that he would find forgetfulness in sleep, the em-

brasures of the bridges are not so crowded as they used to be; but they still have their patrons. A group of sleepers on Southwark Bridge is shown in the photographic reproduction on page 360. Perhaps the most pitiful sight of all is found in the long rows of sleeping outcasts lying in their misery and rags hard by the monument to England's hero of the sea, and in the shadow of the nation's great gallery of art.

In Blackfriars Road the change from the brilliant light of the bridge to the gloom of the streets is striking. But here there still is life. The tramcars run the long night through, and at 2 a.m. the belated wayfarer may for the modest sum of a halfpenny be borne drowsily to the Elephant and Castle, and go far beyond if he wishes it.

To the Elephant, where in the daytime and up till midnight there is ever a surging throng, the small hours bring comparative peace. But there are frequently instances of discord. A man and a woman whose domestic relations are strained sometimes exchange civilities which end in a struggle and a scream. The woman is flung down —sometimes knocked down—and the man lurches away. The screams of his victim do not draw a crowd—there is no crowd to be drawn; but here and there across the road a man will stop and listen, then shrug his shoulders and walk on. Over the water it is not considered wise to interfere in domestic differences at two in the morning.

At most of the coffee-stalls a little crowd is gathered. Some of the customers are genuine enough—men returning from late, or going to early, work. But there are dangerous loafers around the steaming urns and the ever attractive light, and it is not advisable to study character at a coffee-stall in the middle of the night.

In the East-End the dead of night is of short duration. It is almost difficult to define it. Before the last shops in the Ghetto have closed, and the home-returning loiterers have disappeared from the broad thoroughfares in Whitechapel and Stepney, great vans and waggons have begun to make their way almost in procession towards the Docks. Towards the Docks, also, there drifts a sauntering crowd of men who are going to take up their places outside in the hope of

ARRIVAL OF THE NIGHT MAIL (PADDINGTON).

OPPOSITE THE NATIONAL GALLERY : A NIGHT SCENE.

being taken on for a job when the big gates open and the work of the day begins.

Just as the late west is thinking of bed, the early east is up and afoot. In Lime-house and Poplar there are streets which are as busy in the dead of night as some West-End thoroughfares are at eight in the morning.

From the back of the Surrey Theatre to Waterloo Bridge is a broad thoroughfare which is intersected by a number of streets. From some of these emerge from time to time young fellows who are first cousins to the Lambeth Hooligan. The thoroughfare itself is quiet after 2 a.m., but as you walk along, keeping a wary eye on the side streets and the corners, in the shadow you hear a wild scream of "Murder!" ring out, followed by

cries of "Police! Police!" Down one of these streets a man or a woman is perhaps being done to death. You glance up the long road towards the welcome lights of Waterloo, but you see no sign of anyone whom you would care to ask to go down that street with you and find out what is amiss. The cries grow fainter and fainter, then cease altogether. You wonder if in the morning's papers you will read of another murderous outrage, and you are glad when Waterloo Bridge is passed and you find yourself in the Strand.

For the Strand is fuller than any place you have seen yet. People are coming and going. Cabs and carts and vans are passing and re-passing. The newspaper offices are lighted up. Along Wellington

Street you follow a line of waggons piled high with fruit and vegetables for Covent Garden market. In a street near Covent Garden a gang of men are at work laying an electric cable. From deep trenches and long barriers great sheets of flame flare up and dance in the wind, while the busy workers, now in light and now in shadow, toil on through the night. At the gates of the flower market vans are delivering boxes and baskets of bloom of brilliant hue. The market itself is already gay with flowers and palms, and Covent Garden is rapidly being filled with the boxes of fruit and the baskets of vegetables that will fall beneath the hammer and be distributed over the length and breadth of the Metropolis before the ordinary citizen has given the first yawn of approaching wakefulness.

Outside the theatrical and literary clubs, as one passes towards Leicester Square, there is still a line of cabs on the ranks — the four-wheeler predominates outside one, the hansom outside another. A tired "crawler" creeps along here and there, for the London cabman works through the night in the west, though you may walk a mile to find one in the east and some parts of the north and south.

The Haymarket is deserted, but many of the windows of the Carlton still show the yellow glow of the lights within. A chemist's shop is open, and two assistants are in readiness behind the counter to prepare any medicine that may be wanted. Leicester Square is deserted; Piccadilly is empty. Regent Street is without sign of life, but before one of the great shops filled with the fripperies of fashion and left with lights burning a tattered tramp is standing and gazing interestedly at a beautiful opera cloak marked twelve and a half guineas. What attraction it can have for him it is difficult to surmise. Possibly he is thinking of something else—may be of *someone* else —may be of one who in the days of long ago when he was young and perhaps rich wore just such a wrap when he took her to hear Patti in the "Barber." Who knows?

In Bloomsbury the blackness of night is lit up by a glare that at first suggests fire. But there is no roar and rattle of the fire engine, no hurrying crowd has in the dead of night sprung suddenly into being and rushed to a conflagration as the

NIGHT WORKERS LAYING AN ELECTRIC CABLE.

grandest of London's free spectacles. A turn of the corner and the glare shows itself to be a great building operation. Time is an object, and the builders are working in night and day shifts. Here there is a little party of watchers gathered on the kerb. The spectacle of house building through the night is almost as attractive as a fire.

On through quiet streets and squares which are as silent as the grave and into Euston Road, where life begins again. Here are loiterers and loafers, men walking rapidly with home or work in view, and a little file of cabs, luggage laden, going on to the parting of the ways, north, south, and east and west.

Paddington and other of the great termini, after lapsing into quietude at midnight, suddenly wake up between two and four for the arrival of great mail trains. Inside the station there are cabs and porters. The train rattles in and pulls up sharply. The Post Office staff are instantly busy with small mountains of mail bags. The carriage doors open, and sleepy travellers, some rubbing their eyes and yawning, emerge on to the platform to claim their luggage, to be assisted by porters, who run to and fro under the horses' heads with portmanteaux and travelling bags and heavier packages. Presently the last passenger is in his cab, and it clatters out of the station,

the driver giving the address to which he is proceeding to the ever vigilant constable at the gate.

Further on towards King's Cross, the vast goods station of the Great Northern Railway is the scene of another phase of railway life. In the dead of night this hive of industry is at its busiest, and is a picture that impresses itself on the imagination, and tells a story of England's wondrous trade that no one can look upon without a glow of pride.

From King's Cross and along Euston Road, past the great monument yards where stone and marble effigies stand out weirdly against the night, into the Marylebone Road we make our way, and so, amid a silence which increases as we go, through the gates of the Park, which is hushed in sleep. Here no soul is in sight, nor a sound to be heard until the first flush of dawn appears in the sky and the waking birds break into tentative twitters in the thick foliage that stirs gently in the light breeze that has come up with day. Except for them the Park is silent as the grave, restful as sleep. But the silence is broken for a moment or two. Across the Park from the distant Zoo the dull roar of a caged lion is borne upon the wind.

The dead of the night is over, and the life of the day is at hand.

ASLEEP (SOUTHWARK BRIDGE).

EPILOGUE.

By GEORGE R. SIMS.

THE play is played. Act by act, scene by scene, the great drama of Living London has unfolded itself before our eyes. Its characters, its men, women, and children, have fretted their hour upon the stage. We have smiled at their joys and sympathised with their sorrows. Those to whom was entrusted the task or planning the play, of arranging its startling contrasts in one harmonious dramatic scheme, have laid the great heart of London bare, have shown us the Londoner in his habit as he lives. We have seen him in all his moods and amid all his environments, at every hour of the busy day and in the lonely watches of the quiet night. We have been privileged to look upon him in the privacy of his palace and in the solitude of his cell. We have followed him to strange haunts hidden from the passing world ; we have seen him in his family life and in his public life, in his pleasure and in his pain, the honoured guest at the feast of good things, and raising with a trembling hand the cup of charity to his lips.

In every station of life he has passed before us ; in every trade, every calling, and every profession he has taken his place upon the stage, and lent his characteristics and his peculiarities to the crowded scene.

It was my pleasant task to speak the opening words, and bid the audience welcome when the curtain hid from their eyes the human drama waiting to be enacted. It is my grateful task, now that the curtain has fallen on the last scene, to speak the Epilogue ; to tender, on behalf of all who have combined to make my managerial responsibility a happy memory, sincere and heart-felt thanks for the generous appreciation with which their efforts have been received.

There remains for me now but to express the earnest hope that the promise made in the Prologue has been fulfilled, and that we have succeeded in presenting to the English speaking people a faithful picture of the breathing, pulsing Capital of the Empire— that Living London which is at once the admiration and the wonder of the world.